Voices from the Kavango

KLETUS MUHENA LIKUWA

Voices from the Kavango
A Study of the Contract Labour System in Namibia, 1925–1972

Basel Namibia Studies Series 22

Basler Afrika Bibliographien 2020

©2020 The authors
©2020 Basler Afrika Bibliographien

Basler Afrika Bibliographien
Namibia Resource Centre & Southern Africa Library
Klosterberg 23
PO Box
4001 Basel
Switzerland
www.baslerafrika.ch

The Basler Afrika Bibliographien is part of the Carl Schlettwein Foundation

All rights reserved.

Cover image: Contract labourers from Kavango on their way back to Kavango (Grootfontein), 1954. Photographer: Ruth Dammann

ISBN 978-3-906927-19-0
ISSN 2234-9561

Contents

Foreword by Uma Dhupelia-Mesthrie   vii

Acknowledgment   ix

Preface   xi

Introduction   1
    Historiographical review on the contract labour system   3
    Archival sources   13
    Oral interviews   14

1   Tracing the History of the Contract Labour System in the Kavango, 1885–1950s   24
    Introduction   24
    Early intrusions by traders and hunters   24
    The German colonial regime in Kavango   29
    The South African presence in the Kavango   40
    Labour recruitment by South African officials   44
    The formation of the Northern Labour Organization (NLO) and its operations, 1925–1943   54
    The formation of South West Africa Native Labour Association (SWANLA) and its operations   59
    Conclusion   61

2   "They Used to Buy Us": Labour Migration from Kavango   62
    Introduction   62
    Reasons for contract labour migration   63
    Migration journeys, 1925–1972   72
    Women in labour narratives   92
    Conclusion   96

3   Living and Work Experiences   98
    Introduction   98
    The contract labourers on farms   98
    The South African mines and compounds   119
    Namibian mines and compounds   126
    Conclusion   137

4	Returning Home: Economic, Social Impact and Worker Mobilization	138
	Introduction	138
	Mathias Ndumba Shikombero's life story	138
	Economic and social impact	144
	Mobilizing politically	157
	Conclusion	168
5	General Conclusions and Lessons	170
Bibliography		176
Photographs of interviewees taken by Kletus Muhena Likuwa		187
Index		215

Foreword

It was an affinity of interest in forced removals, homelands policies, contract labour and oral histories that brought Kletus Likuwa and myself together in the years of his postgraduate studies in the History Department at the University of the Western Cape. This bond is revealed in a photograph that I have of the two of us that is displayed in my office till today. These fruitful years produced a new black historian of the Kavango, an area which Likuwa observes has been much neglected by scholars given the difficult conditions for research there. Scholarship on contract labour, in particular, neglected to sufficiently consider the movement from this area and official sources too obscured the numbers from the Kavango subsuming them under Ovamboland figures.

While I have never been to the Kavango, Likuwa, as a member of the Vagciriku community, is a master story teller with a feel for the area. As he traversed through the villages of the Kavango in search of the 'vakacontraka', the contract workers, to interview, the reader gains a feel for the geographical terrain and the villages of Kangweru, Guma, Korokoko, Diheke, Mabushe, Bagani, to name just a few of many that stretch from the western to the eastern parts of the Kavango, to find a place in history. The research is impressive drawing on significant archival sources, in particular, the local files dealing with Rundu but the book shines in its use of oral histories. There is a sensitivity as to how to conduct oral interviews, a talent for the languages of the area such as Rukwangali, Rumanyo and Thimbukushu, and a maturity in analysing the narratives themselves well beyond mining these for information. Likuwa is sensitive to processes of transcription and translation and, to allow the interviewees to be heard, extracts from the original interviews are included along with the translations. He has created a new archival collection through his generous donation of these interviews to the National Archives of Namibia.

Likuwa infuses the category of contract labourer with life in the narrative he constructs. The men have names, biographies and feelings. They express the hopes they had, their disappointments, their coping strategies and their journeys. We learn from Ndumba Shirengumuke of Hoha village, for instance, 'It was in Grootfontein where we got bought'. We learn about the 'don't breathe machines', the x-ray machines at the screening processes, the renaming by the employers and the retaliation as workers privately gave names to their employers, and interactions with the 'missus' on the farms. From the mines to the farms, Likuwa, takes us through these one on one contacts. This is not a local history but a transnational history taking one across the borders into Angola, Zimbabwe and South Africa. We are left with the powerful words of Mathias Ndumba Shikombero who was interviewed at age 76 in Rucara village after working for twenty-two years as a contract labour 'what did we really bring from that contract work? Nothing! There were some simple, ugly blankets with pictures of lions on them'. Likuwa's major oral histories of work may prove his great-grandmother Susana Mate Kamwanga, wrong in her reprimand to him 'you the children of nowadays who only want to record to go and write in books. What will you get out of it? You will get nothing out of it?' The scholarship of Namibia is enriched with this new work on the Kavango and the people of this most northern region have secured their rightful place in the country's history.

Uma Dhupelia-Mesthrie
Senior Professor, History Department, University of the Western Cape
30 March 2020.

Acknowledgment

Great thanks to the Carl Schlettwein Foundation of Basel, Switzerland, for the continuous financial support to this academic project and the publication process. Thanks to Professor Patricia Hayes and Professor Leslie Witz for their unwavering academic support. I am extremely grateful to Professor Uma-Dhupelia-Mesthrie, my academic supervisor at UWC. I remain with a lasting impression of her extreme meticulousness to pinpoint the shortcomings in my academic work and suggest constructive improvements. All the remaining shortcomings or mistakes in this work, therefore, are my sole responsibility.

Thanks to my good and loyal friend Dr. Michael Uusiku Akuupa, for your strong advice and the continuing support you provided towards this project. Thanks to Michael Murundu Justinus Shirungu, Maggy Nepaya and Paulinus Haingura for being good and supportive friends during this academic project. I similarly thank my good friend Shampapi Shiremo (my grandson in line with family tradition), for his constant support and for being a compatriot in our academic struggles and for being centrally vocal about the Kavango in Namibian public history. Let the struggle continue!

To my senior brother Karl Lwanga Muduva Likuwa, you believed in my passion for learning and always hoped that one day I would become a highly learned person. You took me away from my village school of Ndiyona to do high school and eventually undergraduate studies in Windhoek, Namibia. You also continued to support me both morally and financially. To you I say, 'Mbatero naviruwana vyoye vyahafita vadimu vetu, kancu kurukenka rwa Kanyondo!' (Your support and work has pleased our ancestors, I promise at the verge of the deep Kanyondo stream).

To my fiancée Elvira Makena Ndara, thanks for all the unlimited love, support and patience you continue to show tome; it gives me the strength to move on to the end. To my children, Muduva, Kayimbi and Kandjimi, it has been a pleasure seeing and thinking of you growing up all of which has added meaning to the need to complete this academic project.

To my mother, Appolonia Karama Maliti, who raised me and is now in old age but still displays strength by working in her field and wishes we could always live and work the field together, I remain greatly indebted. My late father Felix Shindimba Likuwa who inspired me through his Rumanyo language writings to become a writer like him. I thank him for having been a good role model and may his soul rest in peace.

Great thanks to all the former Kavango contract labourers for sharing their life experiences which have helped to bring this academic project to fruition, to them I say, 'kunaviruwanene twe vino vana vetu na vanantjoka vakumeho' (We did this for our children and the youth of the future).

Preface

Voices from the Kavango derives from an observation and understanding that there has been silence about the experiences of Kavango contract labourers. It remained necessary to speak with former Kavango contract labourers to explore the way in which their life histories and voices contribute to our understanding of the contract labour system in Namibia. In particular, this book seeks to ask what light do they shed on migration and on new living and working experiences, their experiences with recruiting organizations and local recruiting agents, and the effect the contract labour system had on them? Is it possible to view the migration of the Kavango workers as a progressive step, or does the paradigm of exploitation and suppression remain the dominant one?

Oral interviews were carried out among the former contract labourers and their narratives were used empirically for information about their experiences and attention paid towards analysing these narratives for meaning. Archival sources further provided insight into the colonial views about contract labourers and the operation of the system itself. This book points to the slow inclusion of the Kavango into the contract labour system. It draws attention to the silencing of the Kavango in the contract labour system, partly due to the marginal numbers of participation from former Kavango land in comparison to the participating figures from former Ovamboland, but also due to the earlier method of counting the numbers of Kavango contract labourers under the 'Ovambo' label by colonial officials.

Although contract labourers made their own decision whether to leave home to get recruited, they did so because of the compelling 'ruhepo', (poverty/hardship) which resulted from the stringent colonial laws. Labour narratives point to many journeys both within and outside Namibia with the aim of acquiring money by working under the colonial economy so as to purchase clothing, which they lacked locally and to accumulate wealth to address 'ruhepo' (poverty/hardship) within their communities. As contract labourers embarked on their journey they became aware of the collaboration between the colonial officials and recruiting agents in the control and exploitation of contract labourers. From the perspective of contract labourers, the contract labour system was nothing but slavery. They felt treated like property to be sold. Contract labourers' naming of employers became a way of dealing emotionally with this mistreatment. The memory of the 'missus' on the farms lingers on mainly because contract workers related to their home experience of the submissive role of women and, therefore, would have found it traumatizing to be shouted at by a woman. The labourers adapted to new colonial times and a new rhythm of labour, such as bells and whistles. They developed good inter-ethnic relations among themselves.

Contrary to the literature, the workers' relationships with the location residents was not always bad.

The impact of the contract labour system was such that contract labourers gained benefits, but they are quick to point out that these benefits were small and non-lasting and not worth their suffering, exploitation and the loss they endured, which always necessitated their continuous return to contract. The book points to this cycle of entrapment for contract labourers, which eventually led to the political mobilizing of workers by SWAPO activists. The workers' mobilization extended to the Kavango and resulted in rebelliousness against SWANLA and its institutions. While this book hopes to contribute to ending the silences about the Kavango's engagement within the contract labour system, it points also to the need for future research highlighting women's narratives about life in the Kavango, as well as postcolonial labour migration to the charcoal and grape farms which, as narratives of the former Kavango contract labourers show, continues.

Some of the lessons can be discerned from the voices of contract labourers for post-colonial Namibia such as the ruhepo (poverty/hardship) of workers and their families results not just from ecological factors (lack of rain and recurrent drought or animal diseases), but also from political factors (such as the control and denial over access and distribution of the local resources by the political authorities).

The post-colonial migration of opportunity seekers from former Kavango and Ovambo lands are partly a result of colonial underdevelopment of these areas and fewer opportunities for access and distribution of local resources. These factors compelled many to migrate in the hope of acquiring opportunities to accumulate wealth with which to address their problems.

The narratives of the experiences of contract labourers provide a lesson that when an existing economic setup such as the contract labour system became oppressive rather than providing a solution to the problems of wealth creation and ending "ruhepo", the workers began to mobilise politically to overthrow the colonial system. Therefore, when considering the post-colonial narratives that Namibians must still wage the struggle for economic independence, the migrant workers in post-colonial Namibia must learn to establish viable political partnerships that work to end their suppression and exploitation and, instead, help them create wealth and end their "ruhepo."

It therefore remains a task for future research to compare and contrast the past struggle of workers to the present and analyse what economic reforms have taken place for the workers in Namibia's post-colonial economy and how far such economic reforms remain useful or detrimental to the workers' struggle.

Introduction

The systematic official organization of the Contract Labour System (CLS) in Namibia took root with the institutionalization of CLS in the early 1920s and only ended in 1971–72 after which recruitment was taken over by labour bureaus in the respective former homelands of Ovambo and Kavango under new labour agreements. Contract labour was an insitutionalised system under which recruiting agencies or institutions recruited labourers to work in the central and southern part of Namibia usually for six to eighteen months. Under this system, any men above the age of sixteen years or mature enough to work and not having any disabilities could be recruited. Once recruited, the labourer had no rights over the type of employment or to negotiate the salary. The recruiting agency effectively sold these labourers to various employers and the labourers remained bound to their employer for the contractual period and were expected not to break the contract. The contract labour system was a colonial strategy to regulate the flow of labour for the colonial economy by cutting down on the tendency of labourers to choose employment on the basis of better wages and in this way control and reduce their tendency to strike.

This book studies contract labourers' engagement with the contract labour system. In particular, it draws on oral sources, a review of literature and archival sources, to explore how the life histories and the voices of the contract labourers from the Kavango contribute to our understanding of the contract labour system in Namibia. In particular, it asks what light these narratives shed on migration and on new living and working experiences, on workers' experiences with recruiting organizations and local recruiting agents and the effect of the contract labour system on labourers and community life. It asks: is it possible to view the migration of the Kavango labourers as a progressive step, or does the paradigm of exploitation and suppression remain the dominant one?

The book points to the gradual inclusion of the Kavango into the contract labour system. Although contract labourers made their own decision to leave home to get recruited, they did so under compelling "ruhepo" (poverty/hardship) that resulted from the controlling activities of the colonial officials. Labour narratives point to many journeys both within and outside Namibia to earn money to purchase clothing, which they lacked locally, and to create wealth as a means to address "Ruhepo" (poverty/hardship) within their communities. As contract labourers embarked on their journey they realized the collaboration between the colonial officials and recruiting agents who controlled and exploited them.

From the perspective of contract labourers, the contract labour system was nothing but slavery as they felt treated like property to be sold. The naming of employers by contact labourers became a way of dealing emotionally with this mistreatment. The memory of the "missus" lingers on centrally because labourers related to their home experience of the submissive role of women and, therefore, they could have found it traumatizing to be shouted at by a white woman. The labourers adapted to new colonial times and a new rhythm of labour such as bells and whistles. They developed good inter-ethnic relations among themselves. The impact of the contract labour system was that contract labourers gained benefits, but these benefits were small and non-lasting and not worth the suffering, exploitation and the loss they endured, while necessitating their continuous return to contract. The book points to this cycle of entrapment for contract labourers, which eventually led to the political mobilizing of workers by South West Africa People's Organization's (SWAPO) activists. The contract labourers' mobilization extended to the Kavango and resulted in rebelliousness against SWANLA and its institutions.

While this book hopes to contribute to ending silences about the Kavango's engagement within the contract labour system, it also points to the need for future research highlighting women's narratives about their place under the contract labour system history, as well as about the postcolonial labour migration to the charcoal and grape farms which, as narratives of the former Kavango contract labourers show, continues. For the first time, the voices of the contract labourers about the contract labour system are explored and herein exists the uniqueness of this book.

The book is structured as follows: the general introduction provides the background, higlights and significance of the contract labour system. It further provides the empirical research methods used to collect and analyse data by specifically highlighting the use of oral sources, archival and a review of literature as key sources. Chapter one explores the development of the contract labour system in the Kavango and explains the foundation for participation in the contract labour system which was laid down by colonialism through early European hunters and traders. It explains the colonial labour demands made on the Kavango and what strategies the colonial administration used to extract labour and why, despite the creation of a market of consumption for European goods in Kavango, scant numbers of men went for contract work during the German colonial period compared to the South African colonial period. This chapter explores the formalization of the contract labour system from 1925 to 1972 through the formation of official recruiting organizations and their activities in the Kavango. It underlines the centrality of colonialism in the development of the contract labour system.

Chapter two deals with labour migration from the Kavango and shows why the contract labourers saw it as a system where they were a purchased commodity. It compares recruitment figures from the Kavango and Ovamboland to indicate that there was never the same interest attached to labour migration from the Kavango as in former Ovamboland, and that while the labour migration figures improved during the South African colonial period compared to the German period, generally, labour migration from the Kavango was always low. The chapter provides the reasons for migration by contract labourers and the labour migration journeys. It also explores the place of women in the labour narratives of men and addresses their role in the contract labour system. Rather than relying solely on the colonial documents in the archives and on written sources, this chapter integrates them with oral life histories.

Chapter three is about the living and working places of contract labourers. It explores the experiences of contract labourers on farms, mines and compounds. The aim is to explain how their experiences in these places shaped the development of a political culture. Furthermore, it looks at the political mobilization of workers in their communities against SWANLA and the contract labour system, which culminated in the general workers' strike of 1971–72 and led to the abolition of the contract system and to the new labour arrangements.

Chapter four explores the contract labourers' views of the contract labour system and what impact it had upon them and answers the question whether the engagement into the contract labour system was a progressive step, or whether the notion of exploitation remained dominant.

A general conclusion chapter seeks to draw the major threads of the book together to highlight the contribution oral histories from the Kavango make towards understanding the contract labour system in Namibia. In addition, it points to what independent Namibia faces with regard to addressing the challenges of the former contract labourers. Such post-independence family hardships can be explained better when placed in the historical context of the voices of contract labourers on their engagement under the contract labour system in Namibia.

Historiographical review on the contract labour system

A body of literature exists on the contract labour system in Namibia, but this is based largely on research on former Ovamboland. Richard Moorsom was a pioneer scholar on the contract labour system in Namibia. His works date back to the 1970s but in 1997 these were assembled into one solid volume.[1] His work focuses on exploring a peripheral society at the time when contacts with white settlers, companies or colonial officials were minimal or

---

[1] R. Moorsom. (1997), *Underdevelopment and labour migration: the contract labour system in Namibia*. Chr, Norway, Michelsen Institute, Bergen.

nonexistent and argues that even in such conditions Ovambo and Nkumbi society underwent a process of underdevelopment essentially similar to that of other African people who became impoverished labour exporting peasantries.² Moorsom provides an analysis of the political economy of Namibia and investigates the origins of an institutionalized structure of labour exploitation, the contract labour system, which he argues was central to colonial power and profit. He argues that the central interest of colonial authorities in human resource was their labour power and that after the 1904 rebellion by the Hereros, Nama/Damara groups, the level of recruitment from the ranks of the dispossessed consistently failed to meet the aggregate labour demand of colonial capital and the state.³ This motivated both the German (1885–1915) and South African (1915–1990) colonial regimes to conserve the remaining subsistence areas for labour recruitment purposes. His work further explores the workers' strike against the contract labour system and discusses some background factors conditioning the consciousness of the Ovambo contract workers and he makes a few tentative observations on the general significance of the strike for its participants.

Stals' doctoral dissertation dealt with the contacts between the whites and the Ovambo in South West Africa from 1850 to 1915.⁴ He focused on the people of Ovamboland and the first travellers and traders among them between 1850 and 1870 and how the latter contributed to the depletion of the Ovambo natural resources and led to the impoverishment of the Ovambo population. He explores the arrival and activities of missionaries in Ovamboland from 1870 to 1883 and their eventual expansion up to 1915 as well as their intermediary roles in the contract labour system. He explores the relation between the Ovambo and the German colonial government from 1885 to 1915 and shows how the German government used them as labourers in South West Africa from 1898 to 1915 by signing protection treaties and securing the cooperation of Ovambo chiefs.

Silvester's doctoral thesis focused mainly on the relationship between black pastoralists and white farmers in southern Namibia and he indicates how the white farmers, with the legal support of the colonial state, dispossessed the black pastoralists of their land and compelled many into becoming labourers for the white farmers. He touches on how migrant farm workers from the northern part of Namibia, who worked for the white farmers in the south, aspired to escape the farming sector and enter other higher paid sectors of the labour market.⁵

---

2 *Ibid.*, p. 12.
3 *Ibid.*, p. 20.
4 E.L.P. Stals. (1967), Die aanraking tussen blankes en Ovambo's in Suid Wes Afrika 1850–1915. M.A Thesis, Universiteit van Stellenbosch.
5 J.G. Silvester. (1993), Black pastoralists, white farmers: the dynamics of land dispossession and labour recruitment in Southern Namibia, 1915–1955. PhD Thesis, University of London).

Allan Cooper has pointed to the trend in Namibian historiography on the contract labour system where scholars have focused mainly on the South West Africa Native Labour Association (SWANLA) as a recruiting labour organization between 1944 and 1972, but have given inadequate attention to its predecessors, the Southern Labour Organization (SLO) and Northern Labour Organization (NLO) which operated in the period between 1925 and 1943.[6] His analysis confirms the centrality of the diamond industry for explaining the nature of contract labour, and much of Namibian politics itself, during the twentieth century in Namibia. He shows how and why the discovery of diamonds in Namibia was profoundly important for the territory and especially how and why it transformed the political fabric of Ovambo society. He argues that it is instructive to review how SWANLA emerged as a conduit for contract labour in Namibia. His study uses archival documents from the SLO and the NLO to reveal how the contract labour system was created and institutionalized in Namibia beginning in the 1920s. He analyzes the effect the contract labour system had on political traditional authorities in Ovamboland, and how the diamond industry specifically was served by this manner of labour recruitment.

A publication by the International Defense and Aid Fund (hereafter IDAF) explained the nature of the labour control system in Namibia and its origins in colonial rule and how the violent expropriation of land by the white minority laid the basis for the migrant labour system for Namibians within the police zone.[7]

Goldblatt discusses the history of Namibia from the beginning of the nineteenth century and deals with the nature of colonialism.[8] He explores the process of land settlement by white farm settlers on crown land under a colonial land settlement scheme and shows how this was dependent upon an adequate supply of local labour. His book explains the dearth of labour for the colonial economy after the Herero and Nama uprisings (1904–1906) and how these necessitated a development of labour policies to regulate the supply of contract labour in Namibia. He provides an understanding of the process of land dispossession of Africans in Namibia under which arable land had been given over to white settlers and also the policies that were soon developed to induce Africans to offer their labour into the colonial economy. His book shows that the contract labour system in Namibia was a well calculated step of the colonial government to promote the colonial economy at the expense of most Namibians.

---

[6] A.D. Cooper. (1999), Institutionalization of contract labour in Namibia, *Journal of Southern African Studies*, 25(1): pp. 121–138.

[7] IDAF. (1987), *Working under South African occupation, labour in Namibia*. London, Canon Collins.

[8] I. Goldblatt. (1971), *History of South West Africa from the beginning of the nineteenth century*. Cape Town, Juta & Company Limited.

An edited book on Namibia under the South African rule, discusses the mobility of communities in Namibia and the colonial efforts at containment during the first three decades of South African colonization.[9] The editors explain that although the sealing off of the north was intended to exclude the region from the political development further south, this did not work as contract labour migrants transmitted ideas and thoughts from south to north and vice-versa.[10] This book, however, does not include the Kavango but acknowledges the exclusion and the editors state that it was an initial exploration of the period of South African colonization and the beginning of what they hoped would be the end of a very big silence.

Banghart in his study presented various reasons in order of importance to explain why Ovambo men went on contract work and indicated that the highest percentage went because of poverty.[11] His view of poverty as the central cause for migration of Ovambo contract labourers has been supported by other scholars.[12]

Although Hayes' thesis[13] is not centrally about the contract labour system, she presents substantial information on migrant labour history in Ovambo. She shows that migrant labour from southern Angola and northern Namibia antedated colonial control by twenty-five years and a clear distinction must therefore be drawn between conditions, which initially stimulated migrant labour and later colonial interventions, which maintained and augmented this flow. She argues that migration cannot be reduced to an environmental squeeze, nor was labour migration completely determined by the nature of internal controls. The central areas of causation, whether ecological or social, are therefore not the real issue: it is their interaction. Hayes suggests that the most useful question to ask here is what caused whom to migrate towards labour centres? In addition, the timing is important: what caused whom to migrate when?[14] Such are some of the questions that this book addresses in relation to the Kavango area.

R.J. Gordon has drawn attention to the centrality of mines and their compounds for understanding the economy of southern Africa and its society. He laments the scarcity of public knowledge about life in the compound which he sets out to explore. Using the para-

---

[9] P. Hayes et al. (eds.) (1998), *Namibia under South African rule: mobility& containment 1915–1946*. Oxford, James Curry Ltd.
[10] *Ibid.*, pp. 24–25.
[11] P. Banghart. (1969), 'Migrant labour in South West Africa and its effect on Ovambo tribal life'. M.A Thesis, University of Stellenbosch.
[12] J.B. Gewald. (2003), Near death in the streets of Karibib: famine, migrant labor and the coming of Ovambo to central Namibia, *Journal of African Studies*, (44): p. 221.
[13] P. Hayes. (1992), A History of the Ovambo of Namibia, c. 1880–1935. Doctor of Philosophy in History, University of Cambridge.
[14] *Ibid.*, p. 146.

digm of the normative and interpretive he seeks to answer the question as to why a high number of labourers were leaving contract at the time when the economy had high recruitment needs and he shows this was due to the set up of the mine structures which oppressed the worker.[15]

In another piece of academic work, R.J.Gordon used archival documents, written books and articles to explore the impact of the Second World War (1939–1945) on Namibia, which also features a rape case in the Kavango.[16] His aim was to explain what impact military service had, both economically but, more importantly, on consciousness? He asks how important were the external stimuli for the development of nationalism? His article shows that the massive stealing and rape by military recruiting officials in the Kavango made Chiefs discontented and turned them against further military and labour recruiting activities, a situation which contributed to the demobilization and harsh punishment of those Kavango soldiers who were found guilty. He shows that the unwillingness of the colonial administration to pay the black ex-service men for their war efforts frustrated them and increased nationalistic and anti-colonial feelings. Furthermore, Gordon shows how the knowledge that the Second World War was fought for freedom was reinterpreted by contract labourers and applied to their own situation to mean the freedom to choose the type of employment and employer.[17]

Some authors have drawn attention to the origin of the workers' resistance to the contract labour system and eventually to colonialism. Tommy Emmet, for example, examines the beginning of resistance and the development of the feeling of nationalism in Namibia during the South African period. He analyzed the nature of colonial rule and labour control during the early years of South African control in Namibia, the expropriation of land for white settlement through land settlement laws and its disastrous effects for blacks. He argues that climatic and ecological conditions created the conditions for labour migration from Ovamboland and southern Angola and fluctuations in labour migration from these areas were closely tied to the supply of food in the area. He explores the exploitative nature of labour policies on contract laborers and the conditions they encountered in the working and living environments on the mines and how these led to the popular resistance.[18] Emmet's work is useful, it shows that the root of popular nationalism in Namibia emerged from the

---

[15] R.J. Gordon. (1977), *Mines, masters and migrants: life in a Namibian compound.* Johannesburg, Ravan press (Pty) Ltd, 1977.
[16] R.J. Gordon. (1993), The impact of the Second World War on Namibia. *Journal of Southern African Studies,* 19(1): pp. 147–165.
[17] *Ibid.,* pp. 148, 162.
[18] T. Emmet. (1999), *Popular resistance and the roots of nationalism in Namibia, 1915–1966.* Basel, P Schlettwein publishing, pp. 176–177.

contract labour system and thus presents the contract labour system as a central feature in the political history of Namibia.

There are other accounts by foreign evangelists working in Namibia which touched on the contract labour system such as was the work by Rauha Voipio. Voipio sought to present a view of the system from those who experienced it. Her methodology though was limited to questionnaires which were sent to various Evangelical Lutheran church congregations in Ovamboland in the early 1970s. She shows that the dislike of the contract labour system was strong even before the 1971–1972 worker strike.[19]

There are also works on the contract labour system sympathetic to SWAPO and the liberation cause which have mainly tended to look at the exploitative nature of the contract labour system on Namibians and therefore explains the SWAPO armed struggle in that historical context. For example, Gillian and Suzanne Cronje draw attention to the conditions under which Namibia's black labour force lived and worked and the implications of the apartheid economy for family life. They document the resistance to South African rule, the origin of SWAPO within the contract labour system and how the apartheid authorities exploited "tribal" sentiments to split and weaken the liberation movement. This book explores the strategies during the South African rule to induce labour for the colonial economy on Namibians. They show the importance of the Christian missions for the contract labour system in that missions were required to urge all Africans under their influence to seek employment in South West Africa.[20]

Autobiographical writings exist which explore contract labourers' personal experiences with the contract labour system and show how such experiences made them join SWAPO in the fight for the liberation of Namibia.[21] A similarity in these accounts is that most, if not all, were written by former contract labourers who became freedom fighters and as such their stories do not show that there were any positive aspects of the contract labour system. They instead point to how the exploitation of the contract labour system was central to their eventual political stand against the system and colonialism as a whole.

---

[19] R. Voippo. (1981), Contract work through Ovambo eyes. In R.G. Green, K. Kiljunen, M.L. Kiljunen (eds.), *Namibia the last colony*. Essex, Longman, pp. 116–120.

[20] Gillian and Suzanne Cronje. (1979), *The workers of Namibia*. International Defence and Aid Fund for Southern Africa, London.

[21] V. Ndadi. (1989), *Breaking contract: the story of Vinnia Ndadi*. Bunbury, IDAF; J. Ya Otto. (1982), *Battlefront Namibia: an autobiography*. London, Heinemann; H. Shetyuwete. (1990), *Never follow the wolf: the autobiography of a Namibian freedom fighter*. London, Kliptown; S. Nujoma. (2001), *Where others wavered: the autobiography of Sam Nujoma – my life and participation in the liberation in the struggle of Namibia*. London, PANAF books; D.K. Ausiku. (2005), My own life stories: is this God's work or Satan's scheme? (Unpublished manuscript, Canada, copy right no. ISBN 0-1038934.

Hishongwa provides a historical perspective on the contract labour system and its effects on family and social life in Namibia. Her small but insightful book describes the exploitative nature of the contract labour system and shows how and why the Namibian workers protested against the contract labour system and why many workers in Namibia united and joined SWAPO, the liberation movement. Her book is useful for an understanding of how the contract labour system impacted on the family and social life of the contract labourers in Ovamboland. However, there is room for expanding on this small beginning. Her passing comment on the abuse of alcohol by contract laborers, for instance, brings forth the need to explore further the history of alcohol usage in communities and whether the contract labour system encouraged alcoholism.[22]

Kane-Berman has traced the development of the contract labour system in Namibia and the eventual factors that led to the 1971 strike by contract workers. He explores the twin policy objective of contract labour system of meeting the white controlled economy's demand for labour, while at the same time keeping to a minimum the number of non-employed Africans in "white areas" through the application of labour laws and pass laws in Namibia and how these affected the contract labourers and their families. The report shows that the labour force in compounds was prohibited from political and trade union activities, which depressed wages and contributed to the general workers' strike of 1971. The report is limited to the Ovambo contract workers' experiences.[23]

G. Bauer's thesis analyzed the development of labour unions for workers and of their status in independent in Namibia.[24] Bauer provides some useful information on the 1971–1972 general workers' strike, how it evolved and what impact it had on contract labourers, especially in Ovamboland.

This review of the literature points to how the 1970s was a significant moment for the production of narratives on the contract labour system. Many key and influential accounts emerged from this period. Since then there have been a few works which focused on explaining the contract labour system and worker's resistance.

The historiographical review points to several silences and neglected areas of exploration. Firstly, the South African colonial authority was a central political agent behind the genesis of contract labour system in Namibia, its aim was to ensure that there were always adequate numbers of labourers to exploit the minerals and maximize profit. Yet, despite its centrality, there has been inadequate focus on its role and interaction with recruiting agents

---

[22] N. Hishongwa. (1992), *The contract labour system and its effects on family and social life in Namibia*. Windhoek, Gamsberg Macmillan.
[23] J. Kane-Berman. (1972), *Contract labour in South West Africa*. Johannesburg, SAIRR.
[24] G. M. Bauer. (1994), The labor movement and the prospect of democracy in Namibia. PhD Thesis, Wisconsin Madison.

in labour recruitments. Secondly, the focus of the literature has been largely on Ovamboland. The Kavango as a supplier of contract labour is neglected. Thirdly, very few have drawn on oral histories of contract labourers. In these written accounts, the contract labourer as a person who has a family history, who engages in the economy and who verbalizes what this meant for him is missing. This book thus seeks to explore these personal narratives of those from the Kavango. The need to draw on oral narratives from the Kavango arose from an observation during my personal discussions with old men when I was a teacher in the Kavango (2002–2003 and 2006–2007). Many of them spoke of having worked as contract labourers and complained of family hardships and of the continuing recruitments from the Kavango to the farms in the former police zone. An interest developed to understand their experiences of the contract labour system drawing on these voices.

In general, the Kavango has been a neglected area of study in Namibia. Kampungu argued in the 1960s that the Kavango did not appeal to many researchers. They regarded the Kavango ethnic groups as having strayed away from their original home and to have broken away from either the Ovambo, or other Angolan ethnic groups which they resemble linguistically and culturally. This belief about the Kavango consequently engendered the idea that a scientific investigation of the Kavango people would not serve any purpose since they are better studied through the other larger groups from which they are believed to have broken away. The hardship involved in travelling to Kavango was another reason for the neglect of the study of the Kavango, as researchers were unwilling to make such a difficult journey.[25]

Despite the concerns raised by Kampungu there were unpublished colonial sources on the Kavango. These included official documents from visiting colonial officials, the Catholic and Finish missionaries and the permanent colonial staff such as the Natives Affairs Commissioners.

Since the 1960s, however, a few doctoral studies on the Kavango have emerged. The PhD thesis by Romanus Kampungu was the first academic work by a local scholar. It dealt with the marriage customs among the Kavango people and yielded valuable information on Kavango pre-colonial history.[26] Several students from University of Stellenbosch and Port Elizabeth completed their doctoral works on the Kavango in the 1960s.[27] A linguistic

---

[25] R. Kampungu. (1965), Concept and aim of Okavango marriage customs. Doctor of Canon Law, Pontifical University of Propaganda Fide, Rome, pp. 8–89.
[26] R. Kampungu. (1965), *ibid*. Concept and Aims of Okavango Marriage Customs. Doctor of Canon Law, Pontifical University of Propaganda Fide.
[27] Studies supervised by Bruwer included those by M. J, Olivier. (1961), Inboorlingbeleid en administrasie in die mandaatgebied van Suidwes-Afrika (PhD Thesis, University of Stellenbosch; J. L. Bosch. (1964), Die Shambiu van die Okavango: a volkundige studie. (PhD Thesis, Stellenbosch University; L.L, Van Tonder. (1966), The Hambukushu of Okavangoland: an anthropological study of a South Western Bantu People in Africa (PhD Thesis, University of Port Elizabeth.

study by Willem Mohling in 1967 focused on the Vagciriku language.[28] As Akuupa comments, the scholarly studies of the 1960s "without doubt assisted in the construction of the imagined colonial Kavango identity and nation".[29] The 1981 publication by Gibson and his colleagues on "the Kavango people[30]" was "in many ways a repetition of the works of Bosch and Kampungu".[31] More academic works emerged in the 1980s. In 1983 Josef Brian Diescho provided an analysis of the Odendaal Commission of enquiry into South West Africa Affairs 1962–1963 and its impact on the Kavango.[32] In 1992 Herbert Ndango Diaz's doctoral thesis analyzed the "Tjakova" myth of the Kavango people.[33] Samuel Kavheto Mbambo's doctoral thesis in 2002 dealt with the various indigenous knowledge systems of the Kavango with specific focus on the traditional healings among the Vagciriku people of the Kavango.[34] An anthropological research study was undertaken by Mattia Fumanti in 2003. He focused on "the process of elite formation and the making of the public space in Rundu against the background of a wider transformation in post-colonial Namibia, which puts forward an alternative view of the youth in intergenerational relations, so often stereotyped as resistance, rebellion and protest".[35]

There are also published history articles and books on the Kavango by M. Fisch, (1983, 1984 and 1994), Fleisch and Mohling (2002) and Inge Brinkman 1999.[36] Other published archeological articles are by Sandelowsky which studied the artifacts uncovered in the Kavango.[37] Meredith Mckitrick's article of 2008 critically engaged with notions of power and identity of the riparian communities of the Kavango.[38]

---

[28] W. J. G. Mohlig. (1967), Die Sprache der Dciriku: phonologie, prosodologie und morphologie. (PhD Thesis, University of Cologne, 1967).

[29] M. U. Akuupa. (2011), The Formation of 'National Culture' in post-apartheid Namibia. (PhD thesis, UWC). p. 114.

[30] D. G. Gibson, T.J, Larson, C. R, McGurk. (1981), *The Kavango peoples*. Wiesbaden, Steiner Verlag GMBH.

[31] M.U. Akuupa, *ibid.*, p. 114.

[32] J. B. Diescho. (1983), An analysis of the Odendaal commission of enquiry into South West Africa Affairs 1962–1963, with specific reference to its findings, recommendations and implementation in respect of Kavango. M.A Thesis, University of Fort Hare.

[33] H. N. Diaz. (1992), A definitive edition and analysis of the Tjakova myth of the Kavango. PhD Thesis, University of Cape Town.

[34] S. K. Mbambo. (2002), Heal with God: indigenous healing and religion among the Vagciriku of the Kavango region, Namibia. PhD Thesis, Utrecht University.

[35] M. Fumanti. (2003), Youth, elites and distinction in a northern Namibia town (PhD Thesis, University of Manchester, p. 10.

[36] M. Fisch. (1983), Der kriegszug der Tawana zum Kavango' *Namibiana*, 4, (2): pp. 43–71; M. Fisch. (1984), Die Kavangofischer im nordosten Namibias. Jagdmethoden, religios-magische praktiken, lieder und preisgedichte. *Namibiana*, 5 (1): pp. 105–169; M. Fisch. (1994), *Die Kavangojagter im nordosten Namibias*. Windhoek, Scientific Society.

[37] B.H. Sandelowsky. (1979), Kapako and Vungu-vhungu: Iron Age sites on the Kavango River, Goodwin Series (3) Iron Age Studies in Southern Africa *Southern Africa Archaeological Society*, pp. 52–61.

[38] M. McKittrick. (2008), landscapes of power: ownership and identity on the middle Kavango

Akuupa's argument that since Namibia's independence, the Kavango region remained in a constant struggle to position itself in the national discourse of history is relevant. One significant boost for Kavango studies has come from the efforts of Professor Patricia Hayes who since 2004, through the generous funding from the Carl Schlettwein Foundation of Basel Switzerland, assisted students from the Kavango region to pursue post graduate studies at the History Department at the University of the Western Cape. As a result, several theses were completed in History.[39] The Anthropology Department has similarly produced several theses.[40] Other local scholars such as Haingura (2017) completed a PhD in Bantu linguistics focusing on a critical evaluation of Rumanyo.[41] While there has been some encouraging development in the literature on the Kavango since Kampungu's pioneering work, the Kavango's engagement with the contract labour system and the narratives of its labourers remains a huge lacuna despite the small attempts by this author since 2016 to publish on contract the labour system in Namibia.[42]

River, Namibia' *Journal of Southern Africa Studies*, 34 (4), pp. 785–802.

[39] See K.M Likuwa. (2005), Rundu, Kavango: a case study of forced relocation in Namibia, 1954 to 1972 (MA thesis, University of the Western Cape); A.H. Nambadi. (2007), The Kavango legislative council, 1970–1979: a critical analysis. MA thesis, University of the Western Cape; H.K. Karapo. (2008), Living memory in a forgotten war zone: the Ukwangali district of Kavango and the Namibian liberation struggle, 1966–1989 (MA thesis, University of the Western Cape.

[40] These include M. M. J. Shirungu. (2016), The use of medicinal plants to treat mental illness in Kavango East and West regions, Namibia. PhD Thesis, University of the Western Cape; M.U. Akuupa. (2011), The formation of 'National culture' in post-apartheid Namibia: a focus on state sponsored cultural festivals in Kavango region. PhD Thesis, University of the Western Cape. M.U. Akuupa. (2006), Checking the Kulcha: local discourses of culture in Kavango region of Namibia. MA thesis, University of the Western Cape; M.J.M. Shirungu. (2010), Cultural and social factors impacting on the programme to prevent mother to child transmission (PMTCT) of HIV in Namibia: a case study of the Kavango. MA thesis, University of the Western Cape.

[41] P. Haingura. (2017), A critical evaluation of the development of Rumanyo as a national language in Namibia. PhD thesis, University of the Western Cape.

[42] See for example, K. Likuwa. (2016), The contract Labour System during the South African Colonial Period in Kavango. In M Kudumo & J Silvester (eds.), *Resistance on the banks of the Kavango River*. Windhoek, Museums Association of Namibia, pp. 29–52; K Likuwa (2015), Colonialism and the development of contract labour system in Kavango. In J. Silvester (ed.), *Re-viewing resistance in Namibian History*. (Windhoek, UNAM Press); K Likuwa. (2014), Contract labourers from Kavango on farms in Namibia, 1925–1972, *Journal of Namibian Studies* (16): pp. 47–60; K Likuwa & N Shiweda. (2017), Okaholo: Contract labour system and lessons for post colonial Namibia. *Mgbakoigba: Journal of African Studies*, 6 (2), pp. 26–47; Likuwa, K.M. & Shiweda, N. (2018), Native recruiters activities along the Kavango River boundary in north east Namibia, 1925 to 1943. *Journal of Namibian Studies*, (23), pp. 87 –100.

Archival sources

Many scholars have pointed to a need to engage more critically with archives making it the subject of study rather than simply mining these for information.[43] The archival sources were one significant source for this book, but these were used cautiously. Stoler has argued that the Archive is a "technology of rule". The colonial state produced information so as to better control its subject.[44] While Stoler has argued the necessity of reading the archive "along the grain" and this is an important academic project, this book continues in the tradition of scholars who have long used archives reading it "against the grain".[45] The archive provides insight into the state's goals, its activities and the knowledge needed for control of the colonial subject.

There are several collections at the National Archives of Namibia (hereafter as NAN) in Windhoek that were perused. These included the Administration (hereafter ADM) files which contained official documentation by the South African colonial administration regarding the Kavango. It included information on WENELA recruitment from the Kavango, monthly reports on labour conditions inside Namibia in the 1950s, monthly reports on labour conditions and on the treatment of labourers in Namibia, reports on labour conditions of the northern district of Kavango, transportation of contract labourers between Grootfontein and Runtu and between Runtu and Katwitwi area etc.

The files in Native Affairs of Tsumeb (hereafter NAT) collection dealt with recommendations of the farm labour commission, notes on attesting officers regarding the issue of permits to employ Extra Territorial and Northern Natives, (hereafter E.T. and N) their control and repatriation, employment of A and B class labourers by farmers, etc. There are also the Natives Affairs of Rundu (hereafter, NAR) files that contain letters of correspondence between the NLO officials and the Natives Affairs Commissioner of the Kavango ranging from the period between 1925 and 1942. Among other things, it includes the following: letters of correspondence regarding the recruitment and activities of runners for the NLO in the Kavango, activities of labour escorts from Kavango to the police zone, recruitment of Rhodesian and Angola natives, classification of labour recruits, presentations of gifts between Kavango Chiefs and colonial administration officials, testimonies of labourers regarding conditions under which they had been recruited, tribal trust fund for the Kavango Native territory, native recruiters, etc.

---

[43] See for instance A.L. Stoler. (2002), Colonial Archives and the art of governance: on the content and form. In C. Hamilton et al., *Refiguring the archive*. Cape Town, David Phillip, pp. 87–109.
[44] Stoler. (2002), *ibid.* p. 92.
[45] *Ibid.*

The South West Africa Administration (hereafter SWAA) collection includes among others, reports on the Kavango expedition by the chamber of mines in 1924, reports by the accounting officer on the expenditures on Kavango recruits, labour supply and statistics from the Kavango, examination, vaccination and repatriation of medically rejected labour recruits, recruitment of minors, improvements on recruitment of Kavango workers, deserters, returning labourers' complaints, special guard for labour, unemployed Africans in Ovambo and Kavango Native Territories, arrangements for the new Rundu labour recruiting station, passes to African women who are wives of labour recruits, the supply of passes and rations to labour recruits, memoranda on native labourers, monthly distribution roll list of native labour, etc.

Despite all this rich archival material, a reliance only on these will lead to the production of history from above.[46] The colonial archives cannot represent the feelings, beliefs and interpersonal relations of the ordinary people. In South Africa, historians have been careful about relying on government records because of the colonial and later apartheid biases of such records. Archival materials have been subjected to changes, careful selections and exclusions. The illusion of the official state archive as a site of knowledge production has been questioned and instead additional means of acquiring sources for history are required. These alternatives include literature, landscape, dance, art and oral interviewing. For the purpose of this book, oral interviewing was chosen.

Oral interviews

Oral interviews were carried out among the former contract labourers from Kavango. I carried out oral interviews from July to September 2009 within the Kavango area of Namibia with a plan to have an adequate representation of interviewees from across the area. To do so, oral interviews were conducted from the Ukwangali area at Nankudu village in western Kavango to the Mbukushu area at Kamutjonga village in the eastern Kavango.

Although the Kavango of Namibia is the area where oral interviews were carried out, the term Kavango (unless specifically differentiated) will apply to both the Namibian and Angolan sides of the Kavango River that extends to the Kuito River. When the former contract labourers crossed the Kavango River interchangeably they did not consider it as crossing two different countries. The contract labourers' narratives challenge the idea of the Kavango River as a national boundary and therefore to limit the writing of the history of their experiences to either side would be limiting the way in which they want their history represented.

---

[46] C. S. Rassool. (2004), The individual, auto/biography and history in South Africa. PhD Thesis, University of the Western Cape, p. 23.

Kavango (which means small place among the Shambyu and Gciriku people) was originally used to refer to the river. The Hambukushu people offer another explanation and suggest the name "rware rwa Kangumbe" (the river of Kangumbe) as the original name of the river. This is in reference to their narratives that Kangumbe was the man who led the party of hunters that tracked an injured elephant and discovered the river after which the Hambukushu people settled at the river. Many theories about the meaning and usage of the word Kavango exist alongside each other and are contested.

During both the German (1885–1915) and later the South African regime in Namibia (1915–1990) "Okavango" was used by the colonialists to refer to the river but since the 1970s the "O" prefix was dropped and "Kavango" was used as a collective colonial identity label to refer strictly to the Kwangali, Mbunza, Shambyu, Gciriku and Mbukushu ethnic groups under one homeland. All other African people in the Kavango homeland were regarded as immigrants. The map below shows the Kavango area from the local people's perspective extending as far as the Kuito River.

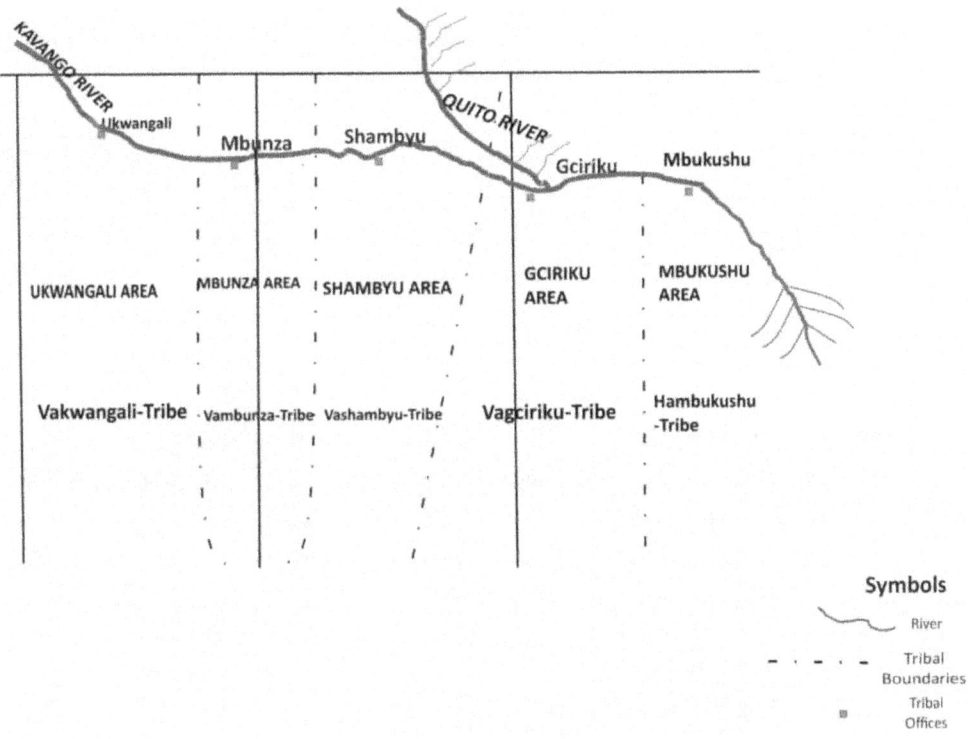

Map 1: Courtesy: Karoline. M. Karupu, Windhoek, 2020. Original map taken from H.N. Dias, (1992), a Definite Edition and Analysis of Tjakova Myth of the Kavango, PhD thesis, University of Cape Town, p.13.

The narratives of former contract labourers were used empirically for information about their experiences and attention was given towards analyzing these narratives for meaning. These interviews are not meant to be seen as attempts to "fill a gap" left by an archive as the archive represents just a "sliver and not total knowledge".[47] However, oral interviews are a crucial alternative to state produced knowledge through the archives. Oral interviews were carried out with a focus on historical change.[48] Through people's oral histories one is able to learn more about their communities since individual experiences are shaped by the development of a lifecycle and the ways in which external crises and situations have impinged on this.[49] The use of oral sources, however, has its own challenges. Oral sources are open to modifications, selections and exclusions similar to the documentary record. They are not mutually exclusive of written sources and "they have common characteristics as well as autonomous and specific functions which only either one can fulfil. The undervaluing and the overvaluing of oral sources ends up by cancelling out specific qualities, turning them either into mere support for traditional written sources, or into an illusory cure for all ills".[50] Oral history was not used as a means to an end but as an alternative to exploring the memories of contract labourers about their experience of the contract labour system, their feelings, hopes and aspirations. It provided an insight into the contract labour system in Namibia as experienced by the workers, which an archive could not do.

This book does not speak for the contract labourers or give them a voice as "this outdated rhetoric ignores how people do speak out in their daily lives".[51] Rather the book speaks about the contract labourers. It is a presentation of contract labourers' experiences and how they remember those experiences. Experience in a broader sense is what happens to people as they move on and engage with their daily life activities and gaining an understanding of these experiences is important towards making meanings of forms of change over time.[52]

I interviewed thirty people. Although two of the interviewees (Theresia Shidona and Mate Susana) were women, the study focused on men who had direct experience of being contract labourers. These two women were sisters and are my great grandmothers and they were interviewed separately during one of my various visits as a grandson who was interested in their life stories and stories of our extended family. Their life stories were useful as I

---

[47] Hamilton *et al.* (2002), *Refiguring the archive*, p. 17.
[48] R.L. Miller. (2000), *Researching life stories and family histories.* London, SAGE publication, p. 22.
[49] *Ibid.*
[50] A. Portelli. (1981), The peculiarities of oral history. *History Workshop Journal* (12), p. 97.
[51] S. Field *et al.* (2007), *Imagining the city: memories and cultures in Cape Town.* Cape Town: HSRC Press, p. 11.
[52] S. Field. (2001), Remembering experience, interpreting memory: life stories from Windermere, *African Studies*, 60(1): p. 127.

used them to make interpretations about community traditional life in the Kavango during the South African colonial period.

Oral interview researchers must always expect the unexpected in their field work which may impact on their field work process. During my stay in Ukwangali area for instance I hoped to get as many interviewees as possible under the guidance of my friend, a teacher at a school but it turned out differently. My friend relied on his father to introduce me to former contract labourers in the area. As it turned out his father informed us that all the old men whom he considered "capable" of narrating the contract labour system history had moved away into the bush villages far from our reaches. Disappointed, I tried other means the next day but only secured two interviews. Hayes had a similar experience during her fieldwork in Ovamboland in 1989 to 1990 where more elderly informants tended to be located deep in the rural interior away from these roads and conurbations.[53] This shows that having links with people in a particular area of research does not always translate into automatic access to oral sources as other factors such as distance and accessibility of oral sources could impact on that process.

I was an insider researcher in the Kavango region in the sense that I was from the Kavango region and could speak and relate to all my interviewees in the various Kavango languages and had family members from all ethnic groups that I could relate to during my sojourns in those areas. While an insider researcher may expect advantages, this is not true in all situations. Bozzoli wrote about the women of Phokeng about the forms of consciousness they express in their histories. She indicates how her interviewer Mmtantho Nkotsoe in Phokeng was able to draw out of her subjects' stories of home and work that many white, or male, or outsider, researchers might struggle to obtain, even using the most scientific methods. Although Mmantho Nkotsoe was a trained historian and sociologist to the women she was interviewing she was seen as a kinswoman, a young girl, a child to some, who wanted to know the stories of the past all of which proved to be her strength.[54]

Such an advantage of being an insider researcher and of being regarded by interviewees as their kinsfolk was also displayed in my case. During my research in the Vagciriku community of which I am a member, it certainly became far easier to secure interviews but that did not leave out room for challenges. My success in Gciriku area was accorded to the fact that my mother lived in Gciriku area and was known by many people. All that I needed to secure an interview was not necessarily an official letter for research purpose but rather a family introduction to the interviewees about my names and those of my parents, which

---

[53] P. Hayes. (1992), A history of the Ovambo of Namibia, c1880–1935. PhD Thesis, University of Cambridge, p. 3
[54] B. Bozzoli. (1991), *Women of Phokeng*. Johannesburg, Ravan Press, pp. 6–7.

clan I belonged to etc. Such an introduction made many feel that I was a part of them and not an outsider. But this advantage as an insider was not always the case as at times an introduction was not enough to create a full attitude of openness in interviews. The limited openness could be explained by perhaps their feeling that I was not a closer family member rather than as a lack of clarity on their part as to the intention of my research. At times interviewees are known to tell interviewers only what they believe interviewers want to be told and very often what they say to interviewers may depend on their changing attitude towards the interviewer.[55] Such a possibility is not ruled out in my experience of oral interviewing of contract labourers in the Kavango where I had to work very hard to try to create a good rapport between myself and the interviewees.

The other reason for success in Gciriku area was that my uncle Mberekera owned a car (the Indian made Mahindra) and he was willing to drive me around anywhere as long as I provided diesel. This proved costly but useful and not only did my uncle act as a driver but he became a field assistant (by default) and in many cases he spoke first by way of introducing me to interviewees which reduced the tension in communication between the youth (the interviewer) and the elderly (interviewees). My uncle's role was consistent with the Vagciriku matrilineal community's custom where a maternal uncle is central to the lives of his sister's children and is expected to speak on their behalf in any situation. To speak first, in the presence of my uncle therefore would have been an act of disrespect, lack of social protocol and a forced takeover of his rightful duty. The above is presented as an example of a challenge to an insider researcher in his/her community to show the existence of family or community social values and protocols which an insider researcher may have to observe and which may have an impact on their oral interview data collection process. The insider researcher is in a better position to call upon common understanding between himself and his interviewees, appeal to common ideas of space, community boundaries, history, hierarchy and culture and may also show more sensitivity and empathy to those interviewees.[56] I had to show sensitivity to local cultural norms in the way I arranged interview sessions. Appointments for interviews were made a day in advance and were usually set for morning hours at nine which was an appropriate time not too early or too late for many interviewees. In the rural setting one had to be cautious and respect the village politics and power structures when arranging the interviews. Usually one has to either go through a member of the Village Development Committee (hereafter VDC) or simply through the village headman for permission to carry out oral interviews in that community. This was the case during my stay in Mbukushu area in the eastern part of Kavango. While at Divundu village, I went with

---

[55] Portelli. (1981), The peculiarities of oral history. *History Workshop Journal*, (12), p. 104.
[56] B. Bozzoli. (1991), *Women of Phokeng*. Johannesburg, Ravan Press, p. 8.

Kayo, a relative from that village who made prior arrangements for me with former contract labourers at Divundu through a VDC member. That morning, however, we met the same VDC member who confronted my relative Kayo and demanded we visit the headman of the village to first get his permission. My relative was disappointed with the VDC member's demand but nevertheless heeded. Permission was then granted.

The interview sessions lasted as long as the interviewees were willing to converse and therefore some interview sessions were as short as forty minutes while others were as long as two hours and thirty minutes. I had to try my best to allow the interviewee to speak more because to be a successful interviewer a set of skills are needed, including an understanding of human relationships such as being a good listener.[57] The difference in the duration of oral interviews could also indicate the value attached to the oral interview sessions by the interviewees. An interviewee may recount in a few words experiences which lasted a long time or spend too much time on brief events. Dwelling on an event may be a way to stress its importance or even to distract attention away from other sensitive issues.[58] Such factors are possible explanations for the difference in the duration of the oral interviews. Some interviewees found my explanation about their right to discontinue an interview if they so wished even during the interview process (as part of the ethical requirement process for research) very strange and laughable. They snapped back that they would not have agreed to an interview if they had not wanted one. A digital voice recorder was used to record the interview while I took photographs with a digital camera at the end of the interview sessions. The idea was to record their stories and make it easy for the interviewer to listen to the recorded interview process later. The use of electronic devices certainly had its own disadvantages. The presence of the recording device and the knowledge that they were being recorded changed the whole environment from a free to serious or tense atmosphere. Some believed the presence of the recording device meant their voices would be aired on the local radio and this was despite having informed them that this would not be the case. In a few cases domestic birds such as chickens made noises and interfered with the interview process.

The oral interview process can at times be used by interviewees as opportunities to educate the young ones (local interviewers) about the culture, history and achievements of their own people and to draw the interviewers in acknowledgment of the failures of the present.[59] The high level of education by the local scholars doing research in their own communities,

---

[57] P. Thompson. (1998), The voices of the past. In R. Perks and A. Thomson (eds.), *The oral history reader*. London, Routledge, pp. 26–27.
[58] A. Portelli. (2009), 'What makes oral history different', *ibid.*, p. 66.
[59] Bozzoli. (1991), *Women of Phokeng*, p. 9.

"while often treated as something to be valued may also be assumed by the local people as rendering local scholars ignorant of local history and culture".[60]

I too had a direct challenge from my great grandmother, Susana Mate Kamwanga, who questioned the effectiveness of the method of recording to collect data from the elders in our community and about the loss of culture by the current generation in comparison to those of the past. After I had requested to record her story she responded that "In the past, when the sun had set, children sat around the fire and the elders told them about their family history and origin. They were not like you the children of nowadays who only want to record to go and write in books. What will you get out of it? You will get nothing out of it".[61] Mate Kamwanga clearly gave me a message that African researchers have lost touch with an appropriate African setting of collecting or sharing oral history. Such criticism evokes the need to find or revive means on how best to reintegrate the African method of imparting information to the western research methods.

I had some specific questions for my male interviewees: why did you go on contract labour, how was your journey, what happened to you upon your arrival at your work destination, what work did you do on contract, what impact did the contract labour system have upon you, what is your feeling about your contract work experiences? I, however, allowed interviewees to freely narrate their life histories. The belief is that community history is embedded in individual life histories and the understanding of individual histories is the basis for understanding and compiling a community history. Despite wanting to provide an atmosphere for free expression to the interviewees, as a historian I was still in charge of the interview stage or process as I chose the topic for discussion, framed the particular questions for discussion and allowed the interviewees an opportunity to speak. "The control of the historical discourse always remains firmly in the hands of the historian: it is the historian who selects the people who are to speak; who asks the questions and thus contributes to the shaping of the testimony; who gives testimony its final published form and, even when accepting that the working class speaks through oral history, it is clear that the class does not speak in the abstract, but speaks to the historian and with the historian".[62] Oral history as a source for historians has several strengths and weaknesses.[63] One of the strengths is that by introducing views from the underclass, opening up new areas of inquiry

---

[60] Ibid.
[61] Susana Mate Kamwanga. (2009-08-11), Guma village.
[62] A. Portelli. (1981), Peculiarities of oral history, *History Workshop Journal*, p. 104.
[63] For an exploration of the weaknesses of the use of oral histories see P., la Hausse. (1990), Oral history and South African Historians, *Radical History Review*, 46 (7), pp. 33–45; P. Thompson. (1998), The voices of the past. In R. Perks and A. Thompson (eds.), The oral history reader. London, Routledge, pp. 26–27.

and bringing out the views of those who have been ignored, oral history makes history more democratic.[64] On the other hand, oral history is certainly affected by the inherent frailty in human memory. Memory is constructed and shaped by a variety of factors and simply mining oral interviews for facts is certainly a limited approach.[65] People have memories which they may consider too risky to disclose to the outside world and the construction of the private/public relationships are therefore crucial in shaping what is remembered, what is silenced or forgotten, what is expressed and how it is expressed and to whom.[66] The problem for oral historians is that people do not keep experience but they build up memories from those experiences and these memories consist of a mixture of images, thoughts and feelings which are built up and passed on in different ways.[67] Oral historians therefore never gain direct access to experiences but only to the words that are used to relay a construct memory of those past experiences.

One challenge for this book therefore was to think of how the contract labourers during the field work process mediated their memory of experiences of the contract labour system to me and in my case this mediation was certainly a dialogue and a learning process. My task was to be humble but show confidence and competency in my work to allow the interviewee to narrate their memories of their experiences more freely. In this book, I tried to explore the meanings behind the narratives rather than just mining these for historical facts or events. The challenge of oral history, however, is that the stories people remember, or choose to tell, show how they would like to remember their experience or how they would like historians to write that history. I learnt not to assume that historians or interviewers capture all experiences of interviewees because from my observation, interviewees only shared little and kept the larger part of their life story to themselves. This was the revealing experience at the end of what I thought was an extensive oral interview session with Bernhard Lipayi Linyando. After I commented by way of thanking him that I was glad that he has shared his life story with me, he responded that he only shared a little bit and left out the majority of his life experiences.[68] What is worth noting for this book is that the unfinished or incomplete oral narrative, as indicated by Bernhard Lipayi, confirms the inherent incompleteness of oral sources and therefore of knowledge production. Since it is not possible to finish off the historical memory of an interviewee, oral history remains unfinished

---

[64] P. Thompson. (1998), *ibid*, pp. 26–27.
[65] P. La Hausse. (1990), Oral history and South African Historians, pp. 33–45.
[66] S. Field. (2007), (ed.), *Imagining the city: memories and cultures in Cape Town.* Cape Town, HRS Press, p. 9.
[67] S. Field. (2001), Remembering experience, interpreting memory: life stories from Windermere. *African Studies*, 60 (1) p. 127.
[68] Bernhard Lipayi Linyando interview. (2009-07-27), Ndiyona village.

work in progress. It also means that "no research can be considered complete any longer unless it includes oral sources where available and, since oral sources are inexhaustible, oral history passed on its own partial, incomplete quality to all historical research".[69]

All the oral interviews were carried out in the Kavango languages namely Rukwangali, Rumanyo and Thimbukushu. In the beginning, oral interview sessions were transcribed into their original spoken Kavango languages and then translated into English which proved time consuming. I later chose to translate only the quoted text to English while working on a transcribed African text for analysis. The process of transcription and translation has its own setbacks as "the most literal translation is hardly ever the best; a truly faithful translation always implies a certain amount of invention, and the same may be true for the transcription of oral sources".[70]

The transcriptions and translations in this book therefore contain their own setbacks and

> [t]hey certainly lack the tone inherent in the voices of the oral interviewees which expressed their emotions about their life experiences and the whispers that emphasize the seriousness or secret nature of some parts of their stories lost during the transition from the oral form to written form'.[71] The importance of the tones 'to indicate emphasis of a point as well as great difficulty, or a wish to glide over certain points are lost in the transition from oral to written text.[72]

An attempt was made at times to listen to the recorded version of the interviews as a way to read meanings of the tone although this remained an incomplete remedy to the situation. There was a question of whether or not to include in this book the original words of interviewees in the Kavango languages or simply present the English translations. I decided to include both the original transcriptions and their English translations because I felt strongly that I cannot claim to explore the missing voices from the Kavango and yet not present it in the language that it was originally spoken, as this would be equal to continuous muting of the Kavango voices in a book that claims to present such voices. Secondly, these were retained so that in future those ardent seekers of the Kavango history will read and hopefully detect new meanings in the African transcriptions which could have been missed in the translation into English. Oral sources were analyzed as a form of "collective memory" and as a construction of the meaning of the contract labour system through an approach which interpreted meanings of people's feelings, emotions and thoughts.

---

[69] A. Portelli. (1981), 'The peculiarities of oral history', p. 104.
[70] Ibid., p. 97.
[71] Ibid.
[72] Ibid.

Only the voices of the interviewees are presented in the quoted oral transcripts used in the book while the voice of the interviewer is absent. This absence is not intended to downplay the central role of the interviewer in the oral narrative process; indeed, I agree too that an understanding of the questions of an interviewer helps the reader to gain insight into the interview process. The reason for the exclusion nonetheless is because the contract labourers spoke extensively about their experiences in non-conformity to the posed questions or at times without being questioned about it. But as a remedy for this intentional exclusion of the interviewer's questions all audio oral interviews and transcriptions have been deposited in the national archives of Namibia in Windhoek under the Kletus Muhena Likuwa collection and should be available to those who wish to get an idea of the type of questions that were posed and how these were answered.

The challenge to oral historians has been sharing their oral data and making it accessible. In the Kavango, for example, despite years of historical investigation by European and African scholars since the 1960s, we still know very little about the oral data behind their work as the whereabouts of their audio recordings as well as transcripts and translations have not been revealed. D. Henige with a similar concern of inaccessibility to the oral data collected by African historians remarked: "These elusive tapes have of course inspired many books and articles but without the evidence on which this legacy has been build, of what value can it be?"[73] I suggest that since so little is known about the Kavango's history, researchers who have done or are still doing research on the Kavango should deposit their collection in the archives or libraries so as to make information and sources accessible to others for useful future debates surrounding the history of Kavango and our methods of oral data collection. I therefore found it right to deposit my oral data collection in the archive instead of seeing it as giving away all my hard-earned oral data to others. I encourage all other scholars who have carried out oral data collection on the Kavango to do the same.

---

[73] D. Heninge. (1982), *Oral historiography*. London, Longman, p. 123.

1 Tracing the History of the Contract Labour System in the Kavango, 1885–1950s

Introduction

The contract labour system in Namibia was a a colonial invention that needs to be explored in the context of the colonial historiography. The advent of European hunters and traders, the Vimbali and Arab slave traders transformed the social and economic lives of the Kavango by nurturing a demand for European goods and also laid the foundation for the peoples' involvement in the contract labour system.[1] This chapter traces the history of the contract labour system which was laid down by colonialism through early European hunters and traders in Kavango. It explains the colonial labour demands made on the Kavango and the strategies the colonial administration used to extract labour. It explains why, despite the creation of a market of consumption for European goods in Kavango, few numbers of men went for contract work during the German colonial period compared to the South African colonial period.

Although labour recruitment in the Kavango had been ongoing prior to 1925, it was unorganized with limited numbers of recruits collected by colonial officials and it was only after 1925 that the the South African administration finally managed to formally organize labour recruitment. The formalization of the contract labour system occurred with the formation of Northern Labour Organization (NLO) and Southern Labour Organization (SLO) in 1925. These were later amalgamated into the South West Africa Native Labour Association, (SWANLA) which recruited labourers from the former Kavango and Ovambo in the early 1940s until the collapse of the contract labour system in 1972. This chapter explores the formalization of the contract labour system from 1925 to 1972 through the formation of official recruiting organizations and their activities in the Kavango. The chapter underlines the importance of colonialism in the development of the contract labour system.

Early intrusions by traders and hunters

Colonialism in the Kavango, as in the rest of Namibia, did not begin with the German conquest of the country in 1885 but included the activities of European travellers, hunters and traders and missionaries prior to 1885 who paved the way for the eventual colonial con-

---

[1] Vimbali (also known as Mambari) were black traders from the confines of the Kingdom of Benquela in Angola who brought European goods, which they acquired from the Portuguese, for trade among the Kavango people.

quest. Although Charles John Andersson was accorded the status of being the first white man to reach the Kavango River by March 1859, further evidence has contested this:

> Andersson was definitely not the first white person to reach the Okavango [Kavango] River. The fringes of Portuguese influence had already touched the Okavango [Kavango]. A traveller, Chapman (1866), also mentions that the hunter Frederick Green and a Professor Wahlberg had in 1855 visited Chief Libebe [Diyeve] in the territory of the Hambukushu people. This same Green and a trade man named Wilson visited Chief Libebe [Diyeve] in 1856. It is known that Libebe's [Diyeve] settlement had quite a number of visits from trades' men.[2]

Kavango formally became part of the German colony from 1885 but the presence of European hunters and traders in the Kavango continued after 1885.[3] In most cases, traders played the role of hunters and hunted large game such as elephants and ostrich because they needed ivory and ostrich feathers for sale and self enrichment in both Europe and America. They offered Kavango kings European commodities in return for permission to kill the game in their areas. A severe outcome of environmental destruction in the north east of Kavango occurred as the European hunters profiteered and came into conflict with the powers of the Kavango kings.[4] The Kavango territory of the upper reaches of Omuramba Omatako, a dry river bed with lush vegetation, was popular and much frequented by European hunters who were based at Karukuvisa in the present day Shambyu district. It was in that part that a renowned hunter, Fredrick Green, killed between 750 and 1000 elephants.[5] Boer trekkers such as Hendrick Van Zyl regarded the Kavango as a true hunter's paradise and broke a world record of killing over 103 elephants in one day and over 400 elephants in 1877.[6] The European hunters and traders sold guns and gun powder and cloths to the kings in exchange for hunting rights.[7] Kings acquired guns, which they distributed to their armies who protected the interests of the kingdoms and also used it to raid others. These trade ex-

---

[2] L.L Van Tonder. (1966), The Hambukushu of Okavango land: an anthropological study of a South Western Bantu people in Africa. Doctoral Thesis, Port Elizabeth University, p.29.

[3] Europeans hunters and traders entered the Kavango after 1885, among them, Faraday, Phillip Wiessel who were killed in Kavango by 1892. See R. S. Shiremo (2010). The reign of hompa Nyangana over the Vagciriku 1874–1924. M.A Thesis, UNAM, 2010, pp. 99–08.

[4] Shiremo. (2010), The reign of hompa Nyangana over the Vagciriku 1874–1924. pp. 83–84.

[5] Ibid., p.86.

[6] See Shiremo. (2010), The reign of hompa Nyangana over the Vagciriku, pp. 83–84. The Boer trekkers came from South Africa (also called Dorsland trekkers) in search of land settlement. By 1878 they reached the Kavango from Ghanzi in Botswana and later in early 1890s they supported Axel Erickson's fight against the Vagciriku of King Nyangana on their way to Angola. Later under the 1925 South African land settlement scheme in Namibia, these Angola Boers (as they were later known) were settled on the farm lands in central and southern Namibia with all financial support for farming.

[7] Shiremo. (2010), *ibid.*, p.120.

changes meant, however, that they gave Europeans a licence to destroy their wildlife. There were cases when hunters did not adhere to the arranged hunting agreement with the kings and in such cases, hunters lost their lives as was the case with Chas Thomas:

> Mr. Thomas was making arrangements with Ovampo [Vagciriku] Chief Nangani [Nyangana] to allow hunters on the north side of the Okavango [Kavango], in his territory. The year previous he had invited Lou Thomas, when in this country, to come back and hunt there. Within a few hours from the river, I met Lou Thomas coming out to meet us with a startling intelligence that C.C. Thomas had been killed by Ovampos [Vagciriku] in the river, while attempting to cross on horseback, in opposition to their wishes on 27 July 1878.[8]

The Vimbundu people of Angola also known as "Vimbali" traded European commodities which they acquired from the Portuguese in Angola and sold among the Kavango in exchange for slaves to sell to the Portuguese or to keep in their households. Andersson observed the Vimbali traders during his visit to King Sikongo of the Vakwangali in 1859:

> At Chikongo's [Sikongo] werf I encountered several Mambari [Vimbali] i.e., black traders from the confines of the Kingdom of Benquela. They brought with them slaves and ivory which they received in exchange with the usual African commodities, beads, guns, ammunitions, etc. I was grieved to find that they had also introduced into the country ardent spirits, which appeared to be extravagantly in demand among the Ovaquangari [Vakwangali]. The Mambari [Vimbali], visit this people regularly once a year, and afterwards push their excursions as far eastward as Libebe [Diyeve]. But, though their route lies in these peddler expeditions for many days along the Okavango [Kavango] River, they never make use of canoes for transporting their merchandise. The ivory is always carried on men's shoulders.[9]

The Vimbali traders carried around "Makupa" (these are large containers filled with European goods) for sale to the Kavango population. Kavango people received goods such as "nguvo da nyime" (lion type blankets), "Mbandwa" (a bundle of cloths), tobacco, beads, alcohol, etc in return for trading family members into slavery.[10] The European goods sold by European traders and Vimbali slave traders to the Kavango people became the same type of goods men from the Kavango aspired to acquire during the contract labour system period. In a matrilineal society such as the Kavango where uncles, who played a central role in the family (as opposed to fathers), sold their nephews and nieces into slavery to the Vimbali traders for whatever reason they saw fit as explained in the following statement:

---

[8] P. Serton. (1954), *The narratives and journal of Gerald McKiernan in South West Africa, 1874–879*. Cape Town, Van Riebeeck Society, 1954, pp. 165–67.
[9] Serton. (1954), *ibid.*, p.237.
[10] See Susana Mate Kamwanga interview. 2009-08-1. Guma village.

> In the past, an uncle would sell to the Vimbundu traders his nephew or niece if he was not on good terms with them. The Vagciriku people are now found in large numbers among the Vimbundu people! Did the Kings also not sell slaves? They did sell so that they could fill their palaces with goods. You the royal people are so wicked![11]
>
> [Kukare nkwirikwa kughulita shimpumba kuvavimbundu ntjene kapi akuyuvhanga navo. Vagciriku weno kukavawana vakayura kuvavimbundu. Nani vahompa navo kapi kavaghulitanga vipika, kughulita vaywide vyuma mu mbara. Muvalingilingi nwe vahompa!]

The result of the slave trade was that the Kavango people got displaced and scattered among other ethnic groups in Angola and likewise people who were captured during raids by Kavango groups have been integrated among Kavango ethnic groups. Susana Mate Kamwanga,[12] who is of royal lineage, provides a description of how the sale of slaves by the kings occurred and the extent of the power of control by the royal clan over the lives of their people:

> The Vakankora royal clan is the hunger clan. If a mukankora royal person had a hold on you in the past, where else would you go? You! Where would you run to? They were kings I tell you! You think we were commoners? Look here, we are the elders, we are the fathers, the mothers and grandparents of those kings. What do you imagine is the Vakankora clan? Who in this country in the past could have had the guts to make decisions contrary to Vakankora clan? If they [Vakankora] decided on anything, then that was how it was going to be. I tell you, in the past we were respected as humans! We are the Kings and who would have dared mess around on us? You think there would still be people remaining in this country today? Aah, you! They would all have been sold off in slave trade to Vimbali people. They would have been sold for cloths [Mate nkuru at his point lowers her voice and speaks in a whispering voice] … that's how they use to be treated. You would see a line of Vimbundu traders coming with their goods for sale. After they have greeted, then the King would go and take a look at their goods and exclaim 'Well, nice clothing, blankets and everything!' The King would instruct those in the palace to pick out the goods and take to his big storeroom. When he had taken enough then he would root out all the slaves in his palace and line them up under the trees. Then he would instruct Vimbali traders 'go and catch that one and that one!' They would go and catch and tie them up on the legs and hands and insert them into 'Vinu' [wooden containers], while the sun was setting down. My dear, they suffered. The slaves were screaming while the traders inserted them into those wooden containers and took them away forever. I have been told about this by my mother and grandmother.[13]

---

[11] Shintunga Unengu interview, 2009-07-31. Rucara village.
[12] Susana Mate Kamwanga was born on 15 October 1915 at Mamono village. She is the daughter of Angela Tunapu and Otho Kamwanga. Her grandmother was Nkayira, the senior wife of king Nyangana who ruled 1866924. Mate has therefore been told of these stories by both her mother Angela Tunapu and her grandmother Nkayira who had both experienced the slave system while living in the palace.
[13] Susana Mate Kamwanga interview, 2009-08-11. Guma village.

[Mukankora ndje sha mukandjara. Ndjara ntjene yinakukwata mukankora. Pakare ntjene mukankora anakukwata oko uyenda? Aah! Pakarendi? Vahompa twe, oveshi vapika? Aah! Vakankora ne vahompa vashirongo vakaliro muno. Mpili mbovo vahompa vanakaromo, vahompane vahompa vene, ngoli vimpempa atwe ne atwe vakurona, tuvanyokwavo tuvashavo, tuvanyakulya vahompa vo! Vakankorane oveshi vare ngoli? Nan! Wakupanga kuvakankora ne kuni wakaliremo muno? Momuvanashitanta vakurona vavakankora momo mmo shikara makura. Nan! Oveshi kudana? Twakalire tuvahompa twe! Oghu kasha atudanene are ngoli? Oveshi ndi mpovalimo muno vantu? Ndi kuvimbali! Yii, ndi to! Vaghure kumakeshe.

[Mate nkuru kunakutameka kughamba kuwowota]. Ngoli mmo kavavaruwananga! Omu ghanakudombayere ngoli makupa ghakughulita. Makura kuyendamo hompa kukenga ashi weni ashi nan! Panayura vyuma vyaviwa vintje, nguvo, kehevi watonda vyaviwa. Makura ame wahompa ashi yendenu mukatoworore vyuma vyaviwa-vyaviwa mukangeneke mundjuwo makura yona ngurangura ntani ngatuyita ngoli rukadona vayatware. Vipika sha! Makura ntani ayenda ogho atumanga ngoli hompa, vyuma navintje adamaghure ngoli akatware mulimundjuwo vakayeyeke-vakayeyeke ngoli dogoro ashi muna gwana? Oghunya ashi yii. Makura ntani kukavafagha ngoli mumbara vapika. Vavafaghe-vavafaghe makura kuvayara ngoli, kuvapaka nage dogoro kunya. Makura ashi 'anwe vavimbali, shapukenu mughupemo mo!' Makura vavo vayende ngoli vakamuwate, kudamunane kupakanga mushinu! Mushinu vashonga ngoli, makura maghuru ghendi ghayimane tupu, namawoko kughashokeka mo ngoli. Liyuva lyalyo kunakangena linakangena, yii, hewa, ruhepo. Ovyo linakangena liyuva vavo kunakutakuma, kuvangeneka, kunakungeneka vanakungeneka, makura pere! Name vyakuntimwitira vamama].

Mate Kamwanga shows that the result of the love for European goods was that kings mistreated their subjects and saw them as objects to be sold off in slavery. Kings had another way to acquire people to swell up their palaces for sale to the advancing Vimbali traders by carrying out military raids on neighbouring ethnic groups in Angola as Shintunga Unengu explained:

In the past they use to go and fight war with the Vimbundu to loot goods to pile up in the palace. Those people depended on war. In the past, the royal people accompanied the army to see what they were looting that side.[14]

[Pakare kavayendanga vakarwane navavimbali vakashakane vyuma vayapongeke mu mbara. Vantu vanya vakolilire kuvita. Pakare vahompaghona kuyenda navakavita vakakenge ashi vintje vanakashakana kunya].

Shintunga shows that the need for European goods encouraged the royals who were in all respects the first class of the ethnic group to accompany raiding parties with the aim of acquiring the looted goods. Gibbons also pointed to these raids by the Kavango groups on the Mbunda people through his recorded observations:

---

[14] Muyenga Shintunga Unengu interview. 2009-07-31, Rucara village.

> Passing through the Makwengari [Vakwangali] country – a people with a bad reputation, which had entrapped and murdered a white man, whom I met on his way thither, three years previously – I reached the confluence of the Kwito, which I traced for over 100 miles. I travelled north, crossing many tributaries of the Kwando and its affluent Luiana. There, the country to a very few miles of the Kwito is drained by the Zambezi system. All this country, to the source of Kwito in the north is sparsely peopled by the Mambunda, a large, ill organized tribe whose lack of unity renders them an easy prey to the more war like Makwengari [Vakwangali] from across the River. There is also a tribe of Bushmen with whom these people live on friendly terms – I imagine for the reason that they give timely warning of the approach of the Makwengari [Vakwangali] raiding parties.[15]

Such raids caused terror among the neighbouring communities who had to live in constant fear and on alert of the advancing Kavango raiding parties. There was also the presence of Arab slave traders among the Hambukushu of Kavango from early times since as Rey explains:

> The Mbukushu are a small though interesting tribe of about 5000 persons living mostly on islands in the Okavango [Kavango] River, their villages being on the mainland nearby. Their numbers have diminished through years owing to the depredation of Arab slave traders from time immemorial and indeed up to 1912.[16]

The colonialists had an interest in the wildlife and other natural resources of the Kavango and thus introduced European goods to the Kavango communities in exchange for permission to plunder their natural resources. The introduction of European goods and the love of it caused kings and their subjects to engage in slave trading with both the Vimbundu and Arab slave traders. This led to mistrust and lack of co-operation among family members, or with neighbouring ethnic groups who lived in fear of attack for slave trade purposes. More importantly, the introduction of European goods and slave trade activities among the Kavango laid the foundation for a new western economic lifestyle among the Kavango which became the foundation for their participation into the later contract labour system in Namibia.

The German colonial regime in Kavango

Despite their interest in South West Africa (SWA), the British at the Cape colony did not annex SWA due to lack of support from the imperial British government in London and they

---

[15] A.S.T. Gibbons. (1901). Explorations in Marotse land and neighbouring regions' *Geographical Journal*, 17(2), p. 122.

[16] C.F. Rey. (1932), Ngamiland and the Kalahari, *Geographical Journals*, Vol. 80(4), p. 305.

thus declared only Walvis Bay as their colonial property and left the rest open to German imperial conquest.[17] The Germans completed the process of colonization of Namibia with the conquest in 1885 to protect their existing economic interest. The German/Portuguese agreement as stated under article No. 1 of the German Imperial Gazette No. 168 of the 21st July 1887 indicated the middle course of the Kavango River as the line of division of a boundary between Namibia and Angola.[18]

There is a difference between the European term "boundary" and the Kavango concept of "murudi" and the local people contest the Kavango River as a boundary between Namibia and Angola. An interviewee indicates:

> A boundary is something that the white people put up whereby one should not cross over it. We do not have such a notion of a boundary. The only notion of a boundary that existed among us in the past was one which defined the extent of the territory of a kingdom, where it starts and ends. You had the defined kingdom of the Hambukushu, Vagciriku, Vashambyu, Vambunza and Vakwangali. A newcomer had to report to the matimbi (king's advisors) for a permanent settlement. This was done to ensure that the king knew you as one of the people who live in his kingdom. But this issue of stopping one from crossing a boundary did not exist among us.[19]

> [Murudi ne shininke osho vatulirepo vamakuwa ashi nakurutaposhi, kapi vyakalireko kukwetu twe vyo vyamurudi wangoweyo. Murudi oghu wakaliroko kwetune wakunegheda shirongo sha hompa, oku watamekera noku washayera. Kuwana shirongo sha hompa wava Mbukushu, Vagciriku, Vashambyu, Vambundja navaKwangali. Mugenda anahepa kukuyivita kwahompa ashi umwe ashi ghumwe wavantu vavape mushirongo. Ngoli vino vyakushweneka muntu ashi nakuvhurashi kupita pamurudi ne kapi vyakalireko kwetu].

While the middle course of the Kavango River was regarded by the colonial authorities as the dividing line for the Kavango territory, Romanus Kampungu indicated that:

> From the standpoint of the Kavango [people] themselves, the Kavango river territory does not only comprise areas within SWA this side of the river but does include also the areas on the other side of the river, Angolan side. It is not unusual that faced with trying circumstances whether general or personal, individual families may cross over from one side of the river to the other.[20]

---

[17] E.P. Stals. (1990), The Commissions of Palgrave, special emissary to South West Africa, 1876–1885. Cape Town, Van Riebieeck Society, pp. xxx–xxxiii.
[18] See, *the German Imperial Gazette No. 168*. 1887. Windhoek, NAN, ADM 30, file 243/3, f1.
[19] Benhard Lipayi Linyando interview. 2009-07-27. Ndiyona village.
[20] R. Kampungu. (1965), Concept and aim of Okavango marriage customs. PhD Thesis, Rome, Pontifical University of Propagation of Faith, p. 6. Romanus Kampungu was born in Kavango. He was ordained as a Catholic priest in 1954. By 1965, he completed a PhD in Cannon laws at Pontifical University of Propagation of Faith, Rome. In 1972 he relinquished priesthood and married Sr. Theresia Katiku, a Roman Catholic sister. He became a prominent figure in the politics of Ka-

The same ethnic groups occupied both sides of the Kavango River and were scattered as far as Kwito River and Limbaranda or Mbunda areas among Vantjeya or Vanyemba in Angola. There were constant migrations of the population across the Kavango River and individuals or families crossed for different reasons. Some people crossed when the main head of the household died and they had to move on to place themselves under the care of another family head of household for guidance and mutual support as is indicated by the personal experiences of Ndumba Shirengumuke:

> My father Shirengumuke was from the lion clan. I am a cattle clan member. My mother is Nyama. I was born at Mabushe, this side [Namibia]. After the death of my mother at Mabushe village after the birth of my younger sister, I was taken to live with Kayambu, my grandfather. I lived with my grandfather Kayambu and Vihemba, the father of Kawana, Shipenga and Kamburu. We lived there but later on Kayambu died and Vihemba followed suit. They were all buried there. My mother has died, and now my grandparents too. Under whose care will I live now? I turned to the cattle clan relatives to Karuli who lived the other side [Angola] in the valley of Kafuro. That was where we went and settled under the care of the elders. After some times, the head of household Karuli died and his mother followed suit. Where shall we go now? We moved on and arrived at Shihungunkuru's homestead at Ncusha. It was in the homestead of Shihungu nkuru where we finally grew up.[21]

[Ame Ndumba Shirengumuke, Shirengumuke waKandambo, Kandambo ka Muhera, Muhera waNtava.Vavava shirengumuke ne mukanyime. Ame nimuka ngombe. Vanane mbo Nyama. Ame kwantjampurukire paMabushe musheli muno. Opo mpo vadohorokera vanane ngoli pa mughunyande wakunkwamita. Opo vadohoroka vanane ngoli opo makura kushapuka kuya ngoli pano anakara ghuno foromani mpo akalire Kayambu ngoli. Kayambu kwakalire vashe vavamama ngoli ovo vashampurukiro vanane Vihemba. Ya, avakandjita nikaye kwaKayambu ngoli navanane Vihemba kwashavaKawana nava Shipenga nava Kampuru, shavo ngoli ogho Kawana. Makura kuyakarangapo ngoli.Pakukarangapo ogho Kayambu anadohoroka mpopano.Kukarangapo nka naye Vihemba anadohoroka.Kuhupako nawa Kapururu Kashova, ogho mughunyavo ngoli, mughunya nakufa Shimbiringwa.Makura ngoli vamama vadohoroka, vanane vanadohoroka, oku nikara kuninko ngoli? Makura Shimbilingwa ngoli naKashova makura kuvyuka ngoli kuno kushikangombe kwaKaruli ngoli kunya mu mbura ya Kafuro ngoli munya. Omo mu mbura ya Kafuro tunayakaramo musheli munya ngoli panya pa ninke pa Kayengona weno opanya ngoli papaghuko weno ndonga musheli munya. Musheli munya mu Shishongo ngoli. Nko twakakalire kuvakurona ngoli. Kukatika oko ayendire Shimbilingwa namughunyendi Kashova, ogho Karuli nturaghumbo anadohoroka, vawina vaKaruli navo vanadohoroka, kuni ngoli oku tuyenda? Kukapita ngoli yo, kuya ngoli pa Shihungunkuru ngoli pa Ncusha. Kuyenda parupadi, mwapita mwararera ngoli. Parupadi vene dogoro kuya pa

---

vango homelands of the early 1970s until his untimely death in1975.

[21] Ndumba Shirengumuke interview. 2009-07-03. Hoha village. Also see Nyambe Merecky interview. 2009-08-06, Shipando village.

Ncusha pa Shihungunkuru mpo tunakulili musheli ngoli dogoro mpo tunashapuka tuyende ku shivanda ngoli].

Some of the early agreements of European imperialists were the Brussels treaties of 1890 which in addition to its work of dealing with ending the slave trade attempted, by international agreements, to control the arms trade in Africa.[22] Germany was expected to uphold this restriction of the sale of guns in South West Africa/Namibia. The restriction of gun sales left kings in Kavango in an angry mood because they were now accustomed to buying guns from European traders and needed more of them. Some European traders in Kavango began to lose their lives in the early 1890s at the hands of the kings as a way to take the guns in their possession.[23] European hunters and traders were no longer seen as partners in trade but as unreliable people. The German administration instead put more effort into the mineral exploitation of Namibia and therefore needed to divert the local people from local trades to working for the colonial economy.

During the early period of the German conquest of Namibia, minerals were discovered in Namibia and these led to the development of infrastructure which required lots of local labour.[24] The colonial authorities constructed harbours such as the port at Swakopmund from November 1889; there were copper mining activities from 1892 at Otavi by the South West Africa Company (SWACO) whose mining rights were later given to the Otavi-Minen-Und Eisebahngesellschaft (OMEG). There was also the construction of a railway line in South West Africa from 1898 and the railway line to Otavi had been completed by 1906. Copper mines were in operation at Guchab and Khan after 1906 and diamond mining followed at Luderitz after 1908 and the increase in white farm settlers in the police zone after 1908 all increased the need for African labour. The German administration made use of the Nama/Damara and Herero people in the south as labourers in the colonial economy, but a labour shortage crisis occurred in Namibia after the 1904–1907 war of these groups against the German administration.[25]

---

[22] R.W. Beachey. (1962), Arms trade in Africa in the late nineteenth century, *The Journal of African History*, 3(3), pp. 451–467.

[23] Shiremo. (2010), The reign of hompa Nyangana over the Vagciriku 1874–1924, p. 120. In 1892, for example, a German trader named Wiesel together with his friend Faraday, a British national, were killed among the Vagciriku and the result was the capture of Chief Nyangana in 1893 by Chief Sekhoma of Batawana to be presented to Mr. Bosman, a British South African Company (BSACO) agent in Botswana who waited in Sekhoma's palace.

[24] O. Kohler. (1958), *A study of Karibib district, South West Africa*. Pretoria, Department of Native Affairs.

[25] The information on the growing need for labour by the colonial economy is taken from E.L.P. Stals. (1967), Die aanraking tussen blankes en Ovambos in Suid Wes Africa, 1850–1915, pp. 190–194.

The new farm settlers needed labourers to work for them, however, the war had decimated a great number of potential Herero and Nama labourers and the administration therefore looked to the Kavango and Ovambo regions to procure migrant labourers. Kurt Von Francois was the first official of the German administration in Namibia to explore the Kavango in 1891 after which many others followed.[26] During their visit to Kavango, German colonial officials recruited men for labour to the farms and mines in the police zone. During the German colonial period, labour recruitments from Kavango were small and were encouraged by the visiting German colonial officials to the area. By 1902, Dr. Gerber attempted to reach agreements with the Kavango kings to encourage men to report for contract labour, but this was futile as Kavango kings did not sign the agreement.[27] Discussions were held by 1909 between German and the Portuguese colonial officials on how they could co-operate to induce more contract labourers from the Kavango.[28] After 1908, the German colonial administration intended to make land available for German settlers in the Kavango in the hope that this would encourage the people of the Kavango to find their way to the centre in search of work on the farms and in mines, and thus they ordered a straight road to be cleared from Nurugas to Casamas.[29] Indications are that men from Kavango got recruited as labourers only after 1909, the last years of the German colonial rule in Namibia.[30]

The people's reaction towards the colonial extraction of labour from the Kavango was based on their economic situation and relations with the colonial authorities. The economic situation of the Kavango people had been influenced by European and American travellers, hunters and traders, the Vimbari and Arab slave traders both before and after the German colonial conquest of Namibia in 1885. A market for consumption of European goods therefore had long been established in the Kavango. Despite the market for consumption of European goods, the majority of people were discouraged from working as labourers during the German colonial period. There are reasons for this lack of interest. Despite the ban on the slave trade by Britain and other European nations, slave trading continued in Kavango up

---

[26] See A. Eckl. (2007), Konfrontation und kooperation am Kavango (Nord Namibia) von 1891 bis 1921, p. 11.

[27] A.P.J. Beris. (1996), *From mission to local church: one hundred years of mission by the Catholic Church in Namibia*. Windhoek, Catholic church, p. 215.

[28] See A. Eckl. (2007), Konfrontation und kooperation am Kavango (nord Namibia) von 1891 bis 1921, p.117. A meeting was held between Von Zastrow of the German and De Almeida of the Portuguese administrations at Namutoni on 09 September 1909 to discuss the Kavango as contract labourers.

[29] Beris. (1996), *From mission to local church: one hundred years of mission by the Catholic Church in Namibia*, p. 215.

[30] A. Eckl. (2007), Reports from beyond the line: the accumulation of knowledge of Kavango and its peoples by the German colonial administration 1891–1911, *Journal of Namibian Studies*, (1), p. 22.

to the end of German colonial rule in Namibia and the Kavango people continued to acquire European goods such as cloths and blankets, which they needed without having to migrate for it as migrant labourers.[31]

Mindful of the exploitation of their wildlife by the European hunters and traders and the ensuing pest epidemic of the 1890s that killed their cattle, Kavango people were still in control of their natural resources and able to make a living. Although the epidemic infected and killed many cattle in the Kavango, the population refused to have their cattle vaccinated and killed a squad of soldiers sent to convince them.[32] The epidemic attacked even wild animals which provided meat for people as Mangondo recalled:[33]

> Innumerable of them were found everywhere even along the river lying dead. The sick animals would be found everywhere easy to be killed even by a child. The plague provided meat for the people who were suffering the loss of their cattle. Those of Gciriku were attacked by this disease at 'epemba' (harvest) at the season of the new fruit and those of Ukwangali during winter.[34]

The Kavango people therefore continued to hunt the game for meat which became easy prey during the epidemic period; they ate from their harvest and also dug and collected wild fruits from the forest and were therefore able to survive in ways they saw fit without turning to recruitment into the colonial labour as a central option.

In most parts of Namibia, it might be argued that the nature of colonial control was that European hunters and traders paved the way for economic control of the local population, whilst missionaries pacified the local inhabitants and undermined existing cultural and spiritual systems, after which followed a permanent military occupation by the German authority. In the case of the Kavango, although European hunters and traders had attempted the first stages of economic exploitation, the arrival, acceptance and establishment of missionaries proved difficult. A missionary settlement and a German military establishment in Kavango came quite late. The people rejected the evangelists from Botswana many times and, by 1883, King Diyeve of the Hambukushu again refused to accept them.[35] The German

---

[31] Rey shows that up to 1912, the Hambukushu of Kavango suffered from slave trade, see C.F. Rey. (1932), Ngamiland and the Kalahari: a paper read at the evening meeting of the society on 6 June 1932, *Geographical Journals*, Vol. 80 (4), p. 305.

[32] J. Duffy. (1961), *Portuguese Africa*. London, Oxford University Press, p. 227.

[33] See Kampungu. (1965), The concept and aim of Okavango marriage customs, pp. 239–240. Mangondo, a member of Vakwangali royal family, was born in 1878 and was the daughter of Nasira who in return was a maternal granddaughter to King Himarwa Ithete of the Vakwangali. By April 1956 when Mangondo was interviewed by Romanus Kampungu at a mission station of Tondoro she was already old and blind. The epidemic of the 1890s in Ukwangali area of Kavango which she narrated to Kampungu was her personal experiences of the epidemic.

[34] Kampungu. (1965). *Ibid.*, pp. 352–353.

[35] T. Magadla & C. Voltz. (2006), (ed.), *Words of the Batswana, letters of Mahoko a Becwana, 1883 to*

colonial authorities had encouraged the Roman Catholic Church since 1896 to establish itself among the Kavango and supported their endeavours as Shiremo explains:

> Major Leutwein who at a later stage became the colonial governor played a critical role in seeing to it that the German Catholic missionaries had an evangelical monopoly over the Kavango region and its people. While at Otjihaenena in the middle of 1896, Major Leutwein who was at the time the German Imperial deputy in the then Sudwest Africa declared in front of the Catholic priest Schoch in the name of the government to open Catholic Missions not only in Windhoek but also among the people of Kavango.[36]

The interest of the German administration in the establishment of missions was apparent when it appointed two fathers for the Windhoek station in 1896 as Klaus Dierks shows:

> October 1896, the Roman Catholic missionary officially begins work in Windhoek with the government appointment of the fathers Bernhard Hermann and Josef Filliung. Both are appointed as priests for white settlers only. The subsequent mission work in northern part of SWA is controlled by the Congregation of the Oblates of the Immaculate Virgin Mary.[37]

The task of the two Catholic missionaries in Windhoek after 1896 was to find a way to expand into the Kavango and by 1903, Father Josef Filliung and Fr. B. Hermann of the Windhoek mission station were on their third expedition to the northern part of Namibia accompanied by Fr., Ludwig Hermandung, Bro., Joseph Bast and Bro., Anselm Reinhard, and they successfully reached the Kavango River at Nkurenkuru in 1903.[38] However this expedition was a failure. The missionaries relied on an agreement that had, allegedly, been made by a German colonial official with the Kwangali Hompa[39] Himarwa Ithete earlier in 1902. When the missionaries finally arrived at Himarwa in 1903, the Hompa denied any knowledge of such an agreement and chased them away as K.F.R. Budack shows:

> In the last week of February, 1903, the Oblate Fathers Hermandung, Filliung and Biegner accompanied by lay-brothers Bast and Rheinhardt left Grootfontein for Kavango. They reached the Kavango near Nkurenkuru on the 18th of March. Himarua, then about 80 years old who was still residing on the Angolan side of the river first

---

1896. Cape Town, 2006, p. 65.

[36] R.S. Shiremo. (2005), The Role of Kavango Kings in the anti-colonial resistance: 1903 the year of unity and resistance' (unpublished paper presented at a conference at Rundu College of Education, p. 4.

[37] K. Dierks, 'Colonial period: German rule' http://www.klausdierks.com/Chronology/contents.htm.

[38] One hundred years of OMI history in Namibia 1896–2005 http://www.rcchurch.na/omi/History.htm.

[39] Hompa is a term in a singular form, used by the people in Kavango to refer to the traditional head of their ethnic group; the plural form would be Vahompa.

contested the existence of the Treaty with Dr Gerber. Later he declared that he did not want any missionaries in his country.[40]

Out of anger and desperation for a mission settlement among the Kavango the fathers summoned a patrol from Grootfontein under Oberleutnant Volkmann which arrived at the river on 12 April 1903. The patrol only succeeded in placing the chief in a worse mood when they told the King that he was standing on German soil rather than his own. An attempt to establish a mission station with Chief Nampadi of the Neighbouring Mbunza tribe also failed and the missionaries had to abandon their aim for the time being.[41] Volkmann with the direct personal involvement of the two Roman Catholic missionaries, Hermandung and Nachwey, attacked and burned down the village of Uukwangali Hompa Himarwa which resulted in casualties amongst the Vakwangali people. The Catholic missionary expeditions to Kavango were not mere spiritual missions but directly connected to the agenda of the German imperial government to extend political power over the Kavango populations. Heinz Hunke, the author of a sympathetic account of the Roman Catholic Church in Namibia, argues specifically as follows:

> The Catholic missionaries did not consider this expedition to Kavango as a mere church mission but as a political mandate as well. This comes out clearly in the letter of the Prefect Natchwey to Governor Leutwein on 17 August 1904 in which he begged the governor to participate in the compensation of missionaries for the following reasons: the missionaries moved to Kavango in agreement with the imperial government; with respect to their political task, they were allowed to draw their equipments from stocks of the government. Prefect Natchwey also prayed the imperial government to honour the memory of the missionary who fell during the expedition as pioneers of culture and cross by granting a mission farm.[42]

Little success was therefore made with colonial labour extraction and migration in the early absence of the missionaries. There was great hostility of the Kavango groups against the German colonial administration similar to that of the Bondelzwarts groups in southern Namibia so that by 11 November 1903, the German colonial administration published a map which indicated the Kavango and the Bondelswarts' home grounds as areas in Namibia where "natives" were up in arms against the German colonial government.[43] The hostility in Kavango against the German administration was partly a result of the Kavango people's vio-

---

[40] K.F.R. Budack. (1976), The Kavango: the country, its people and history. Swakopmund, *Namib und Meer,* Band 7).
[41] Ibid.
[42] H. Hunke. (1996), *Church and state, the political context of 100 years of Catholic mission in Namibia.* Roman Windhoek, Catholic church, p. 10.
[43] Shiremo. (2010), Hompa Nyangana and his reign over the Vagciriku, 1874–1924, p. 128.

lent encounters with the German troops in 1903. In 1903, King Nyangana of the Vagciriku shot and killed a family of German traders who had previously robbed him in trade. Others were injured and escaped but were later killed by the Vashambyu people at the request of King Nyangana.[44] The armed German farmers from Grootfontein district soon afterwards went to rescue the captured German girl named Selma Paasch who was married among the Vashambyu. In order to avoid further revengeful attacks from the Grootfontein based German military troops and farmers, a large section of the Vashambyu ethnic group abandoned the Kavango River in 1903 for safety in western Zambia. These initial encounters between the Kavango people and the German missionaries and troops in 1903 created a bad image of the Catholic missionaries and German colonial administration in the minds of the Kavango people. The attack by the German colonial troops and the Catholic missionaries on the Vakwangali in 1903 and later German attack on the Vashambyu indicates a collaborative effort by the German colonial administration, the Catholic missionaries and white farmers and as such the Kavango population did not distinguish among them.

The 1904–1907 war erupted in central Namibia between the German military troops and the Herero/Nama and the stories of bad treatment and killing by the colonial authorities reached the Kavango through Herero refugees. This added to the distrust of the Kavango of the German colonial authority. The people of Kavango were convinced that the whites had only one aim, to rob them of their land, a conviction that had been enforced by the tales of the Herero refugees.[45]

Captain Franke and the explorer Seiner, who had explored the Kavango by 1906 when peace was returning to most parts of Namibia, reported that the attitude of the people in Kavango remained hostile to the German colonial administration and that it had even been deemed necessary to allot to his expedition an armed escort of 30 troops.[46] This hostility and mistrust of the people of the German administration therefore made the idea of living, let alone working as contract labourers among them unattractive. It seems that this unwillingness by Kavango workers to work for the Germans still existed among some workers long after the end of the German rule. As Gordon shows, during the Second World War period (1937–1945) when rumours were rife of the possibility of the German victory and re-takeover of Namibia, the Kavango workers who worked for Mr. Thomas of Ondundu

---

[44] This event is known as vita vya Handa (the war of Aarnd). There are archival documents relating to this attack or war. See 'Geographische u ethnographische forschungen Caprivi zipfel u Okavango gebiet, October 1902–1906' (Windhoek, NAN, manuscript K.A 12233, file FXIII B4, storage unit 1009).

[45] A.P.J. Beris. (1996), *From mission to local church*, p. 221.

[46] A.P.J.Beris. (1996), *ibid.* p. 207.

mine in Otjiwarongo periodically requested him to send them home before the Germans retook the country.[47]

There was also a lack of a permanent German colonial official in the Kavango to entice labour recruitment and migration to the colonial economy at that time. The German authorities faced infrastructure problems due to the lack of proper roads to travel to the Kavango and also the resistance of the local population, who were reluctant to accept a permanent colonial administration in their area. The Roman Catholic missionaries were accepted in the Kavango among the Vagciriku in 1910 because of Klemens Mbambo who finally convinced his father.[48] Theresia Shidona explains:

> Mbambo was the one who accepted our Djami and Pater Kuiverte who later went to Mbukushu. He said 'I beg you dear father, do not chase the missionaries who have come with the wagon to come and teach the children, do not refuse. Allow them to begin a school to teach our children'. If it was for [hompa] Nyangana alone, they [the missionaries] would have been slaughtered (Shidona is laughing) A-a-A-a! When he saw them red of colour, he thought they were ghosts and not humans, it was just because of Mbambo.[49]

> [Wayavatambulirone Mbambo, ndje wayatambuliro ngoli ghuno Djami wetu naghunya Pata Kuiferte wakunya ku Mbukushu. Ashine perere-penu, ove vava, mwashashwena varuti, muhongi anayo nalitemba. A-a-a-a! Yashonge shure avavanuke vano, yatushonge, yatuyimbite atwe, kapishighushwene. Ndipantjendi Nyangana ndivayapitukire (Shidonankuru kunakushepa). A-a-A-a! Kuvikenga ge-ge-gee shine vimonyo-monyotupu, kapishi vantu, mbyovyotupu mwaMbambo].

Even after allowing the Catholic missionaries settlement in his area, Hompa Nyangana held doubts over the presence and intentions of these missionaries as Father Bierfert indicated:

> One day he came to me and said that he had something heavy on his mind [there was something that worried him] and asked for our help. Thereupon he narrated amply that some years ago, after the unfortunate war with the Germans, numerous Vaherero passed through his land and warned [cautioned] him of missionaries and that one day he would be experiencing the same as they experienced. They too used to accommodate missionaries, but then soldiers came, and these had now taken away their

---

[47] R.J.Gordon. (1993), The impact of the Second World War on Namibia, p. 151.
[48] Klemens Mbambo was the first born of Hompa Nyangana from his senior wife Nkayira. In the early 1890s he was taken captive with his father by King Sekgoma to Batawana. While he was in Botswana, he attended a mission school where he learnt English. Although his father returned later in 1897 to Kavango, he remained in Botswana at the mission school and returned only later.
[49] Theresia Shidona Weka interview. 2003-06-15. Guma village. Theresia Shidona's mother Tunapu and Klemens Mbambo were all children of Hompa Nyangana. This means therefore that Klemens Mbambo was the uncle of this interviewee Shidona and that Hompa Nyangana was her grandfather.

land. At this [King] Njangana [Nyangana] used an expression which in former times was frequently heard in Herero land: 'The wagon has destroyed the Herero people'.[50]

This indicates that Hompa Nyangana was aware of the plight of the Herero people in southern Namibia which resulted from accepting missionaries who in turn collaborated with the German colonial troops to subdue the Herero nation. It shows Hompa Nyangana's logic that accepting missionaries in his area was a stepping stone for physical colonial presence and the eventual loss of power over his land and people and submission to German colonial dominance. One of the historical factors that had rendered Kavango chiefs maintaining a hostile attitude to the Europeans in general, and to the missionaries in particular, had been the hostile relation with the Portuguese under the slave trade. The Africans in the Kavango believed that to fall into the hands of the whites was a dangerous thing and to allow whites into one's land was to draw nearer the source of danger.[51] Seen against this historical context it is easy to see why many chiefs in Kavango were constantly on their guard against accepting white settlers and missionaries in their lands. There existed always an intimate connection between Christianity and colonization so that the people along the Kavango came to look upon the Christianizing and colonizing groups as one and the same people and consequently better not to accept.[52] The Finnish missionaries were only accepted in Kavango during the South African period.[53] The German authorities established military posts in Kavango only in 1911 after the Catholic missionaries established a settlement in 1910.[54] This confirms the nature of German colonial settlement pattern in Namibia as argued by Guido Weigend:

> The missionaries made the natives dependent on the stations, the trading practices selectively favoured certain tribes and the missionaries urged natives to submit to German rule. The missions were a gruesome reality of colonialism in Namibia.[55]

Weigend shows that we cannot separate missionaries at that time from colonialism as they were a part of the establishment process of German colonialism in Namibia. Indeed, this

---

[50] A. Bierfert. (1938), *25 Jahre bei den Wadiriku am Okawango*. Hünfeld: Verlag der Oblaten, p.23.
[51] Kampungu. (1965), The concept and aim of Okavango marriage customs, p. 120.
[52] Kampungu. (1965), *ibid.* p. 122.
[53] As early as 1922 in the region of Nkure-nkuru, there were some Ovambo Finnish Christians from Ovamboland. By 1926 a temporary house was build at the present Finnish mission at Nkure-nkuru to provide shelter for the white missionary who was occasionally visiting Kwangali land with a view to finding a permanent mission station. By 1929 a Finnish Mission Station was founded at Nkurenkuru and by 1938 at Rupara and Mupini.
[54] L. VanTonder. (1966), The Hambukushu of the Okavango land: an anthropological study of south western people in Africa, p. 30.
[55] G. G. Weigend. (1985), German settlement patterns in Namibia *Geographical Review*, American Geographical Society, (2), p. 161.

view is cemented by the following words of one of the founding fathers of Catholic Mission scholarship, J. Schmidlin who argued:

> The mission is one that spiritually conquers our colonies and assimilates them internally. The state may have the power to conquer and annex the protectorates at the external level; yet the deepest goal of colonial policy, the internal colonization, must be implemented with the help of the missions. The state could well enforce physical obedience through punishments and laws, yet it is the mission's duty to bring the natives to spiritual submission and devotion. In this context we may reverse the phrase pronounced by the secretary for the colonies, Dr. Solf, at the Reichstag, 'to colonize is to do mission work' into 'to do mission work is to colonize'.[56]

The South African presence in the Kavango

The German colonial military presence in Kavango (1911–1915) was short lived and was overthrown in 1915 during the First World War (1914–1918). Military operations during the early months of the war had a significant impact on the Kavango. The German magistrate of Outjo and other German officers were shot at the Portuguese police post of Naulila on the Namibia/Angola border and the Portuguese maintained that the first shots were fired by the Germans.[57] The result was the dispatch of a punitive expedition in November 1914 into Portuguese territory under Col., Victor Franke and the complete defeat of the Portuguese at Naulila. An official South African report states that when the news of the shooting of the German officers reached the administration:

> Reprisals were immediately authorized from the German Headquarters on the various Portuguese police posts on the border which was attacked without warning and their occupants killed. Amongst other posts that at Fort Cuangar was attacked and the Garrison killed. The Portuguese assert that the Germans were assisted by Chief Kandjimi and his followers.[58]

Simon Kandere also alludes to the joint attack by the Germans and King Kandjimi Hawanga of Vakwangali on the Portuguese along the Kavango River:

> The Germans came to fight the Portuguese. Hawanga told them 'let me first go across the river and encircle their ammunition store room before you start to shoot your weapons'. He told them that 'when you will hear my gun shot you should also start shooting with your guns. The Portuguese will be running for their weapons and then

---

[56] H. Hunke. (1996), *Church and state, the political context of 100 years of Catholic mission in Namibia.* Windhoek, Roman Catholic Church, p. 10.
[57] SWA Administrator to minister of defense, (1917). Administration of Okavango area: S.W.A. protectorate. Windhoek, NAN, Administration (ADM) 30, file 243/3, part II.
[58] *Ibid.*

I will kill all of them'. He went there and then shot his gun in the air. He indeed finished them off, every time a Portuguese came out he shot him with a bullet and only the Mulatus[59] were spared. All the Portuguese who were there were finished off. The grave yard you see at Nkurenkuru, who do you think killed them? It was Hawanga. He finished them off. You should have seen how the heavy guns were being shot from across. The Germans were shooting from across the River while Kandjimi was on the camp busy killing the Portuguese. No bullet touched him.[60]

[Vandovesi kwawizire vayarwane novaPutu. Hawanga tavatantere asi 'tanko nize nikasikame konzugo zomauta ntani nomuroya matendangongi geni'. Asi 'sinene nomuzuvhu uta royeni matenda', tavapwaga vawize pomauta gawo nivadipage. Eyi gakasikama taroya uta meguru. Hawe sinene a pwaga kohanga navenye tavamanapo opu! Kwakahupirepo tupu yimuratu. Yiputu nayinye yakerepo tayimanapo. Gene mayendo gena omuninki asi yilye gava dipaga navenye, Hawanga gavadipaga. Kwavamene. Tara matendagongi vagaroyepo age kwakuroya Vaputu no hanga kapi tadimukwata. Vandovesi awo kwakambekerere. Apa varoya ngoso matenda age poopo kunakudipaga Vaputu. No hanga nokumukwatasi].

The Portuguese colonial officials lived with grudges afterwards against King Kandjimi Hawanga whom they strongly believed had assisted in the German attack upon, and capture of Fort Cuangar in 1915 and had looted from the Portuguese certain arms, stock and goods.[61] The German victory over the Portuguese along the Kavango during the First World War was short-lived. Shortly afterwards the South African troops under Lieutenant Lawson reached the Kavango and defeated the Germans.

Although the South African Military Regiment (hereafter S.A.M.R.) remained in Namibia after 1915 it was only after 1920 that South Africa inherited Namibia as a League of Nations Mandate. In Kavango, the S.A.M.R. that dislodged the German authorities' control in 1915 did not maintain a permanent military occupation over the former German posts and the Kavango was left as it had been since 1902 to form part of the administrative district of Grootfontein.62 The absence of a permanent South African colonial military structure along the Kavango left some former German officials still roaming around at liberty within the Kavango and continuing to trouble the local people which prompted the return to the Kavango of South African troops on the 23th of August 1916 under Major Brownlee, with the aim:

---

[59] A Mulatu is a concept referring to a person of mixed blood between a Portuguese and a black person.
[60] R.S. Shiremo with Simon Nzamene Kandere, Rundu, Nkarapamwe, 31 July 2005, pp. 12–13. See Shampapi Shiremo collection (Windhoek, NAN).
[61] Frank Brownlee. (1917-01-16), To the secretary of the protectorate, 'Patrol to Nkurenkuru. Windhoek, NAN, ADM30, file 243/3, part III.
[62] The administrator of SWA to the Minister of Defense in Pretoria (1917-11-16), Administration of the Okavango area: SWA Protectorate. Windhoek, NAN, ADM 30, file 243/3, part 2.

> To re-assure the natives who it was alleged were being tampered with by German agents and to deal with any German who might be found residing in that area and to establish relations with the Portuguese authorities on the border.⁶³

The South African colonial officials made arrangements with the Portuguese officials, who since the defeat of Germans by South African troops returned to their former colonial outposts to control the Kavango population. The arrangements allowed the people on both sides of the Kavango River to have free use of the river for the purposes of boating, fishing, watering of stock etc. It also allowed the people on either side of the Kavango River permission to cross and re-cross the river freely for the purposes of visiting, business or other lawful purposes with no pass being necessary for such a crossing. It was agreed that no person from the Portuguese territory would be permitted to reside on the South African side of the Kavango without the permission of the Portuguese authorities and vice versa and that any person proceeding from one territory to the other for unlawful purposes or without a pass would be returned to the territory in which he or she resided by the authority of the other territory.⁶⁴

Despite this arrangement for co-operation, the two colonial authorities had a lot of issues to settle to improve their relations. The South African colonial authorities demanded that the German colonial agents who had fled from the Namibian side of the Kavango to the Angolan side should be handed over to stand trial, but, in response, the Portuguese demanded that before they would do this Hompa Kandjimi Hawanga of the Vakwangali should be captured and handed to them to stand trial for the attacks on the Portuguese during the First World War.⁶⁵ The persistent failure of effective co-operation between the South African and the Portuguese colonial authorities strained their relationship and attempt at mutual political control over the Kavango. The South West Africa/Namibia administrator had a conviction that the Portuguese neighbours in Angola were making unreasonable demands to which he felt they were not entitled and this was the source of conflict between the two colonial powers, which persisted between them and was detrimental to colonial collaboration and mutual control of the Kavango. The mistrust and lack of co-operation between the Portuguese and the South African colonial officials presented several Vahompa of the Kavango with an opportunity to skirt around the Portuguese proposal for the creation of separate kingdoms on both sides of the Kavango River.

---

⁶³ *Ibid.*
⁶⁴ Frank Brownlee. (1917-01-16), 'Resume of arrangements concluded between the Commandant Fort Cuangar and the Military Magistrate Grootfontein district. Windhoek, NAN, ADM 30, file 243/3, part II.
⁶⁵ Report by Frank Brownlee. (1917-01-16, To the secretary to the protectorate titled Patrol to Nkurenkuru. Windhoek, NAN, ADM 30, file 243/3, part III.

The incumbent Vahompa became resistant to colonial advances that were against the idea of their existing status as rulers of both banks of the Kavango River and found ways to play off one colonial power against the other as a technique to maintain their status quo. In 1917, for instance, a Portuguese official who had not succeeded in convincing Vahompa of Kavango to leave the Namibian side of the Kavango River and settle on the Angolan side, carried out an expedition to appoint new Vahompa on the Angolan side of the Kavango. However, he encountered opposition and deception from the incumbent Vahompa who were resident on the Namibian side of the Kavango River. In Vagciriku area Hompa Nyangana convinced the Portuguese official that he would like to continue to be the Hompa on the Angolan side of the Kavango. Hompa Nyangana explained that the reason that he did not reside in "Portuguese territory" was because he had been forced to live near the Catholic mission station and that formerly the Germans had demanded this and now the South Africans were making the same demand.[66] Hompa Nyangana proposed that he would send some men to the protectorate authorities and ask permission to return to his old abode on the Portuguese side of the border with part of his people and leave the rest of his ethnic group with a new king on the South African side. King Nyangana, however, did not really intend to do this. As he later admitted to the Portuguese official:

> You have on two occasions tried to get me to trek over the river to live in Portuguese territory. I again tell you that I will not do as you wish me to do. I shall remain in British territory.[67]

In Mbukushu area, Fumu[68] Disho on the Namibian side of the border warned the Portuguese official that, if another Fumu was going to be appointed on the Angolan side of the Hambukushu, he vowed to fight against that.[69] Major Brownlee, a South African official, complained about Portuguese attempts to reconfigure traditional authorities: "I conclude from the former letter that the Portuguese authorities at Cuangar are looking for trouble and that they are constantly irritating our natives".[70]

The above indicates that the South African colonial authorities opposed the Portuguese strategy and were not ready to condone it. After 1917, a detachment of the South African

---

[66] Col. Jose Carregado Vianna, (1917-12-10), To the military magistrate of Grootfontein. Windhoek, NAN, ADM30, file 243/3, part II.
[67] Major Frank Brownlee. (1918-04-24), To Lieut. Hahn of Ovamboland administration, statements under oath Windhoek, NAN, ADM30, file 243/3, part II.
[68] Fumu is a singular term in Mbukushu language for a hereditary traditional head of the ethnic group of which the plural form is Hafumu.
[69] Col. Jose Carregado Vianna. (1917-12-10), To the military magistrate of Grootfontein. Windhoek, NAN, ADM 30, file 243/3, part II.
[70] Major Frank Brownlee. (1918-01-26), To the secretary for the protectorate, affairs at Nkurenkuru. Windhoek, NAN ADM 30, file 243/3, Part II.

military force occupied a post at Nkurenkuru along the Kavango River and constant military patrols along the river became a measure of political control over the area. The patrols are indicative of the competition for control of the population along the Kavango River between the Portuguese and South African colonial administrations. It indicates that kings in Kavango felt their power over their territory threatened and were thus compelled by the precarious political situation to align with one of the colonialists as a means of continued survival through colonial patronage. This meant, as we shall see, supporting the colonial needs for the extraction of men from their area as contract labourers.

Labour recruitment by South African officials

During the South African military occupation of Namibia (1915–1918), military patrols to the Kavango gathered information for the administration with regard to the estimated figures of the population hoping to induce a flow of labour from these localities.[71] The visiting colonial officials to the Kavango suggested to the administration that:

> With a little water development on the routes, a fairly good supply of native labour would be available for farms or other work from Okavango [Kavango]. During the rainy season both these routes are easily negotiable, but it is during the dry time that long stretches are without water and the natives are afraid to venture them.[72]

The South African authorities were therefore faced with a lack of sufficient infrastructure to facilitate labour extraction. Since the takeover of Namibia by South Africa, the recruitment of Africans in the Kavango, as during the German colonial occupation of the area, was carried out by the visiting colonial officials and labour shortage in Namibia was a phenomenon for the South African colonial economy as it was for the Germans.[73] The South African colonial administration complained that the position of labour was unsatisfactory. The country was crying out for labour as all industries were handicapped owing to the acute shortage which made mining almost impossible and was arresting the progress in the country.[74]

One of the explanations by the colonial officials for this labour shortage was that the large numbers of settlers that were coming into the country at the time increased farm-

---

[71] Extract from Grootfontein annual report Number 3370. (1917-01-29). Windhoek, NAN, ADM 95, file 2794/8.
[72] Deputy Commissioner of South West Africa Police. (1917-01-29), To the secretary for the protectorate 'native labour supply from Okavango. Windhoek, NAN, SWAA 2407, file a521/10.
[73] 'The union of South Africa. (1924), Report. Windhoek, NAN, JX/0220, p. 21.
[74] 'The union of South Africa (1925), Report. Windhoek, NAN, JX 0220, pp. 34–35.

ing, mining and industrial concerns which led to increased demands for labour. Another general impression by colonial officials about the scarcity of labour was that "the natives" were idle and lazy and though fit for labour refused to work. The colonial officials linked the unwillingness of the local people to work to the availability of food and argued that local men went to contract labour when there was lack of food but were disinclined to enlist for contract labour when food was in abundance as the following quotation of 1925 on the Kavango seems to suggest:

> The natives in this area have enjoyed a season of prosperity. The exceptional rain produced excellent crops with the result that little labour was forthcoming from this area during 1925.[75]

Chiefs became an important influence on labour supply in Namibia.[76] The approach of the South African administration was that of co-option of the traditional leadership and indirect rule through them. Colonial officials presented gifts to the Kavango kings and presented the message of goodwill from the South West Africa/ Namibia administrator as a way to buy the friendship of the kings and their people. The colonial officials carried the message about the establishment of a new colonial administration to kings who in turn responded to the administrator.[77] Apart from the colonial officials carrying out labour recruitments during their visits to the Kavango, Kavango kings were encouraged to send men on contract work. Remuneration by colonial authorities to kings was a useful colonial strategy to extract migrant labour. Some kings undertook personal visits to the administrative centres of Grootfontein and Tsumeb to claim their monthly remuneration. During one of his visits to Grootfontein in 1923, for example, King Kandjimi Hawanga of the Vakwangali died and was buried there.[78]

The colonial officials had high prospect of obtaining more labourers from the Kavango and ordered that an eye be kept on the men who were reporting for work to ensure their proper treatment so that a good report of labour conditions may be taken back by them.[79] The administration requested more labourers from the Kavango and remunerated kings who heeded to the request as is evident in a letter by Brownlee:

> I beg to inform you that in response to a message from me to Chief Kandjimi requesting that labourers should be sent here, 57 boys were promptly sent, and these have

---

[75] 'The union of South Africa. (1925) Report. Windhoek, NAN, pp.27–28 and 31.
[76] E.P, Stals. (1990). *The commissions of Palgrave*, p. 217
[77] Frank Brownlee. (1917-01-16), To the secretary of the protectorate 'Patrol to Nkurenkuru' Windhoek, NAN. ADM 30, file 243/3, part III.
[78] See Native Commissioner (Windhoek, NAN, SWAA, 2083, A. 460/19).
[79] *Ibid.*

been apportioned to farmers in this district. Four messengers accompanied the boys, and these will be paid at the rate authorized by you. As Kandjimi is not in receipt of a subsidy, he has been supplied with goods to the value of L.2.00 in recognition of his services, and as an encouragement towards sending further labourers. Kindly approve of my action.[80]

Remunerated kings continued to send labourers in small numbers, and these were distributed to mines and farms as the following indicates:

I have the honour to inform you that today 16 Ovambo [Mbunza] labourers arrived here for work, having been sent down by Chief Karupu. As Karupu is not in receipt of pay from the administration he has been supplied with goods to the value of 10/ as a reward for his services and to encourage him to send further batches of labourers.[81]

The strategy of remunerating the kings to encourage them to send labourers was a common feature in southern Africa. In Malawi for instance, the colonial administration exploited the traditional customs through the form of paying head money to the chiefs, either the traditional ones or those installed by the colonial power to ensure that they made their subjects available for use by the colonists.[82]

Since the 1920s, Kavango kings who had been resistant to colonial domination began to pass on[83] and the colonial administration replaced them with obliging ones who could be deposed by the Native Commissioner at any time as per proclamation No. 15 of 1928 which dealt with installing and deposing of chiefs. This made kings helpless and dependent on the commissioner and helped to centralize the commissioner's power and control over the Kavango population. As a result of these extended powers of the commissioner, the kings in Kavango were brought under control. They were used by the authorities to pass on information and apply colonial laws to their subjects and compel them to sign up for contract labour. Their loss of power to and control by the commissioner made them depend on co-operation as a means of survival. They helped the commissioner collect the tribal tax fund which all young men were expected to pay. The kings assisted the commissioner

---

[80] Frank Brownlee. (1917-05-21), To the secretary for the protectorate, Ovamboland labourers from Okavango (Windhoek, NAN. ADM 95, file 2794/8).

[81] Acting military magistrate. (1917-06-20), To the secretary for the protectorate Ovambo land labourers from Okavango Windhoek. NAN. ADM 95, file no 2794/8. The word 'Ovambo' in the text above is corrected to 'Mbunza' as King Karupu was the King in 'Mbunza area' along the Kavango River and also to show that the use of 'Ovambo' is a colonial misrepresentation of the people from the Kavango.

[82] U. Weyl. (1991), *Labour migration and underdevelopment in Malawi, late 19th century to mid 1970's*, p. 43.

[83] Native Commissioner (SWAA, 2083, A. 460/19). The following kings died in the 1920s period, Kandjimi Hawanga on 19 March 1923, Nyangana waMukuve on 23 December 1924, Ndango waShimbenda on November 1925.

to build grain storage facilities in their kingdom where the recruiting organization stored grains that were given as rations to contract labourers going to the south of Namibia and the kings were remunerated by the recruiting organizations for their services. Despite the kings of the Kavango sending labourers, the mines still experienced a large shortage in the supply of labourers and the administration thought that labourers from the Kavango could be induced to come south through the medium of African messengers.[84] By 1918, the numbers of labourers from the Kavango were reported to be sufficient with some to spare and the colonial authority expressed that a regular supply would be a valuable asset and should be encouraged by every reasonable means.[85]

The constant migration of the population across the Kavango River became a factor that impacted upon labour recruitment in the Kavango. The colonial position of wanting to limit recruitment only to men domiciled in Namibia was problematic. In many cases the local people claimed to be either domiciled or not domiciled in Namibia or Angola just to escape the colonial taxations and the relocation of individuals or families meant the loss of the pool of labour. The division of Kavango between Angola and Namibia meant therefore that the South African authorities relied more on the population on the Namibian side for labour; however, the constant movement of the population across the Kavango River, and the insufficient colonial control of such cross border movements meant that the availability of population on the Namibian side as labourers was unreliable. Besides, the tendency of population settlement across the river was to settle next to their hereditary king and it meant that any settlement of a king on one side of the river or the other meant the acquisition of more population as potential labourers for the relevant colonial administration. The South African administration thus avoided sending kings or people who crossed the river back to Angola despite the Portuguese/South African colonial agreement of 1917. This is evident in the advice of the Secretary of the S.W.A. protectorate to the Military Magistrate at Grootfontein who was on a mission to settle a dispute between two kings in the Hambukushu area of Kavango:

> If the Ovambo [Mbukushu] chief came there from Portuguese territory it would not be desirable if he is found to be the trespasser to order his return to Portuguese territory. If he is a fugitive from Portuguese territory you should assign him to a properly demarcated area and warn him against any trespassing from there.[86]

---

[84] Frank Brownlee, (1917-06-04), *ibid.*
[85] Frank Brownlee. (1918-03-11), To the secretary for the protectorate. Ovamboland labourers from Okavango. Windhoek, NAN, ADM 95, file 2794/8.
[86] The Secretary of South West Africa. (1919-06-27), To the military Magistrate of Grootfontein titled Re: Okavango matters. Windhoek, NAN, ADM 30, file 243/3, part III.

The colonial authorities spread reports about the Portuguese authorities mistreating the local people as a means to justify the settlement of the Kavango population from the Angolan side to the Namibian side as "fugitives" and thus increase their pool of contract labourers. The South African administration, therefore, was not interested in returning the population from their side as this would have been detrimental to their pool of contract labour.

Companies such as Luderitzbucht and South West Africa Company (hereafter SWACO) had previously received labourers from the Kavango but, in 1920, the government turned down their request for the further supply of labourers.[87] The reason for this refusal was because the companies did not have enough accommodation and also because the government had informed them previously that no further recruitment from the Kavango was to be allowed by their company until the administration had sent a permanent colonial official as a representative to the Kavango for the purpose of reporting on the possibility and advisability of such recruiting.[88] The other reason for turning down their request was because the market for diamonds had shrunk and thus they had reduced their production and the government did not see the merit of their request for additional labourers as they could do with their existing number of labourers from Ovamboland.

As a result, all labourers from the Kavango were dispatched to the Otavi mine and railways and to the farmers. The point to be made is that, although the men from the Kavango were not destined for the diamond mines in the south, the need to send them existed in the 1920s but was hampered by the company's economic setback in diamond production. Before and after the arrival of a Native Commissioner for the Kavango, missionaries were useful agents for labour recruitment in Kavango and Ovamboland. In Ovamboland, for example, missionaries were instrumental in distributing drought relief food which was sent by the colonial authorities to the mission stations not just as a humanitarian act but also to win the trust of the Ovambo and maintain the labour supply.[89] Missionaries were appointed to positions within the contract labour industry as they were seen to be more influential in encouraging their congregation members to go on contract. When it was finally decided, for instance, to appoint a Natives Affairs Commissioner on the diamond fields of the south, this post was given to Herman Tonjes an ex-Finnish missionary in Ovamboland who influenced the number of Ovambo men reporting for contract labour. Tonjes carried out expeditions annually together with Streiwolf to Ovamboland to visit various chiefs to build up friendly relations and to ensure an expansion of migrant labour supplies.[90]

---

[87] Luderitzbucht Chamber of Mines. (1920-08-07), Re: natives from the Okavango. Windhoek, NAN, SWAA 2407/ file A521/10.
[88] *Ibid.*
[89] Stals. (1967), Die aanraking tussen blankes en Ovambo's in Suidwes-Afrika, 1850–1915, p. 215.
[90] *Ibid.* pp. 226–227.

In the case of the Kavango, missionaries provided rations and travelling passes for contract labourers to travel to the southern part for work. They also stored the rifles which were provided to African escorts who took contract labourers to the south. Their role in the contract labour system gave them a double image in the eyes of the local people who saw them as God's people and also as colonizers.[91]

A Native Affairs Commissioner was finally posted to the Kavango at Nkurenkuru village by the South African colonial administration in 1921. He was authorized to act as:

> The agent of the administration in regard to improving and regulating the existing flow of Native Labour for Mines, Railways, and other work as also for building etc. by means of registers, passes, medical examinations etc. and encouraging the Okavango Natives to seek employment at these industrial centres. He will not interfere with existing tribal tenure and customs, except to act as an arbitrator as between Native Chiefs, if requested to do so. Any matter of serious import to be reported to Windhoek. He will use his influence to prevent deliberate and serious crimes – including witchcraft etc, but chiefs and headmen should have all matters pertaining to order and petty offences, as also civil cases, referred to them. He will maintain amicable relations with the Portuguese Authorities in Angola but will not hand over any Natives to or demand Natives from them except under instructions from Windhoek.[92]

The arrival of a permanent Native Affairs Commissioner in the Kavango was a turning point in the colonial relations with the local population as his activities and implementation of colonial policies affected the lives of the Kavango people and changed their lives forever. The first settled colonial representative to the Kavango, R. Dickman, locally known as Kasamane [old one], arrived at the time when men from Kavango were reluctant to proceed to the police zone.[93] This was due to the bad reports they had received from returning labourers about an epidemic which resulted in a high death toll. This the commissioner rejected as rumours as the following report indicates:

> The returning labourers from Mbunza and Ukwangali areas spread rumour to the effect that an epidemic had broken out in the south and that seven natives had died at the Grootfontein copper mines.[94]

---

[91] Shikiri waNkayira interview. (2009-08-08), Ndonga linena.
[92] Secretary of South West Africa. (1921-03-11), To the superintendent for native affairs at Nkurenkuru, Recruiting of native labour. Windhoek, NAN, ADM 30, file 243/3, part III.
[93] Police zone was a term that referred to the central and southern part of Namibia where contract labourers from Kavango and Ovamboland went for work and where there were stringent police controls over the Africans.
[94] Native Affairs Commissioner R. Dickman. (1923-12-01), To the Native Commissioner of South West Africa 'labour: Okavango district' (Windhoek, NAN ADM 30, file 243/3, part III).

In fact, in 1919 there were repeated outbreaks of the influenza epidemic. These were preceded by measles that swept the diamond fields with appalling suddenness and severity and resulted in as much as a 20% death toll amongst the workers at some sites.[95] These circumstances at the diamond mines were spread by returning labourers in both Kavango and Ovamboland and this increased fear among them and resulted in less men reporting for contract during the 1920s.[96] In his tour of the Kavango in the Shambyu and Gciriku areas in 1923, the Native Commissioner was unsuccessful in recruiting local men because most of them hid in the forest as he advanced into their villages. The commissioner was convinced by the women's explanation that most men were away in the bush to collect veldkos and this was despite the fact that they had a good rain and harvest the previous year.[97] Previously, most men from Kavango who were recruited at Tsumeb recruiting depot had been posted to work in the Luderitzbucht mines but, after 1923, men from the Kavango demanded to be recruited at the Grootfontein depot as a way to avoid being sent to Luderitzbucht where it was feared the epidemic had broken out. The new commissioner reported that any attempts to force the men to go to Tsumeb recruiting depot presented a great risk of their refusing to proceed to the south altogether and recruitment dropped as there were fears that they might actually be sent to the far south anyway:

> During my last journey along the river, I was informed by various headmen that natives having heard that others had gone to Grootfontein, and from there sent to Tsumeb and later to Luderitz, they now refused to go south.[98]

Faced with the protest of Kavango men against being recruited at Tsumeb depot for the Luderitz area, the office at Tsumeb was removed to Ondangwa and it was agreed that all the labourers from the Kavango would in future be employed in the Tsumeb/Grootfontein area only and that the magistrate of Grootfontein would be responsible for their medical examination, attestation and distribution.[99] The administration encouraged the Native Commissioner of Kavango to make this new arrangement widely known to all the kings and headmen and to instruct all future recruits from Kavango to report to the magistrate of Grootfontein. While this was simply a new strategy of labour extraction to the administration, it was certainly a victory for the Kavango labourers. It points to how people could shape recruiting practices and make decisions that they felt comfortable about.

---

[95] The Union of South Africa. (1919), Report. Windhoek, NAN, JX/0220, p. 6.
[96] 'The Union of South Africa. (1921), Report. (Windhoek, NAN, JX/0220, 1921, p. 12.
[97] Ibid.
[98] R. Dickman (1923-12-01), To the Native Commissioner of South West Africa (Windhoek, NAN, JX/0220.
[99] Ibid.

The commissioner embarked on putting an end to the apparently existing slave practice among the Kavango people.[100] Previously in 1921 Cocky Hahn (alias Kangora/Shongola) who was based in Ovamboland had made a number of visits to the Kavango apparently on a mission to end the "slavery practices" of the kings against their subjects.[101] Hahn received his nickname in Ovamboland because of his personal use of the sjambok to beat the local people. But, as Hayes has indicated, although no written sources exist that testify that Hahn himself personally used force, what is striking is that oral sources affirm that he frequently did so.[102] An oral source from the Kavango also affirms that Hahn personally used the sjambok. During one of his tours in the Kavango, Cocky Hahn was approached by the senior wife of King Nyangana named Nkayira with a case in which a man held her sister Nyama and children in "upika" servitude across the Kavango River on the Angolan side. Her granddaughter Theresia Shidona elaborates:[103]

> When Kangora came at this 'Unyondo' tree which is situated at the river side, my grandmother immediately went to meet Kangora and said 'Muranda has kept my young sister captive with all her children, he has made them 'vapika'. Kangora exclaimed 'Eee! That's exactly the kind of things I came for, good!' They slept, in the morning they went to collect them and brought them here. There was also another case at the same time of Mbangu who kept Shapirama in captive for having killed a person, he was instructed by his master to shoot and so he shot a person. They were all summoned here in that big Unyondo tree, hey! At the time of Kangora, I was also a witness and saw it all, I was a young girl. Then Muranda undressed and lied down on his knees and hand so that he was beaten while naked. Mother! That Kangora! He beat him until the buttocks were now becoming smaller and smaller until they were now just so small, Mother! Oh, no![104]

> [Ovyo anaya shimonyo-monyo Kangora, palighunyondo li lya kaliro kunya kumukuro, vamama kare kava kakuvhukumina kwaKangora ashi "Muranda wamuna mughunyande, mpwali kwendi navana vendi. Wavamuna ghupika" Ame waKangora "Eee! Vyavone mbyo nayere, yaa!" Kurara poo, ngura-ngura avavayendere kuyavatura. Ogho Mbangu ngoli naye nka wamunino ngoli Shapirama anaroyo muntu, kwamurenkire ntilyendi ashi roya, nko kumuroya, naye vanakamushimba. Mughunyondo muu, tati! Opo paKangora ne natuvantje vyakumona ngoli, atwene weno shimpe tjure, tjure kurapaghuka. VaShikonga na Mukonda na Kayando, navantje ana vashimbi ashi "vakaye navo". Makura oghu Muranda kushutura muromba ne nko kupakera panya nkokurara ngoli vavashepure matako-tako. Nane! Kangora! Ashi "ghombomana".

---

[100] 'The Union of South Africa. (1923), Report. (Windhoek, NAN, JX/0220, pp. 18–19.
[101] Theresia Shidona Weka interview. (2009-08-11), Guma village.
[102] P. Hayes. (1992), A history of the Ovambo of Namibia, 1830–1935, pp. 292–293.
[103] Theresia Shidona Weka was born at Mamono village in Namibia on14 May 1914 at and passed away in November 2009. She was the daughter of Angela Tunapu and King Josef Kamutuva Weka. Shidona was the granddaughter of Nkayira and King Nyangana.
[104] Theresia Shidona Weka interview. (2009-08-11), Guma village.

Mbangu naye kushutura likeshe, kushutura ruvya, ashi "vombomanenu namuvantje" Atwe kunakuvakenga. Ntani ngoli dimurungaa. Kava toghonanga vantu, nan! Kutoghona! Matako kaghadidipa- kaghadidipa, Kaghadidipa-kaghadidipa, mpo ghana kuyahura ngolipane, nane! Hee, a-a! Navantje kare kavavaghupuko, vanayashungiri kunyonga yavamama Nkayira. NavaNyama wakuyita vanane Nandjira vanashungiri. "Tundenuko ngoli muyekuno! Kumumunanwe, ashi oko ngakamumuninane kuni? Ogho Muranda gho! Shipungu shimwe-shimwe ntjo shakumunina muntu ndi? NanJ.

The establishment of courts by the commissioners and the provision of flogging were promulgated in 1928 in chapter three of Proclamation Number 15 of 1928. Colonial flogging had been practised by colonial officials in both the Kavango and Ovamboland earlier than that. In the Kavango, people who were found guilty of slave practices were stripped naked and given public floggings and fined by the Commissioner. These punishments were great public humiliation for most of the people. The employment of the term slavery as an equivalent of the local term "upika" by the colonial officials to describe what practically represented to the Kavango groups the relationship of servant to master or debtor to creditor, was unfortunate. As was later realized by the colonial officials, there was nothing in the nature of the generally accepted term slavery which could be equated to the local term "mupika".[105] Instead, the term mupika (singular) or vapika (plural) could refer to a subject, or a servant.[106] The vapika at times voluntary pledged themselves and their children as security for some debt or obligation and the period lasted only whilst the obligation existed. These vapika had their own fields, their own cattle and vapika of their own, they could marry anyone, exchange masters at their own will and were allowed free movement to settle from one territory to another. For the colonial officials however, slave practices included the presence of many people in large homesteads and the king's palace. In the numerous meetings held by the commissioner of the Kavango, he informed the chiefs and their people that the administrator was extremely upset to hear that people were being bartered or sold like cattle, and ordered that the practice must henceforth cease.[107]

The colonial action of putting an end to slavery practices among the local population was more of a colonial strategy for labour control than a humanitarian action. One impact of the commissioner's campaign against slavery was that homesteads with large families and other dependents were broken down. People were compelled to reduce the number of people in their homesteads or palaces and build smaller independent households. This increased the number homesteads and of the household heads who had to enlist for contract

---

[105] 'The Union of South Africa. (1923), Report. (Windhoek, NAN, JX/0220), pp. 18–19.
[106] Ibid.
[107] Ibid.

labour to be able to support their new independent households.[108] Throughout the 1920s fewer labour recruits were forthcoming from both the Kavango and Ovamboland and this led to a serious labour crisis between 1923 and 1925.[109] The diamond mines in Namibia especially were complaining of labour shortages, but the colonial administration lacked infrastructural capacity to extract more labourers from the Kavango. The administration was not prepared to take the sole responsibility of recruiting and their alternative in view of this problem was to stop recruiting from the Kavango altogether.[110] The Administration convened a meeting in Windhoek on 6th September 1923 with the representatives of the mines who recommended that a representative of the mines visit the Kavango area for the purpose of investigating the roads, water supply and most likely centres for obtaining recruits.[111] However, despite efforts by the Luderitz Chambers of Mines and OMEG to implement the proposal for expedition it was not executed apparently on the grounds that:

> The number of natives in that area is very limited, and even supposing the expedition was successful in combing out one or two hundred more labourers this would not materially affect native labour supply and unless a good case can be made out, it is regretted the permit applied for cannot be granted.[112]

The above seems to indicate that the refusal of permission was that the population of Kavango was too small, but such a conclusion excludes other factors such as the lack of interest and the protests of Kavango men. The men from Kavango therefore continued to be allocated only to the Tsumeb and Grootfontein mines while the diamond mines in the south were to receive Ovambo exclusively so as to meet the wishes of the local people of Kavango. As the general manager of a mine explained:

> If the very same boys are allocated to the copper mines and Ovambos thereby released for the diamond mines, everyone, including the natives themselves, has all reason to be satisfied.[113]

---

[108] Kumbwa interview. (2008-07-09), Bagani village.
[109] T. Emmett. (1999), *Popular resistance and the root of nationalism in Namibia, 1915–1966*. Basel, P.Schlettwein Publishing, pp.174–175.
[110] The secretary of South West Africa. (1926-07-02), To the administrator of S.W.A, 'Native labour recruitment-Okavango natives. Windhoek, NAN, SWAA 2407, file no. A 521/10.
[111] Sgd. M Otzen. (1924-02-23), To the inspector of mines. Windhoek, NAN, SWAA 2407, file no. A521/10.
[112] The secretary for South West Africa. (1924-03-31), To the secretary for Luderitz Chamber of Mines, 'investigation of native Labour resources: Okavango. Windhoek, N.A.N, SWAA 2408, file F/521/11.
[113] The general manager of Luderitzbucht. (1924-11-27), To the secretary of South West Africa, 'Re: native labour' Windhoek, N.A.N, SWAA 2408, file F/521/11.

The formation of the Northern Labour Organization (NLO) and its operations, 1925–1943

Since the labourers from the Kavango after 1923 were no longer in favour of working at the diamond areas of Luderitz in the south of Namibia, the authorities in Namibia had to consider this boycott and come up with a new strategy for ensuring a continued supply of labourers for the diamond mines in the south and recruited labour from South Africa, Bechuanaland and Basutoland[114] An outstanding feature of the first ten years of South African rule in Namibia (1915–1925) was the ability of the northern areas (Kavango and Ovamboland) to resist the pressure of the colonial state to extract a migrant labour force.[115] The colonial administration therefore needed to find internal solutions to address as a matter of urgency the labour demands of the diamond areas and the white farmers' needs. The colonial administration finally convened all the major stake holders in the economy at a conference in 1924 to address the labour supply crisis. The outcome of the conference was the formation of two recruiting organizations, the Northern Labour Organization (NLO) and the Southern Labour Organization (SLO) in 1925 which began the official organized recruiting of contract labourers from the Kavango and Ovambo respectively. The ethnic and economic rivalry relationship between the German owned copper mines in Tsumeb and the coastal diamond mines, owned by British/South African capital was part of the reason for the creation of the two (NLO and SLO) recruiting organizations which supplied labour to the copper and diamond mines respectively.[116] However, it is important to recognize that it accommodated the 1923 demands by Kavango men not to be recruited in the danger ridden diamond mines of the south. The SLO agreed with the diamond mines of the south to draw contract labourers from Ovamboland while the NLO got permission from the administration to supply northern mines and industrial concerns and farmers in the territory with African labour from the Kavango. NLO undertook the first expedition to the Kavango in December 1925 to establish rest camps on the migrant routes (These were the Gciriku-Muramba matako-Nuragas-Karukuvisa and thence to Grootfontein route and the Nkurenkuru-Grootfontein or Nkurenkuru via Ntsintsabis thence to Tsumeb route). A representative of NLO, Mr. E. Schoenfelder (locally known as Katjire), who was sent to report on labour conditions in the Kavango returned in 1926 and by 1927 Mr. Bertrand of

---

[114] T. Emmet. (1999), *Popular resistance and the root of nationalism in Namibia, 1915–1966*, pp. 176–177.
[115] *Ibid*, p. 79.
[116] J. Silvester, M. Wallace and P. Hayes. (1998), Mobility and containment: an overview, 1915–1946. In P. Hayes (ed.), *Namibia under South African rule, mobility & containment, 1915–46* (Oxford, James Currey Ltd), p. 39.

the NLO reported that they were obtaining all the recruits that they could possibly expect to get from Nyangana area.[117] Although the NLO obtained men from Angola and Northern Rhodesia (Zambia) as contract labourers this was not supported by the administration as the following indicates:

> The administration does not desire that natives from outside the territory be recruited. A copy of your letter is forwarded to Mr. Eedes and he is being requested to see that in future headmen do not allow natives to cross over and settle in South West Africa.[118]

The labour organization was therefore at pains to identify and recruit only people who were domiciled on the South West African/Namibia side of the Kavango and this impacted negatively on their recruitment process as is shown by the NLO secretary to the administration secretary:

> We can assure you that all our recruiting is and until the administration removes the recent restrictions will be confined to the Ovambos and the Okavango [Kavango] tribes. As regards these latter we should like to beg his honour the administrator to allow us some latitude. We should point out that the natives of these tribes are, as regards domicile, exceedingly mobile and unstable. A village which is this week or this month on S.W.A. side of the river may, by next week or next month, have shifted with all its inhabitants to the other side of the Okavango [Kavango], or vice-versa. Six important groups from Diriko [Gciriku] area have transferred themselves to the Portuguese side within the last twelve months or so. These changes of domicile are so frequent that it is impossible for us to be certain in every case whether recruits desiring contracts are technically domicile or originated in this territory. But we view with apprehension the present trend of the natives from the South West African to the Portuguese side which will remove so many of them from our source of labour supply, if the present restrictions are to be maintained in all their severity.[119]

In view of this threat of migration and loss of potential labourers a need for stringent control over the labour supply was necessary and the colonial authority in Namibia passed the Northern and Extra Territorial Native Control (NETNC) Proclamation No. 29 of 1935 which finally allowed control and recruitment of labour outside Namibia and indicated a change of heart to their earlier policy of refusing NLO to recruit outside Namibia.[120] The proclama-

---

[117] The Northern Labour Organization. No year. Windhoek, NAN, SWAA 1/1/46, 2426, A521/26 (V.5).
[118] 'Illegal recruiting, administrator to the managing secretary of NLO' (1935-12-14).Windhoek, NAN, NAR 1/1/55, file 11/1/2.
[119] 'NLO managing secretary. (1935-11-28), To the secretary for South West Africa Windhoek, NAN, NAR1/1/55, file 11/1/2.
[120] 'Circular on Control of Extra- Territorial and Northern Natives. (1936-01-08). Windhoek, NAN, NAT 1/1/54, S/U-20, file 25.

tion defined a "native" as one whose parents is an aboriginal and it required the compilation of a register of all "natives" in the territory. The policy of the administration was to prevent the detribalization of the Kavango and Ovambo people. In pursuance of this policy such Africans were normally to return to their homes periodically.

Proclamation No. 39 of 1935 required all Africans from Kavango and Ovamboland to possess an identification pass to be recruited in the police zone and discouraged further issuing of visiting passes to them. Visiting passes were no longer issued to Africans to limit their movements to the urban areas only for employment purposes and thus control the Africans as reserves for colonial labour. It was agreed that a metal tube container as used in Northern Rhodesia should be issued to the African labourers to carry their identification passes. These Africans were mainly recruited by companies such as SWACO and the Otavi Minen Und Eisenbahn Gesellschaft (OMEG) of Tsumeb, Otavi and Grootfontein areas. The series of colonial regulations that were provided in 1935 did not only prevent the Africans from Kavango and Ovamboland from moving permanently to the city but it helped to channel migrant labour at reduced wages.

Act No. 32 of 1937 declared the Kavango as a Native Territory and a tribal fund tax was introduced to be paid by any man who belonged to the Kavango Native Territory. Tribal fund tax was a colonial strategy for labour recruitment which targeted only matured men who were not physically challenged to report as contract labourers for the colonial economy.

The Native Commissioner continued to be a central recruiting agent and did all that was in his power to ensure a great supply of contract labourers. He created a camp in each of the area of the five ethnic groups where he used to convene meetings to inform people of colonial policies. In his meetings in 1937, he provided men with certificates in metal tubes to identify them for tax payments. He levied and collected tribal tax of a rate of 5/- on all males over the age of eighteen years as from the 1st of October every year.[121]

The system of administration in the Kavango was quite different to that in Ovamboland. There were no headmen or sub headmen, and the administration therefore had to create new "tribal" administrative structures. The colonial administration divided the Kavango into six tribal administrative units each with appointed native recruiters (also known as labour headmen) whose service may be withdrawn at any given notice.[122] The kings usually recommended their next of kin for positions of native recruiters and they were subject

---

[121] The Chief Native Commissioner in Windhoek. (1938-01-23), to the Assistant Native Commissioner of Rundu. Windhoek, NAN, NAR 1/1/55, file N4/3/2.

[122] By 1939 the following were the native recruiters, Phillipus Mudiro for the reserve area, Shivanda for Kwangali, Kasiki for Mbunza, Frans Kashasha for Shambyu, LinusShashipapo for Gciriku and Muyatwa for Mbukushu area.

to the orders of the Native Commissioner and their kings.[123] These native recruiters did not have a fixed salary but were remunerated depending on the number of recruits they enlisted and escorted to the police zone. Native recruiters therefore created their own links within communities for more potential labourers to report to them for work. Since some of the potential labourers had to cross from Angola, they needed boats to be able to cross as the Kavango River had a lot of crocodiles and other dangerous reptiles. The NLO did not have boats to ferry potential recruits across the Kavango River and depended on local boat owners. NLO remunerated boat owners for each recruit ferried by deducting small amounts from the salary of the designated labour headmen and this caused conflicts between the local boat owners and the labour headmen.[124] The native recruiters or labour headmen became well respected figures within their communities and others like Langhals Kanyinga accumulated wealth.[125]

The NLO previously enjoyed the sole role of recruiting in the Kavango and Angola until this role was challenged by an Anglo-American recruitment association named Witwatersrand Native Labour Association (WENELA) which recruited men for the South African gold mines and the tobacco farmers of Southern Rhodesia (Zimbabwe).[126] WENELA had a recruitment office at Shakawe in Botswana with Mr. Matthias Davis as their recruiting agent. When WENELA began its recruitment operations into Angola and Kavango Native territory by the late 1930s, more Kavango men chose to be recruited by WENELA for the South African mines and the Zimbabwe tobacco farms. The WENELA native recruiters in Kavango were seen actively looking for more people to recruit in Kavango and only increased the fear of the NLO in Namibia.[127] The fear by NLO was that because WENELA paid higher wages than NLO, labourers therefore chose WENELA causing the NLO to fear losing control over their recruiting area. The recruiting activities by WENELA in the Kavango were seen as illegal as WENELA had no formal agreements as was indicated by the Assistant Native Commissioner of Rundu:

---

[123] Langhans Kanyinga. (1936-01-02), Declaration. Windhoek, NAN, NAR 1/1/55, file 11/1/2.
[124] See report on the conflict between native recruiter for Sambyu area, Kashasha and Mbandje, a boat owner at Runtu, in, 'native recruiter, Sambio area' (Windhoek, NAN, NAR1/1/55, 11/7).
[125] He was a native recruiter in the Vagciriku territory during the German and early South African period. For more on the story of Langhals Kanyinga's fortunes and wealth see a Rumanyo biographic novel by A.H. Kanyinga. (2002), *Liparu mu Sancana* (Windhoek, Gamsberg Macmillan).
[126] In 1934, WENELA established a depot at Maun, in Ngamiland for recruitment of Batswana and other natives such as Angolas and Barotses. Within a short time the number of such recruits warranted the establishment of a WENELA station at Muhembo border.
[127] No author. (1937-02-04), Native recruiters: Okavango recruiters. Windhoek, NAN, NAR 1/1/55, file 11/7.

I beg to inform you that no organized recruiting of the Kavango Native Territory is being undertaken by Mr. Davis on behalf of the Johannesburg Gold mines. In any case, it is not possible to prevent S.W.A. natives from going to the Union via Bechuanaland if they wish to do so. It seems an established fact that that during the last 3 to 4 weeks, a number of natives from this side of the river left their kraals going to Muhembo to be recruited there for the Rand. Many boys from the Kavango Native Area intend going as well.[128]

The NLO's pool of labour was therefore threatened and it had to consider new strategies for labour recruitment. The administration on behalf of NLO finally reached a consensus with WENELA that NLO will limit its recruitments in Namibia while WENELA will limit its recruitment operation to Angola.[129] The new restriction was justified as follows:

In view of the fact that no surplus labour exists in either the Union or South West Africa, any exodus of labour will have a detrimental effect on both the Union and South West Africa as the case may be. Should the doors be thrown open to facilitate a free flow of labour, the labour position in South West Africa will most definitely deteriorate since experience has shown that natural flow of labour will tend to favour the Union. Hence, the present position actually protects the interests of the South-West-Africa employer. For this reason, it was agreed that South West Africa natives will not be employed in the union and that such natives who enter the union clandestinely would be returned to South West Africa.[130]

The administration in Kavango used the kings to inform their subjects that men were no longer allowed to get recruited in South Africa and as such, some local people concluded that it was their kings who were responsible for this. As Shikombero shows:

It happened like this. It was later decided by King Shashipapo that 'I do not want my subjects of Gciriku territory to continue going to Djwaini (Johannesburg mines) because people are dying there when the mine collapses. I no longer wish you to go'. That was when we people use to go there at the recruitment centres and register ourselves as Angolans because if you said you were a Gciriku person you were not permitted.[131]

[Weno mmo vyashorokire. Muruku ayarenkire hompa Shashipapo ashi kapi nashana vantu vande vamugciriku vayendange ku Djwaini mbyovi vantu kunakafa ngudu, mina kumbanduka. Kapi nashana nka ashi muyendangeko. Vantu mpo kavarenkanga ngoli kuyenda vakakutjangite ashi vaAngora, ntjene aghutwenya ashi mugciriku nakukupulitirashi]

---

[128] No author. Native labour recruitment-Okavango natives. Windhoek, NAN, SWAA 2407-A521/10/2.
[129] No author. 1944-06-28), Rest camps on the Okavango River. Windhoek, NAN, SWAA 1/1/46, 2426, A521/26 V.5.
[130] Ibid.
[131] Mathias Ndumba Shikombero interview (2009-07-28), Rucara village.

The decision to stop Namibians from going to the South African mines was not the kings' decision and the local people's view of making the kings central in this restriction indicates that there was a thin dividing line of co-operation between the kings and the colonial authorities in the labour recruitment process. But as Shikombero's interview shows people subverted these restrictions. Despite the agreement with WENELA, the NLO continued to lose labourers as more men preferred South Africa rather than Namibia. This threat over the pool of labour from the Kavango forced NLO to expand its recruitment among the Ovambo for the northern mines and farms of Grootfontein, Otavi and Tsumeb and not limit the Ovambo labourers to the diamond mines of the south as was by then the practice.

By the early 1940s, the SLO which operated solely in Ovamboland felt its position threatened by the recruitment operation of NLO in Ovamboland and demanded that the South West Africa administrator be allowed to expand its recruitment jurisdiction to include recruiting for farm work from both Ovambo and Kavango areas though this was against the mutual agreement between NLO and SLO operations.[132] The administrator's response was that if the NLO was allowed to recruit in Ovamboland it would not object to the SLO being allowed to recruit in the Kavango area, provided the SLO was restricted to its own mining requirements and that this would result in a duplication of service if the SLO was allowed to recruit for farm labour.[133] These advances of the NLO into Ovamboland, the complaints and demands from SLO with regard to its wish to expand recruitment for farm and mine labourers from Kavango, encouraged new talks for the possibility and the need to form a recruiting organization which would operate in both Kavango and Ovamboland to recruit for the mines and farms of South West Africa/Namibia.

The formation of South West Africa Native Labour Association (SWANLA) and its operations

The South West Africa Administration considered it expedient under these strained relationships that the two recruiting organizations (NLO and SLO) should amalgamate their business into one. By 1942 therefore a constitution was drafted for the new concern which would take over the business of both the NLO and SLO in terms of the amalgamation agreed upon.[134] By 1943 therefore, NLO and SLO merged into South West Africa Native Labour Association (hereafter SWANLA) with the following objectives:

---

[132] No author. Suggested revision of agreement between NLO and SLO for the recruitment in Ovamboland and the Kavango. Windhoek, NAN, SWAA 1/1/46, 2426, 521/26, V.5.
[133] *Ibid.*
[134] No author. (1942-11-24), Amalgamation: Northern Labour Organization Limited and Luderitz Chamber of Mines recruiting'. Windhoek, NAN, SWAA 1/1/46, 2426, A521/26, V.5.

To recruit and distribute African labour; to carry on business in the recruiting areas as retail general dealers and hawkers; to watch, protect and further the interests of the employers and of the recruited labourers; to purchase or otherwise acquire, sell, lease or hire any movable and/ or immovable property; to lend or invest money with or without security, and to borrow money or mortgage bond or otherwise; to use profits to centre a reserve fund; to reduce recruiting charges subject to the improvement relating to recruiting, to the reduction of recruiting charges; to do all such other things as the Association may consider to be incidental or conducive to the above stated objectives.[135]

SWANLA had its main offices in Rundu and Ondangwa and a recruiting depot in Grootfontein. The underage teenagers from Kavango, Ovamboland and Angola were also recruited by SWANLA and engaged to do farm work and, although an order was granted to prohibit the practice of underage recruitments after 1948, it continued.[136] The labourers from Angola and Zambia came to Namibia with underage relatives and, since they could not return home alone or be left uncared for, they were permitted to proceed south for employment.[137] In view of these circumstances it was proposed that an additional class "D" should be created for these underage labourers who could be supplied for light farm work or domestic services in towns to employers recommended by the Magistrate.[138]

By the 1950s, a new proclamation was promulgated which authorized the Northern and Extra- Territorial Natives on expiry of contracts of service to enter into new contract with the original employer, or with others as long as a strict condition was observed whereby a total period of service did not exceed two years.[139] Originally contract labourers were recruited for a contract period of 12 months but in the 1950s this was changed to between 18 months and two years with the right to renew it for an extra six months.[140]

The evolution behind these new extended labour contracts was a result of the lack of labour and the need to make the best out of the available labour. In Kavango traditional rulers were against this new policy of engaging their men on 18 months' contract.[141] But this change of the duration of the contract period was a self-sustaining strategy of the colonial economy and was implemented regardless of the opposition of the Africans. The colonial

---

[135] The draft constitution of SWANLA. Windhoek, NAN, SWAA 1/1/46, 2426, A521/26, V.5.
[136] M.J, Oliviers. (1961), Inboorlingheid en administrasie in die mandaat gebied van Suid Wes-Afrika. PhD Thesis, Stellenbosch, pp. 276–277.
[137] The Native Commissioner of Rundu. (1945-06-11), To Chief Native Commissioner. Windhoek, NAN, SWAA 1/1/46, 2426, A521/26 (V.6).
[138] Ibid.
[139] Circular letter. (1950-10-16), To agents of SWANLA. Windhoek, NAN, SWAA 1/1/46, 2426, A521/26.
[140] M.J. Oliviers. (1961), Inboorlingheid en administrasie in die mandaat gebied van Suid Wes-Afrika, p. 307.
[141] Ibid.

administration shrugged it off and believed that the Kavango people will sooner or later come to accept it.[142] The labour narratives in the subsequent chapter on labour migration indicate that the long duration of contract work remained a cause for concern among contract labourers until the end of the contract labour system by 1972.

Conclusion

This chapter has emphasized the centrality of the colonial administration in the development of the contract labour system in the Kavango as the colonial officials remunerated the kings to compel their subjects to go on contract work. The early recruitment attempts in the Kavango were weak because people had access to resources. During the German colonial period the lack of physical structures and permanent administration officials coupled with the local people's hatred of the German administration contributed to the low labour migration response from the Kavango at that time.

The chapter shows that the Kavango men had some agency and made decisions as to where they would not go as when they resisted being sent to the death ridden diamond mines of the Luderitz area through the Tsumeb recruiting depot. The refusal effectively defeated the administration's wishes and compelled the administration after 1925 to limit the distribution of contract labourers from the Kavango to the mines and farms in the northern and central areas of the police zone.

The greater organization of labour control during the South African colonial period through the formation of SLO and NLO was not very effective although it was an improvement compared to the German colonial period. Although NLO re-organized labour supply from the Kavango, the continued complaints of labour shortage indicate ineffectiveness which finally compelled its merging with SLO into SWANLA by the early 1940s. How effective SWANLA was in securing labourers from the Kavango is one of the questions addressed in the subsequent chapter. It focuses on contract labourers themselves and their accounts of reasons for migration and their migration journeys.

---

[142] *Ibid.*

2 "They Used to Buy Us"[1]: Labour Migration from Kavango

Introduction

Colonialism was central to labour migration from the Kavango. The introduction of western clothes by Europeans and black slave traders created a need for western clothes but the colonial prevention of trading activities and the game protection cut off local supplies for clothes and exerted pressure on the Kavango men to migrate as contract labourers. Labour migration from Kavango during the German occupation period was low and totalled only 122 men between 1910 and 1913.[2] This is in contrast to Ovamboland which recorded 9 295 labourers in 1911, 6 076 in 1912 and 12 025 in 1913.[3]

The table below while not a comprehensive statistical compilation, shows the extent of the disparity in migration from the Kavango and Ovamboland in the 1920s, the 1940s and 1950s. It shows that despite the operations of NLO and later SWANLA, the numbers reporting for contract labour system from the Kavango were low. However, the table also indicates that recruitment by SWANLA (1943–1972) was better than its predecessor NLO (1925–1942).

Year	Kavangoland	Ovamboland
1924	346	3273
1925	243	3269
1926	355	4033
1941	639	4060
1942	351	3137
1943	539	6659
1959	1033	14960

Table 1: SWANLA recruitments compiled from, "The annual report of SWA Administrator of 1938–40 on labour recruitments from Kavango", (AKA 552, N1/15/6-2 and. from "The Union of South Africa report on labour recruitments" (JX0220, 1924, 1925 & 1926), labour recruitments 1938–1940', AKA 552, N1/15, 6-2 and from SWAA 1/1/46, A521/26 (v.5).

---

[1] This is the statement which was made by interviewees about their view of the contract labour system. See Ndumba Shirengumuke interview (2009-07-03), Rucara village and George Mukoya (Shamandimbe) Weka interview. (2009-07-27), Rucara village.
[2] A. Eckl. (2004), Konfrontation und kooperation am Kavango (Nord Namibia) von 1891 bis 1921 (PhD Thesis, University of Cologne, 2004), p. 120.
[3] See M.J. Oliviers. (1961), Inboorlingheid en administrasie in die mandaat gebied van Suid Wes-Afrika. PhD Thesis, Stellenbosch, p. 253.

This trend continued for the whole period of the contract system and by 1971 it was reported that there were 43 000 contract labourers in Namibia of which only 3000 were from the Kavango and the rest were from Ovamboland.[4] The statistics for labour migration indicate that the response to labour migration in the Kavango was not the same as in Ovamboland as there was never the same value attached to contract labour migration in the Kavango as in Ovamboland.[5] This chapter seeks to analyze why men from the Kavango, few as they were in comparison to those from Ovamboland, became contract labourers. Further, this chapter draws attention to labour migration journeys. While workers may have been men, this chapter highlights the role of women in the contract labour system as it emerges from these oral history narratives. Rather than relying solely on the colonial documents in the archives and on written sources, this chapter draws substantially on oral histories.

Reasons for contract labour migration

In Ovamboland labour migration is related to the process of pauperization combined with severe short fall in the colonial economies. An era of intensive raiding and impoverishment is said to have resulted in a generational conflict and labour migration became a way for young men to compensate for subsistence economies reduced by rinderpest, famine and raiding with fire arms for slaves and cattle.[6] Drought and the kings' taxation led to men without cattle, and a process of pauperization among the Ovambo was set in motion which the society was incapable of relieving. As raiding and trading were increasingly curtailed by the expansion of the colonial system, a form of culture transfer in favour of migrant labour occurred.[7] Moorsom provides an analysis of how workers from Ovamboland accounted for their movement into contract labour: 59% said it was because of poverty, 20% said it was to help family and 8% wanted cattle, 7% wanted clothes, 1% land, 4 % wished to marry and 1% wanted adventure.[8]

In the Kavango, lack of clothing was the main problem they faced and was central in the labour migration by contract labourers. The love for clothes had been introduced to the Kavango people by colonialists (European hunters, traders etc) and accessibility to it was again

---

[4] J. Kane-Berman. (1972), *Contract labour in South West Africa*. Johannesburg, South African Institute of Race Relations, 1972, p. 5.
[5] M.J. Olivier. (1961), Inboorlingbeleid en administrasie in die mandaad gebied van Suid Wes-Afrika, p. 253.
[6] M. Mckittrick. (1996), The burden of young men: generational conflict and property rights in Ovamboland, *African Economic History*, (24) p. 120.
[7] R. Moorsom. (1997), Underdevelopment, contract labour and worker consciousness in Namibia, 1915–1972, p. 71.
[8] *Ibid.*

curtailed later by the commissioner and police. The mission stations in the area were not providing clothes and the colonial prevention of the killing of animals reduced accessibility to animal skins for traditional clothing and people therefore left as contract workers (not to supplement food supplies as they always had these in abundance) but to acquire money to purchase clothes. This is indicated by Mathias Ndumba Shikombero, a contract labourer whose first contract was to Djwaini (Johannesburg) mines in the 1950s at Mziginya mine. After Johannesburg he soon left for contract work to Angola where he experienced mistreatment at work. After Angola he left for Grootfontein in Namibia and worked at a company in the Tsumeb area. He escaped from contract work and walked back to Kavango because he was unhappy with a low salary as he was used to higher pay in Johannesburg mines. After a brief stay at home he went for another contract to Grootfontein and was sent to Walvis Bay but received the same low pay. By 1971 after the contract workers' strike he returned to Kavango. Shikombero explains the central need for clothes:

> In the past, you could survive even if you did not go on contract work. There was always a variety wild fruits on which we survived. We went on contract work simply because there were no clothes! Those traditional skins which we previously wore were no longer favoured by anyone as we had by then imitated from our friends [the whites]. We were now all interested in the nice clothes of the whites. Where else would you get the skins to make the traditional dress? There was nowhere to get it since the whole forest was now full of the nature conservation officials who protected those animals. Where else would one get a skin dress since you could no longer kill a buck to use its skin and soften it into a traditional skin dress? Previously it was possible because there were no nature conservation officials and that was why it was possible to get a skin to make a traditional dress. But later on when the animals were prohibited, where else could we get animal skins? That was when we just got stuck to wearing their clothing which we still continue to wear.[9]

> [Pakare mpili kapi unakuyenda ku kontraka kuvhura shimpe kuparuka. Mpoghuli mughome, ntimba mpodili, maguni mpoghali, matu, ntjaki vinke, navintje ovyo katuparukanga vene. Kukontrakane katuyenderangako morwa vidwatasha kwato! Odinya dimuromba detu mpwalinka oghu kadinyenenango, ameshi tunahonenesha ngoli kuvaghunyetu? Tunanyenene vidwata vyaviwa ngoli vyavamakuwa. Vipapa vyadimuromba kuninko nka ukavishimba? Kwako, wiya naghuntje vaNatuur ngoli vakukungo ovyo vikorama. Kuni uviwananka ashi kughudipaya mbambi ushunte udwate? Panya pashakare kwatosha ngoli vakukunga, mbyo katukaranga kuwana shipapane kushishuntane kudwata ngoli. Ano murukune vanavishweneke vikorama

---

[9] Mathias Ndumba Shikombero interview. 2009-07-28. Mathias Ndumba Shikombero was born at Mashemeno on 4 August 1933. His parents King Shikombero and Memba were from the Vakankora royal clan. His parents later settled at Makena village where he grew up. He returned to the Kavango after the 1971 workers' strike and never went on contract work again. He lived as a fisherman along the Kavango River afterward.

makura shipapa kuni ushiwananka?Makura kukakatera ngoli mbyovyo vyavo ovi tunakudwata ngoli makura].

It is interesting to note that, although men in the Kavango had to pay the tribal fund tax after the Kavango was declared as a Native Territory in 1937, they did not provide tax payment as the reasons for going on contract work. It is thus less central in their view in labour migration than other factors. The young men felt inferior to a returning labourer as a result of his change in appearance, status and difference to them. The men discussed these issues with excitement as they herded cattle in the valleys. The community also organized feasts for returning contract labourers all of which gave them the impetus to go on contract labour system. The "shiperu" dancing feasts for returning labourers became platforms of entertainment for other men on their way to the Rundu compound.[10]

Some men thought that while during childhood a boy was associated with domestic or family work, manhood required of a man to leave home and search for goods or means to support the family and the contract labour system became the only viable option. It seems that in some, if not many, African community traditional marriage practices were impacted upon as men regarded preparation for marriage as an important reason for labour migration. In the Phokeng area, South Africa, unmarried men are said to have migrated as labourers to earn enough money to pay "Bogadi" (bride wealth) to enable them to get married and that by the 1930s all young men could be said to have gone to the city to work for this purpose.[11]

The need to prepare for marriage must not be spoken about in isolation from the influence and the control that the colonial administrative officials exercised over African traditional marriage practices. Men in the Kavango also provided the need to start a family as another reason for joining the contract labour system. The notion was that a man must acquire money to be able to start a family and maintain it. Some young men therefore went into contract work as preparation for marriage. Men from the Kavango, however, could get a woman to marry without having to go into contract labour system as marriages were arranged by parents. The parents found a wife for the son and negotiated with the parents of the woman. Although the contract labour was not a prerequisite for marriage; the commissioner promoted this idea as a means of labour control. As the following report indicates:

> It is stressed that parents should not allow their daughters to marry youngsters, who, through laziness have acquired nothing on which to maintain a home, a wife and children. Labour ennobles and parents should insist on their sons going out and earn

---

[10] Kamenye Likuwa interview. (2009-08-13), Kangweru village.
[11] B. Bozzoli. (1991), *Women of Phokeng*, p. 84.

cash wages. After all the parents have to rear off their offspring and it is up to the latter to say thanks in a material manner.[12]

As a result of the insistence of the commissioner that the parents should refuse marriage of their daughters to "youngsters" who have not yet gone on contract work, migration into contract labour system became a ritual act of transformation into maturity by some young men in preparation for marriage. Benhard Limbangu Shampapi was a contract labourer who worked at Walvis Bay in 1966 and became politicized by SWAPO before working at a mine in Windhoek. After his return to Kavango in the 1970s he worked for the Portuguese in Angola and got entangled in Angola's civil war. He explains

> In the past, according to the lives of the people of Kavango and perhaps too those of Ovamboland, when you grow up, say around the age of sixteen and above, we would say one has got to go and test himself among the whites before you come back to start a family. You needed to first go and work among the whites to acquire goods such as pots, plates. When you returned from contract work, that was when you began to search for a wife to marry. This was like the culture for men. The reason why I went on contract was because of the need to start a family. I also wanted to acquire money to be able to purchase and wear clothes just as other men were doing. In those times, if you got the luck to be sent to a good white man who paid well, you would acquire money to purchase a cow so that you also accumulate your own wealth, and that was the purpose.[13]

> [Pakare liparu lyetu atwe vakavango pamwe kumwe vene navaWambo.Nange unakuru pamwaka walye murongo nahamboghumwe shitware kumeho ashi kukakutota tanko kuvirumbu, kughuto wopo ngoyawana lipata, nkwandi kuhova tanko kukakutota ghukawaneko vyakuyaghuraghura palipata yira vapoto, visha navintje vinya vyakuyaparukita ngoli namukamali woye. Pakukatunda ngoli oko ntani unakuyashana lipata.Kwakalire yira ndjo mpo vene yavakafumu.Shitambo nayendilireko amene ntjosho sharuhepo rwalipata, nganikashane name nganiyaghuraghure name yanidwate yira momo vanakudwata vaghunyande. Mbyovyoshi pakare nange unakawana shirumbu wakufuta nawa mmo ngaghuyawana maliva ghakuyaghura ngombe, shinenepo ngombe, ghuwane nove kaghugavo koye, ntjo shitambo vene]

There was a tendency in the Namibian colonial archival documents to explain the high or low turnout of contract labourers for contract work on the availability of food in their areas.

---

[12] See report titled 'Meetings with Chiefs and headmen, Annual meeting held at Runtu on 3 January 1952 to 5 January 1952' (SWAA 1852 File 2/16/3/6).

[13] Benhard Limbangu Shampapi, Rucara village, 28 July 2009. Limbangu was born at Lighuyu village (Namibian side of the river) on 24 August 1946. His parents are Garu and Murarero. He worked for the Portuguese after his last contract in Namibia and was entangled in the Angolan civil war which he quit by 1977 and returned with his wife and settled at Rucara village (Namibia) where his parents had settled since the civil war in Angola. He later in 1996 got a job as a hostel worker until he retired in 2006.

Lack of rain and poor harvest was used to explain the high increase in labour migration while high rain and good harvest explained the low labour migration turn out. The oral interviews however indicate the contrary whereby lack of food was never the central factor for labour migration process. In the Phokeng area, South Africa, Nthana Mokale said:

> We went to work because on the Reef on completing school. It seemed that if one finished school one had to go and work. We did not suffer. We had grain in the house and there was always milk from the cows. There was not a shortage of food, and this was the case with other girls.[14]

Similarly, migration of contract labourers from Kavango in Namibia was not a result of hunger and starvation, because men from royal palaces where food was in abundance also became contract labourers. Rather, the need to acquire European clothes which no longer was easily available locally played a greater role in migration.[15] Previously, the elders were the centre of the existence of the young ones and the young ones feared and respected the elders in almost every sphere of their lives but this changed over time. The respect for elders by the youth was previously possible because parents catered for most of their children's needs. The parents made clothing and blankets from animal skins and later provided European cloths and blankets for their children which they acquired through trade and could also provide cattle to the young ones to assist them with accumulation of wealth. Since the parents' access to these goods and local resources were cut off through stringent colonial measures, they were no longer able to provide all of their children's needs. This impacted upon the relations between the older people and the younger people. In some African communities such as Phokeng in South Africa, migrant labour had at least part of its origin in the rebelliousness of the youth against the elders where the youth were unhappy that:

> They must look after the cattle for too long, they must work too long for their parents, and the parents do not give them clothes. They must run around naked; then they leave the cattle and they trek away, so that they will be in a position to earn money to buy clothes and to buy other things for themselves. As a result of all these and other forces, what has begun in Phokeng as discretionary migration gradually gave way to something more permanent and functional.[16]

In the case of Ovamboland in Namibia, McKittrick has dealt with the generational struggle between the young men and the elders as the youth saw options of economic emancipation through labour migration.[17] In the Kavango, while the parents continued to demand that the

---

[14] B. Bozzoli. (1991), *Women of Phokeng*, p. 93.
[15] George Mukoya Weka interview. 2009-07-29, Rucara village.
[16] B. Bozzoli. (1991), *Women of Phokeng*, pp. 84–86.
[17] Meredith Mckittrick. (1996), 'The burden of young men', pp. 115–129.

youth look after cattle, some of the young men too deviated and chose the contract labour system to acquire clothing for both them and their parents. Martin Maghundu, a contract labourer, worked at Kamukaru farms in Grootfontein in 1966, at Walvis Bay in the fish factory by 1969 and later at a beer factory in Swakopmund indicates:

> The reason why we went there [contract work] was because the elders always use to make us look after cattle but they were not providing us with clothes, except for a loin cloth that covers only the front part. There was nothing but only cattle to take for herding with no clothing to wear. Later on we saw that this was plain suffering, especially after we saw that others were wearing clothes. It was then that we said, 'Oh! No, there is something of value this side' and that was when we decided to go on contract work. Previously we had no clothes and in most cases your mother would simply tear a piece from her cloth to give you to wear and that was why we decided that we must go and work on contract.[18]

> [Atwe eyi twayendilirekone kuninga hakuru kehepa kuditha ngombe, kadi hanakukuvhateka, thinyambonyambo vene pithatho thinyambo.Shime dthotho ngombe vene ukadithe kadi hanakukuvhateka, munyima po twayimonine keho eshi, aye okune kunyanda ku.Nopa twayimonine keho omu hanakuvhata hayedthetu atwe, a-a poudi mudyo oko, po twayendire keho.Atwene kuvata thimunyambo, karo kokukudjadjwirako nyoko kukahehe koshovate keho.Munyimane atweneko kuyenda keho.]

Before the introduction of the Lorries as transport in Kavango, the returning contract labourers used to pay for the boat services from the mission stations to transport their acquired goods along the Kavango River. When other men saw the boats full of clothing and compared it to their own lack of it they also felt encouraged to go for contract work. This is closely similar to another example of an incitement for migration by Phokeng women in South Africa after a view of their friends' rooms stocked with furniture in comparison to their own lack of it.[19] In the Kavango the returning labourers looked good in their outfits and other men were impressed and therefore went for contract work too. The returning Kavango contract labourers spoke highly of their places of contract work about what they did there, the type of food they ate etc., and these distant lands became famous among many young men who no longer only wanted to hear about it but wished to experience this. This sharing of experiences in the Kavango is similar to Phokeng returning migrant women in South Africa who narrated about all the good things happening in Johannesburg and thus inciting other women to migrate so as to experience it personally.[20]

---

[18] Maghundu Martin interview. (2009-08-19), Divundu. Maghundu was born at Divundu village in western Kavango.
[19] B. Bozzoli. (1991), *Women of Phokeng*, p. 92.
[20] Ibid., p. 93.

Young men felt too grown up to continue to depend on provisions from their parents and thought they could provide for themselves through the contract labour system. It was a result of their feeling of a reciprocal responsibility as young men that at a certain point they had to take over from their parents' duties and return the supporting hand by providing them with clothes and this could be done by working under the contract labour system.

The European clothes became a part of life of the Kavango people and the lack of it was deemed "ruhepo" (poverty/hardship) while continued wearing of skins began to be regarded by the local people as a sign of "poverty" rather than as "mpo yetu" (our culture). Bernhard Lipayi Linyando went on his first contract in Namibia to a farm at Otjiwarongo and did not reach his homestead after his first contract as he had brought along nothing. He returned from Rundu for another contract to the Outjo area. He worked twice on a farm. The third time in 1964 he worked at the Safari hotel in Windhoek where he extended his contract period and returned to Kavango only in 1966. By 1967 he left for his fourth contract to a mine called Oamites mine near Rehoboth area and stayed until 1968, his last year for contract work. He explains the issue of poverty for the Kavango:

> Our "ruhepo" (poverty/suffering) was about lack of clothing, women's bodies or breasts were bare. The boys wore loin cloth which whoever gave to them. We did not wear all these things for any other reasons but poverty. Culture wise, it was our culture, but we did not really mean it to be culture, it was just plain poverty. If it so happened that as soon as we had arrived, we had our own goods, we would never have been wearing in such a way. It was a result of poverty or lack that we looked around to see what we can possibly wear. That was when we use to soften the skin of a buck to make dress for women with a cloth covering their front part, but their breasts were still exposed. At their head, women plaited it with vihiho (dreadlocks) and smeared it with fat. That was our way of life. I had personally worn a loin cloth during boyhood and would go herd cattle with a bare chest. We wore clothes only after we had gone to contract work. The poverty that we mean here was about lack of clothes, lack of blankets and you had to sleep and be covered under that big skin. That is what we mean by poverty.[21]

[Maruhepo ghetune vidwata kundereko, vakamali marutuutu ndi mashweeshwe. Vamati walye tumunyambo tupu walye ogho anakakushekero, kapishi kwavidwatilire ashi vintje ruhepo. Mpone mpo yetu vene, ano ngoli kapishi mpo yeneyene yatambiro, ruhepo tupu. Ashi ndi tupu twayire navintu vyetu ndi kapishi ngoli mo katudwatanga, ruhepo tupu makura kukenga ngoli ashi vintje tuvhura kudwata.Kushunta ngoli vipapa vya mbambi vyavakamali okuno kakeshe tupu kakumeho.Rutune

---

[21] Bernhard Lipayi Linyando interview. (2009-07-27), Ndiyona village. Lipayi was born at Kadedere village. His father was Linyando and his mother was Mwengere. After his contract labour experiences he joined the South West Africa Territorial Force (SWATF) in 1970. After six years here he quit. In 1978 he secured employment in a secondary school hostel and worked until his retirement. In 2009 Bernhard Lipayi Linyando was a village headman of Ndiyona.

mashweeshwe vene, okuno kumutwene kutakerako vikoka vyavihiho makura kukudama ngoli rukura.Ndyo liparu lyakaliro pakare.Ame munyambone naghudwata kare, kuyenda kungombe rutuutu. Atweko kukadwata mburukweva mpopo twayendire ku kontraka. Ruhepo oro tunatambane nkagi mpoyilimo, vanuke nguvone kwato, nkwendi vakushuntire linya limupapane ushutemo, ndo ruheposha runya]

Returning labour migrants in some African communities felt distinct from the community with their new status through acquisition of European clothes and thus created a view that the African dress was a sign of backwardness and they looked down on those who wore them as was an example of migrant women in Phokeng who looked down on others for wearing "tabarakwe" (traditional floral cloth).[22] Similarly the Kavango people who continued to wear skins instead of European clothes were looked down upon as old fashioned and were cast as outsiders as Shikombero indicates:

> Later on, if you wore a skin dress again, would they not laugh at you? No ways! They will laugh at you when they see how that skin is stuck untidily on you as you walk. Even the children will fear and ask where this person is coming from, they will run away.[23]

[Muruku makura ntjene aghushidwatanka shipapane kapi ngavakushepa? Nan! Kukushepa, lyalyo linakanyatere vene omunya unakayendandi? Ngavatjira nka navanuke ashi nan! Oghune kuni anatundu ghuno? Kuduka!]

Various factors exist as final stimuli for migration into contract labour by men. Some men regarded contract labour migration as an act of "kudanaghura" (playing around). Muyenga Shintunga went for his first contract to Grootfontein in the 1930s on foot under a labour escort Kanyinga and was sent to work in Windhoek in a kitchen. He later went for his second contract to Karibib farms and again for his third contract to Usakos and on a fifth contract to Omaruru at an open cast mine. He later left on contract to Djwaini [Johannesburg] mines. He explains: "We were just playing around! We were playing around that we should go and work"[24] [Atwene kudanaghura! Kudanaghura ashi tukavereke]. The concept "kudanaghura" (playing around) among the Kavango people mainly refers to a simplistic, non-serious oriented engagement in any particular activity for the purposes of fun. The movement into contract labour therefore was not regarded by some of them as a crucial aspect of their lives but simply as an act of play and fun searching. Men migrated because the south was becoming famous as a place of opportunity and they wanted to also try their luck as was the

---

[22] B. Bozzoli. (1997), *Women of Phokeng*, p. 93.
[23] M. N. Shikombero interview. (2009-07-28), Rucara village.
[24] M. S. Unengu interview (2009-07-31), Rucara village. Muyenga Shintunga Unengu was born at Kayova, +- 1915. His father was Unengu and the mother was Ruhepo Shirongo.

case with Shikiri waNkayira, who left for his first contract to Grootfontein on foot with the labour escort Kanyinga and worked at Raison farm before 1936: "It was from my own heart, I wanted to go to the south which they were all talking about and said to be famous where all the elders were going. The reason really was to go and search for good things".[25][Vya kumutjima waumwande vene nashanine kuyenda ku shivanda osho vaghambanga navantje sha fumano vayendanga vakurona navantje. Shitambone kukashana vininke vyaviwa]

Contract labourers went because they hoped "tukawane ugavo kuvamakuwa" (to find/accumulate wealth from the whites).[26] This notion of going "to find wealth from the whites" holds great meaning as it indicates the labourers believed the whites had the wealth and therefore the only way for them to get some of it was by going there through the contract labour system. Since many faced the hardship of lack of clothes they became easily enticed and migrated because of the hearsay of the possibility of earning a lot of money. The underage boys had to find ways to get on contract work as they could not under normal circumstances be allowed by their parents and some therefore ended up on contract simply because they followed behind and cried for the older boys to take them along. In the Phokeng community:

> The historical circumstances of the coming of migrancy meant that people embraced it as much as they submitted to it; that they could, within admittedly narrow limits, choose occupations as much as have them forced upon them; and that they could think of themselves as actors as much as people acted upon. They saw their coming to the city as their own will and a means to raid the city for resources they needed to fulfill their dreams.[27]

It is a different scenario in the case of the Kavango, Namibia. Here labour migrants did not embrace the contract labour system although they submitted to it because of the difficult circumstances imposed upon them by colonialism. Although they personally chose to leave their homesteads and go to the recruitment centre, they did so as a response to the economic and social hardships that resulted from the colonial activities upon them. Although they originally hoped, under the difficult circumstances that contract labour system could be a means to gain money to address their hardships, their narratives of labour migration show that this hope faded away. Their voices therefore are not of happiness, although they include expressions of joy about some of their achievements, but of melancholy and sometimes of anger about the contract system and its colonial exploitation set up as a whole. As

---

[25] Shikiri waNkayira interview. (2009-08-08), Ndongalinena village. Shikiri waNkayira was born at Hoha village, ± 1918. His mother was Nkayira.
[26] Muyenga Shintunga Unengu interview. (2009-07-31), Rucara village.
[27] B. Bozzoli. (1991), *Women of Phokeng*, p. 97.

they embarked upon the migration journey the contract labourers observed and became aware of the co-operation of the recruiting organization, the colonial administration and the employers in their subjugation and exploitation. The following section focuses on migration journeys of contract labourers both outside Namibia to Angola, Zimbabwe and South Africa, and within Namibia to the police zone.

Migration journeys, 1925–1972

In some African communities, traditional chiefs were responsible for sending off some members of their chiefdom to contract or migrant work so that they would bring back some goods to the chief upon return. Such was for example the case in Phokeng where a tradition of male migrancy had long existed whereby regiments of young men were sent out to work by the first chief Mokgale right from the earliest days of the Kimberley mines.[28] Closely similar, in Ovamboland, some labourers had to ask the tribal leader's (chief) permission to go and work in the south and they then had to give a share of their earnings to the chief upon return.[29] In the case of the Kavango it was different. Usually the idea to leave for contract work was discussed at "shinyanga" a gathering space around the fire where all members of the homestead gathered in the evening for relaxing and discussing their experiences during the day and where everyone also gathered in the morning to greet each other before they went for their daily work.[30] The members were therefore accountable to their family members and not to the chief for their labour migration, although they had to be registered as coming from the area of jurisdiction of a particular chief. There were cases where underage boys escaped to go on contract labour without their parents' consent and therefore did not discuss their plans for migration at "shinyanga". As is indicated by their life narratives some contract labourers had been on contract labour outside Namibia as far as Djwaini (Johannesburg), Salisbury (Harare) and Angola and then went on contract labour within Namibia as a way to continue the exploration which they had begun elsewhere. The following political map of Namibia, which shows neighbouring countries such as South Africa, Angola and Zimbabwe indicates countries where labourers from Kavango went to work.

Despite the presence of Namibians in South African mines, the history of labour migration of men from Namibia does not feature greatly in South African literature of foreign migrant labourers to that country.[31] This could be because South Africa did not have official

---

[28] Ibid., p. 84.
[29] Stals. (1967), Die aanraking tussen blankes en Ovambos in Suid Wes Africa, p. 192.
[30] Nyambe Merecky interview. 2009-08-06), Shipando village.
[31] D. Yudelman. (1984), *The emergence of modern South Africa*. David Philip, Cape Town, p. 269.

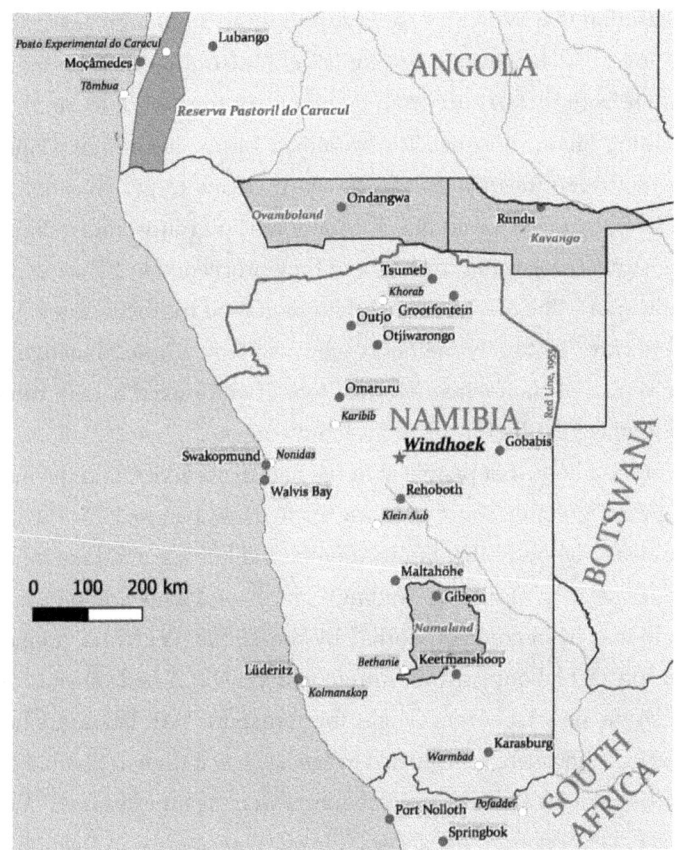

Map 2: Namibia 2020. Cartographers: Falk Griemert & Bernard. C. Moore.

recruiting agreements in Namibia for the South African mines but also because, unlike other countries, the numbers of contract labourers from Namibia were minimal.[32] Although a number of authors have written about their experiences of contract labour system in Namibia, very few of them mention that Namibians have also worked in South Africa. A small beginning has been made by Ndaoya.[33]

From oral histories it appears that the contract labourers preferred going to Djwaini rather than seeking work within Namibia. This is ascribed to their view of higher pay in the South African mines. There was also the view that Djwaini was the destination for strong men.[34] After 1944 arrangements were finally made between WENELA and the South West

---

[32] Ibid.
[33] L.N. Ndaoya. (2000), Oshiwambo-speaking migrant workers on the Witwatersrand gold mines from 1940 to 1969. UNAM, B.A thesis, p. 1.
[34] Maghundu Martin interview, (2009-08-19), Divundu village.

African administration that WENELA could recruit up to 3000 men a year for the mines in Johannesburg.³⁵ By 1947 however, the colonial administration in Namibia again resorted to preventing men from its territory from going on contract work to South African mines as this was draining labour destined for Namibian farms and mines. Contract labourers however faked their identities by registering as Angolans to get recruited. Kavango contract labourers to Djwaini (Johannesburg) usually left in groups and walked to Muhembo police border post near Botswana from where they proceeded to Shakawe where they got the WENELA transport. The men provided their own food for the journey. Men were given Mahangu meal to carry by family members who also took a little Mahangu meal and kept it safe until the return of the men when they took it and mixed it with the new pounded Mahangu meal to make the first meal and celebrate return.³⁶

There were other taboos that people at home had to observe when the men left for contract work to Djwaini (Johannesburg) as a means to avoid bad luck for the labourer. It was expected by the absent labourer that family members at home should not be angry with him during his absence so as to please the "vadimu" (ancestors) who would in turn protect him on his journey to and from contract work.³⁷ By the 1940s, WENELA transport was introduced to collect contract labourers from Rundu and WENELA had various camps along the route from which the new labourers caught the transport.³⁸ All labourers had to be examined at Rundu before they were transported to Shakawe and then to Maun. From Maun they went up to Francistown. In Francistown, labourers were again examined. A belief emerged that if none of them experienced headaches during their sojourn in Djwaini, it was a result of the medical injection they received during medical examinations in Francistown.³⁹ In Francistown, contract labourers were transferred onto trains and taken to Mafikeng where they arrived in the early hours. At the entrance in Mafikeng, there was a large stone monument which labourers were informed was an image of a late king. From Mafikeng, labourers arrived in Johannesburg at Mzilikazi station in the morning. As the contract labourers arrived in Johannesburg in the early hours, they were woken to look at the bright lights of

---

³⁵ R. First. 1963, *South West Africa*. Middlesex, Penguin Books, pp. 26–27.
³⁶ Mathias Ndumba Shikombero interview (2009-07-28), Rucara village.
³⁷ Anselm Likuwa Mukoya interview. (2009-08-04), Ndiyona village.
³⁸ J. Crush et al. (1991), *South Africa's labor empire, a history of black migrancy to the gold mines* (USA, West View Press, pp. 37–39.
³⁹ G.M. Weka. (2009-07-29), Rucara village. George Mukoya was born at Nyondo village in 1926. His father was King Kamutuva Weka and his mother was Mantjodi. In Namibia he went for his first contract work to Grootfontein in 1950 and worked at Tubusis farm. During his second contract in Namibia he worked on a farm in Karibib. His third contact was at Wesa [Uis] mine. During his fourth contract which was his last time on contract, he worked in Swakopmund and returned home in 1967. By 1970 he worked at the construction company that built many offices and schools in Kavango.

Johannesburg. Some were left with no words to explain the difference of the bright lights of Johannesburg to the abundance of stars in the night skies of their home villages. George Mukoya Weka first left for contact work to Djwaini (Johannesburg) in 1948. He provides his experience of the arrival in (Djwaini) Johannesburg:

> When we arrived there–hey-that was truly Djwaini! As we were arriving, they woke us up 'wake-up-wake up and look, you have arrived in Djwaini.' When we looked up those lights looked like the way we see stars in the sky. Then they said, 'yeah, you have arrived now'.[40]
>
> [Pakukarupuka ngoli okone–eee- ashi yinone Djwaini shiri. Nkokuno tupune makura ashi 'yaa, rambukenungoli, rambukenu mukenge munatikingoli mudjwaini'. Kukengako okone yiramomutwakenganga ntungwedi, odo ramba, 'vavo ashi 'yaa, tunatiki ngoli'.]

At Mzilikazi, Kavango labourers met other labourers such as "Mambogwani, maNdaghu, maZulu, maSwazi, maXosa, maBwatja, maTanganyika, maPedi, maNyasa and maPondo".[41] The new labourers were led by policemen to the compound after which they were stripped naked and paraded at the medical examination centre and were moved from one office to provide urine and feaces for medical examination.[42] When labourers spoke of this practice of medical examination, they usually said it with a lower voice, a sign that it was not to be spoken about loudly as it was shameful. In some instances, such as that by George Weka, it was accompanied with a quick laughter which expresses a continued disbelief of a shameful practice that was practiced upon them. This must be similar to what Jeeves indicated whereby new recruits at the depot in Johannesburg received cursory medical examinations by being paraded with all of the other recent arrivals past a medical officer.[43] Afterwards each contract labourer made a pledge for work by touching on the red pen in the hand of the white official.[44] This notion of touching the red pen as a sign of a pledge could in actual fact be the process described by Jeeves in which a labour bureau inspector interviewed the recruits to explain again the terms of the mine contract which had been negotiated at the time of recruitment.[45]

Mzilikazi depot was the centre for distribution of contract labourers to various compounds and work destinations such as "Spring mine, Western Reef, Daggafontein, Diepfontein, Spaarwater and Welhedag mine".[46] According to WENELA recruitment procedures, those graded

---

[40] G.M. Weka. (2009-07-29), Rucara village.
[41] M.N. Shikombero interview. (2009-07-28), Rucara village.
[42] Interview with G.M. Weka, Rucara, 29 July 2009.
[43] A.H. Jeeves, *Migrant labour in South Africa's mining economy: the struggle for the gold mines' labour supply 1890–1920* (Johannesburg, Witwatersrand University Press, 1985), pp. 21–22.
[44] Interview with G. M. Weka, Rucara, 29 July 2009.
[45] Jeeves, *Migrant labour in South Africa's mining economy*, pp. 21–22.
[46] Interview withTheodor Kupembona, Guma village, 6 June 2001.

A were fit for underground mines, B was fit for surface work and C was unfit for all mine work.[47] During recruitment each labourer was provided with a number tag on his hand as a form of identity so that in the case of death underground it was easy to trace and identify him. All labourers who died were buried there and only a death notice was sent home. Workers believed that during recruitment each had their grave site prepared with their recruitment number on.[48] This belief suggests that contract labourers believed their enlistment for contract work to South Africa was an act of signing up one's life to dangers and death.

The duration of contract work was about seventeen months. It was the policy of the South African government that foreign Africans may neither migrate permanently to South Africa, nor bring members of their families or relatives and that at the termination of their service contract they had to be repatriated to their respective countries of origin.[49] Contract labourers from the Kavango therefore had to return after their contract expired and they were extremely excited because the fear of mine deaths that they lived with was over and left behind. Some labourers made a show about the end of their contracts by tying up their knee protection covers and boots to a rope which they pulled behind them on the ground. When fellow contract labourers saw these they said "anaposile-anaposile" (he has completed-he has completed).[50] The returning contract labourers had to report at "sangwenya" (office) the next day morning for record purposes after which they were transported to Mzilikazi centre from which they returned to the Kavango. The returning labourers were known as "magayisa" and deserved respect from "manyowani" (newcomers) who were expected to give way to the approaching "magayisa" which was almost like a rite of passage.

Despite the advantages of going to the South African mines some labourers later became discouraged after the plane was introduced to take them from Shakawe to Francistown. The plane made them sick and they could not stand the plane flying in the sky and they expected it could fall down anytime.[51] Some of those who wanted to return to Djwaini would drop their goods at home and immediately return to contract.

Some contract labourers from Kavango went to work in Salisbury in Zimbabwe. The contract labourers to Salisbury were those who were rejected for the South African mines in Francistown at the labour recruitment centre. Contract labour recruitment centres became places of displacement and disappointment for many contract labourers as they were separated from their friends. They were, however, also centres of new engagements and

---

[47] 'WENELA recruits' (SWAA 2397, A521/10).
[48] G.M. Weka. (2009-07-29), Rucara village.
[49] W.J. Breytenbach. (1972), *Migratory labour arrangements in Southern Africa*. Pretoria, Africa Institute of South Africa, p. 18.
[50] G.M. Weka interview. (2009-07-29), Rucara village.
[51] Mathias Ndumba Shikombero interview. (2009-07-28), Rucara village.

friendship ties with people from other areas. There was a feeling of melancholy and despair among contract labourers who were sent to Zimbabwe as they had not intended to go there and were separated from friends.[52] Medical rejects remained high in Botswana and presented a negative image for recruiting levels as it showed that migrants who travelled long distances with much hardship could not count on securing employment.[53] In order to counter this setback, WENELA developed a farm labour scheme to provide employment for large numbers of these rejects with the Rhodesian farmers.[54] Contract labourers in Francistown felt it pointless to refuse the offer to Salisbury as they had already come that far from home.[55] To some, working on Zimbabwe farms became the means to prepare for an eventual contract work pass to Djwaini (Johannesburg) mines.[56]

Apart from the labour work in Zimbabwe, new opportunities prevailed for contract work in Angola. In the 1950s, the Portuguese in Angola needed contract labourers to work on new American supported development projects in the interior of Angola and the colonial administration recruited men from Kavango as contract labourers. As the following report of the commissioner at Kavango indicates:

> A lorry for the purpose of carrying labour recruits from the Kavango River to the interior of Angola has been established. The administrator at Fort Cuangar reports that American capital for the development of Angola is coming in. The development will cover new railways, European settlements on irrigation schemes, irrigation dams on the Kunene, tree planting for securing an adequate supply of wood fuel close to the main railways and so on.[57]

Large groups of men from the Kavango enlisted for contract work in Angola in the 1950s.[58] The contract labourers to Angola were collected by a Portuguese truck at Ukwangali Portuguese post and those from Mbukushu and Gciriku areas had to walk at least about 170km to reach their point of departure for contract work. Contract labourers travelled through many places in Angola to reach Benquella where wood cutting work awaited them. From Ukwangali Portuguese post along the Kavango they went to Kayundu (Angola) and moved on until Menonge from where they later arrived at the district of Silva Porto/Bie.[59] In Silva Porto/

---

[52] Nyambe Merecky interview. (2009-08-06), Shipando village.
[53] Crush et al. (1992), *South Africa's labor empire*, p. 467.
[54] Ibid.
[55] Shintango Karenga interview. (2009-08-05), Korokoko village and Nyambe Merecky interview. (2009-08-06), Shipando village.
[56] Nyambe Merecky interview. (2009-08-06), Shipando village.
[57] The Native Commissioner, Okavango. (1952-03-24), To the Chief native Commissioner in Windhoek, 'monthly reports for January and February 1952' (NAR 1/1/55. A579/1.
[58] Mathias Ndumba Shikombero interview. (2009-07-28), Rucara village.
[59] Ibid.

Bie they got into a train which operated on coal. Someone had to keep on throwing wood to keep the coal burning for the train to move. They later reached Bella Vista, from Bella Vista to Singwali from Singwali to Kahara from Kahara to Nova Lisboa from Nova Lisboa to Longondjo from Longondjo to Eleti up to Lobito, where they stayed for five days, and then on the sixth day moved on to Benquella.[60] Many contract labourers thus had prior experience as contract labourers outside Namibia before contracting within Namibia.

Inside Namibia, contract labourers from the Kavango travelled to various places. During the early South African colonial period, migration from the Kavango was usually under the escort of the visiting colonial officials in the area and later through labour escorts and eventually through organized recruiting agencies. Contract labourers regarded labour migration as a tightly controlled process, which exerted overt control over them as all their personal and family details were recorded at Rundu and reproduced and kept at Grootfontein recruiting centre. In the beginning, migration from the Kavango to Grootfontein took a long time due to the lack of transportation. Despite exceptional cases where some labourers got a lift with the Catholic missionaries' transport between Grootfontein and Nyangana mission station, for a very long time, the migration process of labourers was on foot which usually took about seventeen days of travel to Grootfontein.[61]

The journey by foot has parallels with the migration from Ovamboland. In the latter case because most men went to search for work during the periods of hunger, they were weak and the journey was too much for them to bear.[62] White farmers along the way accused them of destroying poles and pumps and refused to provide them with water.[63] During the rainy seasons, some streams overflowed and could not be crossed and many Ovambo labourers are said to have drowned or lost their property there.[64]

In the Kavango, during the journeys to Grootfontein contract labourers had to bear the burden of carrying their load of goods on their shoulders and provide for their own meals and they were also hampered by Bushmen attacks and thirst.[65] Neither the administration nor the NLO were prepared to set up permanent water points on the migrant routes from the Kavango to the police zone and labourers usually drank water from the Bushmen water holes and were always in conflict with them. Later on, the NLO representa-

---

[60] Ibid.
[61] In 1931, a returning contract labourer Nehemia Mbamba got a lift from Grootfontein to Nyangana mission station from which he travelled on foot to Nkurenuru in western Kavango, See, P. Toivanen. (no year), Namibia, Kavango, Ngapi nare? unpublished script. University of Stellenbosch library, TEOL 266.416881 TOI.
[62] Stals. (1961), Die aanraking tussen blankes en Ovambos in Suid Wes Africa, 1850–1915, p. 197.
[63] Ibid.
[64] Ibid., p. 198.
[65] Shikiri waNkayira. (2009-08-08), Ndongalinena village.

tives worked to encourage migration from Kavango by cleaning up existing water places. The administration finally agreed to sink boreholes in search of water in the most drought-stricken stretches of the two main routes leading north to Kavango on condition that the recruiting organization would supply and maintain the necessary pumping plants, storage tank etc.[66] Several bore holes were sunk between Nurugas and Karukuvisa with varying levels of success, of which the Kano vlei proved the most viable . A windmill, pump and tank were erected, and boring operations were soon in progress in the stretch on the Tsintsabis-Kurinkuru road.[67]

The colonial administration appointed an African policeman named Langhals Kanyinga to live along the "Muramba matako" (the valley of buttocks) labour route which later acquired a name "Ndonga ya Kanyinga" (the valley of Kanyinga). His task was to control the Vacu (San) and also to work as a labour escort. There were labour escorts for other areas of Kavango too. Labour escorts were provided with rifles and bullets to protect the labourers from Vacu and any other dangers during the migration to or from contract work. They would leave their rifles at the control border post before crossing the police zone and would only retrieve them upon their return. These would be handed over for safe keeping to the missionaries in Kavango from where they would be collected upon their next journey.[68] There were cases where headmen did not carry a rifle during escorts and migrant labourers put pressure on their headmen and mocked them through songs for their reluctance as was the case with headman Kanyinga who sometimes did not carry along a rifle. The migrant labourers mocked him in a song on their traditional flutes: "Kanyinga, so foolish of you, go and bring the rifle".[69](Kanyinga we pauyero karete uta). Kanyinga apparently had a strategy to control Vacu (San) from attacking labourers and therefore did not need to always carry the rifle. Instead he brought along dagga herbs to provide to Vacu whenever they asked for a smoke.[70] The excessive dagga smoked by Vacu made them pass out soon afterwards into a deep sleep and thus provided contract labourers ample time to move away from the easy reach of the Vacu. Such a strategy was not, however, applied by the contract labourers on their return journeys as dagga usage was prohibited in the police zone. It was on these return journeys that they were prone to Vacu attacks. Vacu continued to attack migrant labourers and the administration was left with the serious task of finding a lasting solution. Interviewees from the Kavango allege that the NLO officials at Grootfontein took a

---

[66] 'The Northern Labour Organization' (Windhoek, NAN, SWAA 1/1/46, 2426, A521/26 (V.5).
[67] Ibid.
[68] 'Native recruiters for the Okavango [Kavango] area (1937-02-04). Windhoek, NAN, NAR 1/1/55, 11/7.
[69] Anselm Likuwa Mukoya. (2009-08-04), Ndiyona village.
[70] Ibid.

step further by arresting and killing the leader of these Vacu. They then forced his followers to eat up the leader. Shikiri relates this extraordinary story:

> The "Vacu" (San) never went to the police zone for work, they were just living quietly in their bush. In the past, Vacu use to kill contract labourers and they were later pursued by the whites and arrested. The king of those Vacu was taken for trial at Grootfontein where he was killed. His corpse was boiled in a huge pot and his followers were compelled to eat up their leader. Since then, Vacu also began to establish good links with Grootfontein.[71]

> [Vicu vyamuwiya vyavyone nakumonakoshi kushivanda, vyavyo pore muwiya wavyo omo. Vyavyo karene mpopanya kavadipayanga vaka kontraka makura kuvayendera ngoli vavirumbu vakakwate ogho hompa wavone makura avamutwara hompa wavo kushivanda vakamudipaye. Avakamutereka makura kutininika vantu vendi vamulye dogoro vakunyena-nyene. Makura kutunda opone ntani kumona Vacu vamuwiya vakundame ngoli navo kuShivanda].

The annual report of 1925 indicates an incident in which a group of Vacu attacked returning labourers but were captured by the colonial police and taken to Grootfontein to stand trial. As the following indicates:

> The Bushmen who inhabit the dry stretches between the Okavango [Kavango] and the Police Zone gave some trouble. They attacked parties of returning labourers, wounding several, and followed that up by an attempt to overawe and intimidate the Bunja [Mbunza] tribe in their own area. The movement was suppressed by Chief Muduni, without serious conflict with the Bushmen, and later a police camel patrol was successful in capturing some of the Bushmen who were concerned in attacking the returning labourers, and took them to Grootfontein for trial. Since then all has been peaceful.[72]

Portelli has made the point that "oral narratives are always psychologically true" and that this truth may be equally as important as factually reliable accounts.[73] His argument can be applied in this case. We do not know if these oral narratives of barbaric atrocity by colonial officials are true. What is important, however, is that it indicates the labourers' views that the colonial authorities and NLO were gravely concerned about Vacu attacks on labourers and took steps to stop these. It signifies how the image of "Vacu terror" lingers on in Kavango memory.

---

[71] Shikiri waNkayira. (2009-08-08), Ndongalinena village. A similar story was given by Anselm Likuwa Mukoya. (2009-08-04), Ndiyona village.
[72] 'Union of South Africa Annual, (1925). Report. Windhoek. NAN, p. 35.
[73] Portelli. (1991), What makes oral history different. In R. Perks and Thomson (ed.), *The Oral History Reader*, p. 68.

There were two border control posts from Kavango to the police zone. One was the Nurugas border control point which was an entry point to the police zone of Grootfontein for the labourers from the eastern part of Kavango, and the other one was Tsintsabis border control point between Ukwangali area and the police zone of Tsumeb, which was an entry point for the labourers from the western part of Kavango. Before labourers reached the police border points, they had to dip their feet in a medicine bowl the labourers referred to as "D.P." which the colonial authorities apparently intended to clean them of all the diseases of the Kavango area and prevent the spread of it to the police zone.

A former contract labourer Shindimba Shihungu wanted to go to Djwaini (Johannesburg) mines but was rejected at Rundu for being too young and was instead sent to Grootfontein and worked at Outjo farms. After returning home he left for a contract to Djwaini (Johannesburg) mines. After returning from Johannesburg, he left for Windhoek on a mission to purchase a horse which he exchanged in Kavango for many cows. He then left for his second contract to Grootfontein in the 1950s and worked at Omaruru at a company that transported cattle. After Omaruru he left for another contract to Windhoek which was his last time on contract work. He presents his experience of the disease control at the border check point:

> We usually followed the route of Karukuvisa and whenever we reached Karukuvisa we were all treated with D.P. medicine apparently to remove all the diseases from Kavango because we were going to stay in another environment. The D.P. medicine was dissolved in a container of water where each labourer had to dip their feet apparently to remove all the diseases of the Kavango so that we do not take it that side to the whites.[74]
>
> [Kupita yinya ndjira yaKarukuvisa, ovyo tutika kunya ku Karukuvisa tanko nka vatu dipe. Kutudipa ashi lihamba lyaKavango litundeko, ashi okunya tunakuyenda tukakareko, nako peke. Mumema vaturamo mutondo waD.P. moomo tulyatangemo natuvantje mpadi-mpadi ashi lihamba lyaKavango litutunde manashi tulitwara munya kuvamakuwa].

Despite the fact that the contract labourers were checked for diseases during their journey to the police zone, the same exercise was not performed upon their return to the Kavango. The colonial authorities were clearly only worried about the spread of diseases to the white man's area rather than from the white men area to the Kavango. In the official view the Africans were the carriers of diseases into the white man's area. Apart from the D.P. disease control measures, the labourers were inspected for security purposes by the police at the

---

[74] Shindimba Ndumba Shihungu interview. (2009-08-06), Shipando village. Shindimba Ndumba Shihungu was born at Nyondo village. His parents were Shihungu and Wayera. Upon his final return to Kavango from contract work, he worked as a tailor in a Portuguese shop until he later crossed and settled at Ndiyona village (Namibia).

police border posts of Nurugas which separated the Kavango area to the police zone. As Shihungu explains:

> At Nurugas police border post, they would inspect us to ensure that we did not carry along any unwanted thing. Nurugas police post was the border with Grootfontein and was the place where the presence of the police began.[75]
>
> [Pavaporosi paNurugas kutu sefa ashi walye tunashimbi vyakupira kupulitira. Pa Nurugas ne mpo pa mururani na shivanda, mpo vatamekera va porosi].

These inspections ensured that contract labourers did not carry illegal goods detrimental to the security of the colonial state. After 1936 when the office of the Native Commissioner operated from Rundu, all new labour recruits began to report at his office. The office became a social space where songs drawn from the personal experiences of some men were composed. One interviewee narrates that a traditional song such as "pull myself up to as far as Rundu, my hip is paining"[76] (Sikokave ure wa Rundu, nyonga zange kukora) developed when a man on his way to the office of the commissioner which was built on an elevated level, stumbled and hurt his hip but nonetheless had to move on and reach the office at all costs.

At Rundu, the contract labourers slept at a labour compound that consisted of thatched roof houses, situated near the river side but later in the late 1950s another compound was constructed further away from the river with permanent brick structures. A policeman guarded the entrance to the compound. His duty was to see to it that no illegal people entered the compound. Illegal people included SWAPO cadres who wanted to mobilize support among contract labourers. The policeman controlled the movements of people in and out of the compound and allowed labourers to leave the compound only at certain given times. He allowed the labourers to leave the compound and visit their families in the surrounding settlements of Rundu such as Mangarangandja or Nkarapamwe. He also permitted men to go and collect firewoods in the bushes.

Inside the Rundu compound there were black workers who wore uniform and directed manyowani (new ones) where to sleep. The presence of a white official at Rundu compound was to do office work. He mainly recorded new labourers but was usually assisted by black workers. The numbers reporting at Rundu compound were always very small and contract labourers waited for a week or two for the number to increase before they were sent to Grootfontein. The contract labourers detested the weeks of waiting at Rundu and regarded it as an act of sitting around for nothing as little care, if any, was given to them. Labourers were not provided with bedding and they had to cook for themselves. As an interviewee

---

[75] *Ibid.*
[76] Mberekera interview. (2007-01-20), Kambowo village.

explains "We carried our own blankets to the compound at Rundu. We were only provided with maize meal and salt. They feared that if they gave us clothes, we would escape and return home immediately. We also use to cook for ourselves".[77]

At Rundu, contract labourers also provided unpaid labour every day for Mr. Venter, a SWANLA agent. Contract labourers believe that they were made to do all this manual work simply because they were "kashuku kamudoli" (derogatory word for new recruits) who could be treated in any disrespectful manners in comparison to "vaghunguli" (the finishers/returning contract labourers). As Shihungu further explains:

> We worked at Rundu compound and after five we were always given 'mahangu' cereal to pound for our meal. Yes, that is how it uses to be at Rundu, you had to pound mahangu for one's porridge, my God! While you waited at Rundu to be enlisted for contract work, there was other manual work you had to do such as removing grass from the office of the commissioner whom at that time was baas Mare. Usually we worked at Mr. Venter who was in charge of the compound. Mr. Venter was the SWANLA agent, but we worked for him for free. What could we do about it, we were all 'kashuku kamudoli' [new comers] what will they pay us for? What about the mahangu we were given to pound for our meal, did it not come from Mr. Venter? That was it. We were only given 'mahangu' cereals to go and pound after work and cook for ourselves. All new labourers who were going to work for the first time were called "kashuku kamudoli" and those who were returning from contract work were known as "vaghunguli" [the finishers].[78]

> [Mukaruwane pa Rundu po ovyo munakaya pa ses uur kumupa mahangu ghamakukutu mutwe mulye. Yii! Kutwa! Pa Rundu pa opo pakalire ndi? Nan! Ove? Kutwa! Karunga ncu! Ngura-ngura mpovili tanko vakamuruwanita kunya ku mberewo. Mukadjupaghure mushoni, ndi vakamupe kehe viruwana vene mbyo mukaruwana kwa komisari ngoli akaliropo baas Mare. Mukaruwane tanko nka kogho kamukomboni ngoli Venter, mbyovyoshi ndje wa swanera ngoli. Amuruwanite ngoliko mavoko-voko anwe ne vakashuku kamudoli ashi mulyoko? Ogho mahangu munakutwane ashi ghare ngoli? Kapishi ngo gha Venter gho? Mutwe mahangu, mukashuke naghumwenu ntani mupike ngoli naghumwenu mulye mpopo ngoli. Navantje vanya vanakuyendo rwakuhoverera ku shivanda ne va kashuku kamudoli, ovanya vakukavyuka mboko ngoli vaghunguli].

The South West Africa Administrator appealed to the recruiting organizations that more adequate rations should be given to recruits at Rundu and that such rations should include meat, fat and vegetables (mainly wild spinach obtainable at small cost in the Kavango and carrots).[79] As an experiment, it was suggested that the organizations should issue 1lb of

---

[77] Bernhard Lipayi Linyando interview. (2009-07-27), Ndiyona village.
[78] Shindimba Ndumba Shihungu interview. (2009-08-06), Shipando village
[79] S.W.A Administrator (1950-10-03), To W.N.L.A district manager at Francis town. Windhoek. NAN. SWAA 2423, A521/26.

meat and vegetables to all recruits.⁸⁰ Such suggestions were not implemented and contract labourers at Rundu continued to receive only mahangu meal and salt.

A contract labourer was examined twice, first in Rundu and then again in Grootfontein; the testing procedure was extremely degrading and embarrassing for contract labourers.81Labourers at Rundu were taken to a hall surrounded by a short wall made of reeds near the SWANLA shop to be medically examined naked by a male testing officer. The labourers were again sent to the hospital to what they called the 'wahahesera' (don't breathe) x-rays machines to test if they had tuberculosis (TB). They called the x-ray machine as the 'don't breathe' machines because labourers were usually asked to breathe in and hold it for seconds while an x-ray was taken. They underwent all these medical testing processes to determine their health status so that only the healthy ones were selected. An interviewee describes the testing process:

> You stayed there for a week to be stripped naked in a surrounded wall where you were tested. You ran around naked and then he would order you to stop. He then doctored you and looked at you on every part of your body. He ordered you to bend down and up. After he was done with examining and recording you, he then sent you to the hospital to the 'Don't breathe' machines (X-rays) where they checked if you had T.B after which you returned to the compound and slept. Early morning, they took you to the SWANLA office to be recorded again. When that was done then they loaded you in the lorries for the journey. At our time the buses were introduced, and we went by bus.⁸²

> [Kutika mu Rundu kwakarangamo viruwana. Vamutjangaurae, vanamana kumutjangaura kukara mpopo pamweya shivike. Makura vamushutaghure rutu-rutu. Mpolili lirapa vadikireko weno. Makura vamushuture rutu-rutu mpopo vamukona-kone muduke ngoli-mudukaghane-dukaghane mawoko-woko moomo mulirapa ove kwato osho unadwata. Mudukaghane ntani vamurenka ngoli ashi yimanenu, makura vamukenge ngoli, wakurumana, warenka weni. Kutundapo kuyenda ngoli ku wahesera, vakamukonakone ashi na TB yoye ndi weni. Kurara lyakukyako kuyenda ngoli kushivanda. Ruvede rwetu dado besa dinayatiki ngoli ndo twayendire nado].

Those rejected for recruitment had to bear their own costs of homeward journey. After the medical official examined the contract labourers he provided each successful recruit with a metal alphabetic tag around his hand. Those who had the A symbol were fit for jobs in the urban areas such as mines and domestic work. The B symbol labourers were fit for heavy farm work such as extensive milking, dam building, herding of large flocks of sheep or goats while the C symbol labourers were fit for light farm work such as milking a few cows, herd-

---

⁸⁰ *Ibid.*
⁸¹ SWANLA Manager of Grootfontein. (1953-04-08), To the Chief Native Commissioner in Windhoek medical examinations of recruits at Runtu. Windhoek, NAN. SWAA 2426, A521/10.
⁸² Bernhard Lipayi Linyando interview. (2009-07-27), Ndiyona village.

ing small flocks of sheep, goats and other light herd work.[83] The provision of symbols to labourers at Rundu was only meant for classification purposes and the labourers still remained at loss as to what employer they would be assigned and of their work destination until they reached Grootfontein labour depot where formal recruiting and job designations took place.

Transport was finally introduced by NLO in 1938 from Kavango to the south and Mr. Gaerdes Kemp (locally known as Kemba) was appointed to transport contract labourers and to run the only NLO shop at Rundu. The lorries that transported migrant labourers followed the road from Rundu via Karukuvisa–Tsintsabis to Grootfontein. This was a deep sandy road that slowed down the speed of the lorry and made the journey very long.

Ndumba Shirengumuke was one of the contract labourers to Grootfontein who was sent to a farm in Gobabis to milk cows. After his first contract work he returned home and worked for the Portuguese by transporting their goods in large canoes along the Kavango River to various Portuguese posts. He was later sent by the Portuguese to Luanda where he worked on ships at sea. In Luanda he worked with other labourers who came from as far as Zaire. There he was accused of misconduct and was transferred to Nova Lisboa where Shirengumuke believed he was destined to be killed. After arriving in Nova Lisboa he escaped to save his life and he tells of a long journey on foot through small villages of Angola until he finally arrived along the Kavango River and crossed to the Namibia side where he settled permanently, never returning to the Portuguese side. Shirengumuke explained his experience of the route to Grootfontein: "The lorry moved by constant pushing. Even as it moved, one could just stand along a bush to urinate and then later run after it and be sure to catch it. The route was extremely sandy".[84][Oyo roli ne nkwandi kutindayika.Mpili kunakuyenda-yinakuyenda, muntu kuvhura kuyimana tupu pepi nashishwa utikame, muruku makura uyitjide, ani ndi ndjo ukawana.Ndjira ruvhutu].

The journey to the police zone was usually long and quiet and labourers did not sing as was the case with "magayisa" (the returning labourers) such as the Tjimbundu people and the Nyemba of Angola who sang songs such as "shunga-shunga kom-kora" (dance-dance, more).[85] Shindimba Shihungu explained that this was so because labourers on their way were always worried about what will happen to them on contract, where they would work and whether they would survive and return home while the returning contract labourers were happy to have survived contract work and to return home.[86]

---

[83] The Native Commissioner. (1947-03-28), To District surgeon of Runtu, 'Classification of recruits, SWANLA and WENELA' (NAR 1/1/55, 13/1/1.
[84] Ndumba Shirengumuke interview. (2009-07-03), Rucara village. Ndumba Shirengumuke was born at Katere in 1921. His parents are Shirengumuke and Nyama.
[85] Bernhard Limbangu Shampapi interview. (2009-07-28), Rucara village.
[86] Shindimba Ndumba Shihungu interview. (2009-08-06), Shipando village

The SWANLA lorries caused great inconvenience to the labourers as they did not contain seats or covering roofs and labourers suffered from the heat and rain during summer and had to stand during their long journey to and from the police zone.[87] After these repeated complaints SWANLA replaced the lorries with buses.[88] In the 1950s, a gravel road was constructed between Rundu and Grootfontein and thus SWANLA transport made use of this new road, only stopping at Mururani point which was the new point of entry to the police zone. It was also a veterinary check point to prevent the transportation of animals and any raw meat products from the Kavango as labourers arrived in Grootfontein at a labour recruitment and distribution depot.

Many contract labourers prefer not to use the word "labourer" to identify themselves and instead use the terms "the contracted" or "people". A key image that they construct is one of sale or purchase at Grootfontein recruiting depot. The colonial administration sold people (labourers) to the needy white men (employers) who had placed an order for their required number of people at SWANLA at a fee that went to the colonial administration's coffers. As one labourer indicated:

> It was in Grootfontein where we got bought. What else do you reason it was all about? The white people use to send money to their friends to look and find for them some people. So, money was given to those in offices and when we arrived there we were told, 'o.k. this one needs this number of people'. The money with which we were purchased went to the administration. That is how it was.[89]
>
> [Mu shivandane mmo mwakutughura ngoli kunya navimbapira. Oveshine ndi weni? Ameshi vamakuwa vakone kutumasha vimaliva ashi ngamukantjaneneko vantu makura avatapa kuvaghunyavo kuma mberewo makura kuyane nko vamurenka ngoli ashi yaa oghuno ashana vantu vashi ngandi. Vimalivane makura viyende ngoli kwa hurumende. Ogho mukuwane ndje wakutapa maliva kumberew o ashi muntumineko vantu vashi ngandi. Ngoweyo vyakalire.]

This view is echoed in the choice of words by a white farmer who referred to contract labourers as paid slaves whom he said were sold to various employers by a labour recruiting company called SWANLA.[90] Bartholomeus Someno Katota who served at Shivanda, Outjo, Windhoek and later Walvis Bay points out:

---

[87] 'Vervoer van Ekstra Territoriale en Noordelikke Bantoes tussen Grootfontein en Runtu en tussen Runtu & Katwitwi' (LGR 3/3/4, file N3/13/2, 7 Mar. 1960).
[88] *Ibid.*
[89] Ndumba Shirengumuke interview. (2009-07-03), Rucara village.
[90] The secretary for native affairs. (1950-09-20), To the secretary for South West Africa. Windhoek, NAN, SWAA 1/1/46, A521/26.

> Under contract they use to sell us like cattle. Do you not know what contract labour system was? They use to sell us! Any white man who wanted some people was given. We would even be given to him for eighteen months before we return home. It is Sam Nujoma[91], that Ovambo man, who finally removed contract so that one should move around anywhere as you like. If there was no Sam Nujoma we would still be in contract.[92]

> [Kontrakane yakutughulita yira ngombe. Kapi wayiyiva nanive kontraka? Kavatughulitanga! Keheghu mukuwa anashano vantu kumupa, kuvamupa nka mwedi murongo na ntantu ntani kukavyuka kumundi. Sema Nauyoma, ghunya mu Vambo ndje ayaghupiropo kontraka mposhi vantu vakuyendawire tupu momu vanashana. Ndi naSema shi ndi shimpe mpotuli mukontraka].

It is evident that even labourers from Ovamboland held the view that they were sold and bought under the contract system. Ndadi, a contact labourer from Ovamboland explains:

> Employers buying people [labourers] from SWANLA wanted strong boys able to do hard work in mines and on farms, not young boys unable to lift even a bag of cement. I was sent back like this four times before they finally accepted me.[93]

The contract labour system was viewed as a euphemism for modern slavery as the settlers obliged the colonial authorities to supply them with African labour but did not in return feel any obligations for the welfare of labourers.[94]

A contract labourer Frans Tuhemwe Shevekwa was sent in 1970 to work at a farm in Grootfontein. He returned to Kavango in 1971 but left again for a second contract and was sent to Outjo farms where he experienced great mistreatment. He returned to the Kavango in 1972 but left for Walvis Bay in 1973. He observed the response to labour migration from Kavango compared to that from Ovamboland:

> When I reached the compound [Grootfontein] and saw the returning labourers, those from Ovamboland were as many as the soil. Those friends of ours from the west [Ovambo] use to go in large numbers then us. We from Kavango were few.[95]

---

[91] Sam Nujoma was an Ngandjera man from Ovambo land. He became political and organized contract labourers against the colonial system. He was the president of Ovambo People's Organization (OPO) and later by 1960 of South West Africa People's Organization (SWAPO). He became the founding president of the republic of Namibia on 21 March 1990.

[92] Bartholomeus Someno Katota interview. (2009-08-12), Mabushe village. Someno was born at Ndonga yaKanyinga (Namibia), date of birth is unknown but he said he was born during the reign of King Shampapi (1925–1944). His parents are Katota and Kaharu. After contract work he worked for the Portuguese as a tailor in a clothing shop.

[93] V. H. Ndadi. (1974), *Breaking contract, the story of Helao Vinnia Ndadi*, p. 17.

[94] M.R. Bhagavan. (1986), *Angola's political economy, 1975–1985*. Uppsala, Scandinavian Institute of African Studies, p. 11.

[95] Frans Tuhemwe Shevekwa interview. (2009-07-30), Sharughanda village. Tuhemwe was born at Kayova village (Namibia) in the homestead of Shiremonkuru on 18 August 1946. His parents

[Opo nayatikire mu komboni yashivanda niyamone vaka kontraka, vakuWambo vangi yira livhu. Vanya vaghunyetu vakuutokero kavayendanga vavangi, atwe vaKavango tuvasheshu.]

The Grootfontein depot was the main recruiting and distribution centre of contract labourers from the Kavango and Ovambo in Namibia. All contract labourers met there on their way to and return from contract work. Upon arrival, labourers were dropped at the main gate and were usually led by police officials inside the labour depot compound. Such police escorts were a security measure to ensure that contract labourers did not get lost into the nearby African locations upon arrival but got to the work for which they had been brought to do.

Within the Grootfontein compound, men from the Kavango had separate sleeping sections from those from Ovamboland. Shihungu Shindimba explains, "In the compound, the Ovambo slept separately from the Kavango. That is just the way it was. But the compound was one and was fenced up".[96][Omo mukomboni vawambo kukukarera, vaKavango kukukarera. Mmo tupu vya kalire. Ngoli kombonine yimwe vene, vayidingilika mundarate].

If this separation of contract labourers by colonial officials was meant to avoid communication between the labourers from Kavango and Ovamboland, then it was not successfully implemented as contract labourers intermingled within the compound (especially at the cooking space and by visiting each other at their various sleeping sections) and more so they intermingled at all destinations of work.[97] The next morning after arrival at the Grootfontein compound, labourers reported to the office of the placement officer who distributed them to their various work destinations.

The politics of allocation for the contract labourer was a very complicated one. The new labourers had no knowledge of where they would work before they arrived in Grootfontein. Their destiny for job placement and distribution was left in the hands of white labour officers one of whom the contract labourers came to refer to as "katwe katoka" (white head) in reference to his head which had grey hair. He registered all the newly arrived men.[98] The labourers gave white recruitment officers at Grootfontein names which explained the features or characteristics of those officials. Harold Eedes (also known as Nakare), a former Natives

---

were Mbandara Shevekwa and Mutengo who later crossed and settled on Angola side of the river. His father left for contract work and never returned home. When Tuhemwe returned to Kavango after his last contract in 1974 he found his family had crossed to the Namibian side of the Kavango River because of war. He was later employed in a government hostel, a job he retained until retirement. Since 2018, Tuhemwe has been Vagciriku Chief on the Angolan side of the Kavango River.

[96] Shindimba Ndumba Shihungu interview. (2009-08-06), Shipando village.
[97] Ibid.
[98] Bernhard Lipayi Linyando interview. (2009-07-27), Ndiyona village.

Affairs Commissioner in Kavango who later worked at Grootfontein recruiting depot was named "Shimbungu" (hyena). Bernhard Linyando explains:

> Upon arrival, the next day in the morning we would go to the office of SWANLA to the man we called hyena, Nakare. He was a white man but was named hyena because of his cruelty and it was also then we exclaimed that we have come to face death. He would never let you walk, you always had to run.[99]
>
> [Kukatika, linaki ngurangura makura kuyenda ngoli kumberewo ya Swanera kogho kamuyuvhanga kwaShimbungu, ogho Nakare. Ghuyene mukuwa, ngoli kwamutire ashi shimbungu morwa ukenya. Mmo twakarenkiliresha ashi hawe nani kumfa tunaya. Kwato ashi ghuyende weno, kuduka makura. Mukuwa vene ndjeghunya ayahoviro kuyaruwana muno muKavango ashi Komisari ntani anavyuka nka akaruwane mushivanda, Mr. Eeds ndyo lidina lyendi].

Since labourers knew their job categories as they already received these number tags in Rundu, their objection at Grootfontein recruiting depot was therefore not against the type of employment but rather against the area of employment or a particular employer as the following narrative by Shihungu Shindimba indicates:

> At Grootfontein, they decided that you were going to a particular destination and you did not have a say in turn. I was so unlucky and was sent to Outjo. After we all finished being registered and allocated and had returned to the compound, some Ovambo men heard about my fate and came to enquire as to which boy was allocated to Outjo. When they saw me, they exclaimed 'aah! This one! He is a dead man already, he is already dead!' But I ignored all their expressions. But one friend of mine named Kambombo and another old man protested to being sent to Outjo. The bosses threatened them that they would pay all the SWANLA food and costs so far incurred if they refused. But those two have to stand their ground and said they were not going there. Those two men returned back home, honestly.[100]
>
> [Mushivanda kukupangedera ashi kungandi unakuyenda makura, kulimburura kundereko. Ame ngoli lihudi lyande avakantuma ku Outjo.Pakumana-mana kututjanga niyende ngoli mu Komboni, vaVambo vanayuvhuko nko kuya ashi ogho mumati anakuyendo ku Outjone ghuni? Tupu vankenga ashi, aah, oghu ndi? Kafya nare, kafya nare. Amene kayinatja. Ngoli unyande Kambombo namukondi nka ghumwe, ovo avageye ngoli, vashwenine ashi kapi tuyenda atwe, vanashwena. Ovanya vahona ashi ntjene kapi muyenda ndi kumufuta odino ndya da SWANLA munali. Vavo ashi kapi tuyendako. Ovo vakondi vavyukire nawa-nawa]

Outjo was an area in southern Namibia where the former Angola Boers were settled under the colonial administration settlement scheme of 1925. The Outjo farmers were known by labourers from Kavango as "Mburu da Angora" (Angola Boers). Historically, this was a

---

[99] *Ibid.*
[100] *Ibid.*

group of Boers from South Africa who arrived in Namibia in the 1870s in search for land to settle and graze their livestock. Later, after some armed clashes with some ethnic groups in the Kavango they crossed the Kavango River and settled in southern Angola. It is known that a Boer Commando unit from South Africa led by Axel Eriksson on their way to the new envisaged settlement at Mossamedes in Angola attacked the Vagciriku of Kavango in 1894.[101] After the South African takeover of Namibia, these Angolan Boers requested the South African administration to consider their resettlement in South West Africa/Namibia. By the mid 1920s therefore, the South West Africa administration through a land settlement scheme settled these Angola Boers in the farm areas of Outjo in southern Namibia. The interaction between the Angolan Boer settlers of Outjo and the people from the Kavango therefore dates back as early as the 1890s. Since the Boers there were notorious among the African labourers for extreme cruelty and killings of labourers, contract labourers felt very unlucky to be sent to work there as they feared their lives were in danger. Labourers such as those of category A (for urban work) had some choice of the place of employment but those graded "B" and "C" (for farm work) had no choice left at the Grootfontein recruiting depot. When various jobs available from employers and their destinations were announced to the assembled men, those men of category A who were interested quickly rushed to that particular line as Benhard Shampapi explained:

> It was in Grootfontein we were divided. They would come with a form and then call out that 'from this form here, we need a number of boys to a particular place who are in need of a particular job'. Then the people who desire that particular job enters that particular line and goes to look for their names. That would be the routine, and what remains would be for the farm labourers. Then they would again say 'we need farm labourers', and then they would give orders 'You! Come here!' They would just give instructions to farm labourers because they were minors. They would call out 'come so that we write you, go to that particular farm'. What choice could he possibly make? It was difficult because he was a child. That was the routine procedure until all were placed.[102]

[Omo mushivanda mmo mwakumuhangura ngoli.Kuya naform makura kuyita ngoli ashi foromu yino yinakaropo tunashanako vamati vangandi kushirongo shangandi ovo vanakushano viruwana vya ngandi.Makura vantu kungena mumurayini ovo vanavipango ovyo viruwana makura kuyenda vakashane madina ghavo.Ngoweyo ngoweyo, ovyo vinahupopo vyavakafarama makura ashi tunashana vakafarama ashi ayi, yiya ve, mukafaramane kurenka tupu, twanuke ashi yiyave tukutjange, yenda kufarama ya ngandi, atokore vinke, udito mwanuke.Ngoweyo vene dogoro munakapwa].

---

[101] Shiremo. (2010), The reign of Hompa Nyangana over the Vagciriku, p. 104.
[102] Bernhard Limbangu Shampapi interview. (2009-07-28), Rucara village.

After a labourer was placed in a job he was provided with a blanket (two blankets if you were sent to Walvisbay where it was colder), a long sleeved shirt and one pair of shorts, regardless of the size of the labourer, bread (the quantity depended on the length of the journey) and two cans of jam. They were then provided with a train ticket attached to a permit of employment for each labourer, which indicated their names, the name of the area where they were to work and that of the employer. They travelled by train to their various work destinations.[103] Contract labourers dreaded the coal trains they named "kataghura" (the cutter/breaker) that transported them from Grootfontein to various work destinations because these were cattle transport with a stench and labourers felt their humanity degraded. Ndadi explains the conditions on the "Kataghura":

> There were no buckets or latrines. We just had to wait each time till the next station-if we could-then run to the bush or latrine. Also, there was no water on the kataula; cattle could survive without it for days. Eating dry bread, I got extremely thirsty, which was worse than the hunger.[104]

Labourers, upon their arrival at work destinations, had to hand over the employment and pass permit forms. It and was only returned to the labourer after the contract period had expired and the magistrate of that area had signed the forms to certify the expiration of contract.[105] This measure of control ensured that labourers had no documents available during the contract period to travel elsewhere without the permit of the master and could not change work (unless he breaks contract and leave without the papers).

When the contracts had expired, labourers were given back their pass permit to return to the Kavango and were eligible to re-apply for another labour contract. In cases where the former employer still needed the service of the labourer, he had to apply to the office of the commissioner or magistrate for a re-contract for a labourer and pay the recruiting fee. This only materialized in a case where the labourer was interested and agreed to be re-contracted to the same employer. Upon return to the Kavango, returning contract labourers reported at the church mission stations or at the Native Affairs Commissioner at Rundu before they returned to their various home villages.

The main emphasis on this labour migration section is the centrality of colonialism to labour migration from the Kavango, as it introduced European clothes but later curtailed local means of accessibility to it and insisted that men go on contract labour. The labour migration figures from the Kavango were always lower than Ovamboland and there was never the same value attached to labour migration from these areas. This speaks much to the dif-

---

[103] *Ibid.*
[104] V. Ndadi. (1974), *Breaking contract, the story of Helao Vinnia Ndadi*, p. 18.
[105] Bernhard Lipayi Linyando interview. (2009-07-27), Ndiyona village.

ferences in the central factor for labour migration, the ecological settings and the timing of the physical colonial presence in the two areas. The labour journeys section indicates how labourers had to endure long and tiring journeys to reach their work destinations and how they were subjected to all sorts of human mistreatments in the name of medical or security check ups. The extent of the traversing of national boundaries by contract labourers show how far they were willing to go through a lot of trouble to fulfill their needs, all of which speaks to the severity of the central factors for their labour migration. It also shows the new social networks developed by the Kavango contract labourers in their social integration period with other Africans under the contract labour system. It indicates the vast experience Kavango contract labourers acquired outside Namibia and shows how their responses to contract labour system within Namibia was shaped and informed by such acquired outside experiences. The labour journeys show the colonial administration were anxious to improve labour supplies from the Kavango and put in place water holes on labour routes and dealt with the security threat against labour supplies posed by attacks by Vacu. As it emerges through the oral narratives, women played a great role in the contract labour system, which is an aspect of history that is less well known and to which this chapter now turns.

Women in labour narratives

It is possible from the labour narratives of the men to draw out some idea as to what the place of women was in the contract labour system. Although two women (Theresia Shidona and Susana Mate) who were sisters were interviewed, the interview focused on their life stories and I did not draw them on the subject of the contract labour system. The two were my extended grandparents and were interviewed separately during one of my many visits to them. This study therefore looks at women's role through the male narratives.

In Namibia women were prevented from working in public places unlike their male counterparts and were instead located in the informal sector of the economy, or at home.[106] During the colonial period in Namibia women's mobility was regarded by both colonial officials and the African males as threatening to tradition and order in their communities.[107] Women had to remain home to produce food for family subsistence while men were away on contract. The colonial administration in Namibia viewed the presence of African women in the police zone negatively.[108] It regarded the African women in the urban areas as agents of social con-

---

[106] H. Becker. (2010), A concise history of gender, "tradition" and the state in Namibia. In C. Keulder (ed.), *State, society and democracy: a reader in Namibian politics.* Windhoek, Konrad Adeneur Stiftung, pp. 181–182.
[107] Hayes, 'A history of the Ovambo of Namibia, c. 1880–1935', p. 289.
[108] M. E. Wallace, 'Health and society in Windhoek Namibia, 1915–1945' (Basel, P Schlettwein,

tamination who spread venereal diseases; unmarried women were compelled to undergo compulsory testing, which made women in the urban areas very angry.[109] Hayes similarly shows that women in Ovamboland were prevented from leaving Ovamboland because of the allegedly immoral effects and that this discourse of "responsible patriarchy" was shared by both administration and Ovambo male elders.[110] In Ovamboland, the Christian missions, the commissioner and the chiefs collaborated to impose this way of thinking about women's place.[111]

Similarly, in the Kavango, women were not allowed to leave the area for the south and the colonial administration together with the chiefs collaborated to prevent women from leaving. Labour escorts who did not adhere to this order and took women to the south were fined. One labour escort in 1936 declared under oath:

> I was fined five head of cattle by Chief Shampapi because I took two women down to Grootfontein last year [1935]. These women were not in possession of a pass. I often heard Nakare [commissioner] order that no women were to be taken south and also heard Chief Shampapi give similar orders. The two women bothered me so much that I eventually took them down to Grootfontein.[112]

Women have been viewed either as beneficiaries or victims of the contract labour system.[113] Oral history narratives confirm this representation. Women are said to have benefited when returning contract labourers brought home items such as bundle of cloths to share with other family members.[114] They have also been presented as victims by becoming infected with sexually transmitted diseases from returning contract labourer husbands.[115]

Women also had to suffer the fate of having their traditional braids cut by their husbands who supported the commissioner. It was made easier by the fact that the returning contract labourers during the contract labour period saw that women in the police zone had short hair and therefore they accepted the order of the commissioner and missionaries to have all women in Kavango to cut their "vihiho" (dreadlocks).[116] Yet even in the situation of having their vihiho hair cut, women only chose to be cut after they saw that they could get something

---

2000).
[109] Marion Wallace, 'a person is never angry for nothing' in P. Hayes et al. (ed.), *Namibia under South African rule*, pp. 77–94.
[110] Hayes. (1992), A history of the Ovambo of Namibia, c. 1880–1935, p. 288.
[111] P. Hayes. (1996), Cocky Hahn and the black Venus': the making of a native commissioner in South West Africa, 1915–46. *Gender and History*, (8)3, p. 372.
[112] Langhans Kanyinga. (1936-01-22), Declaration. Windhoek, NAN, NAR 1/1/55, file 11/1/.
[113] Yeboah. (2000), The impact of labour migration on Namibian women, p. 20.
[114] G.M. Weka interview. (2009-07-29), Rucara village.
[115] Yeboah. (2000), The impact of labour migration on Namibian women, p. 20.
[116] G.M. Weka intervieww. (2009-07-29), Rucara village.

out of it in return for their loss. As the following indicates: "At first the women refused but when they finally saw the wives of the king who did it how they were provided with goods such as head scarf and dresses it was only than they also agreed to cut and wash it all off"[117]

Since most men went on contract labour system most parental and family responsibilities at home are said to have been left completely on the women's shoulders.[118] Women, however, drew on the communal institution of "ndjambi" which entailed organizing community members to plough your field after which you invited all the helpers to the beer drinking feast at your homestead.

Some men stayed longer on contract labour much to the dislike of family members and so women found means to keep men, especially their sons, longer at home through the marriage arrangement process. Although tradition and customs in Namibia have been collaboratively utilized by chiefs, colonial officials and missionaries to control women, the women used the opportunities presented to them by the existing traditions to their advantage. The women, especially mothers, played a central role in the search for marriage partners for contract labourers. They were able to convince their sons not to return to contract labour until they have settled the issue of marriage and this was at times a delaying strategy by mothers to keep their sons longer at home. Tuhemwe Shevekwa narrates from his personal experience:

> I stayed there in Tjaisa only for one day. The next day I said 'Oh, no, mummy I am leaving.' Then my mother tried to stop me and said I must wait first to meet the woman they have proposed for me. I told her I cannot wait and I gave them all the presents I bought for the girl and her family. But after further convincing I agreed to stay a little bit longer for my mother to go and bring the girl I was destined to marry.[119]
>
> [Makura anikararamo liyuva limwe tupu, oli makura ame aye, yina ame kunakuvyuka. Vanane avashana kunkonda ashi weni ngoli unya mukamali twakuvandekera. Ameshi, kapi nimutaterera, anivapa navintje vyo nakamughulilire vatape kwamukadona naliro lyendi. Ngoli muruku rwakunkondja anipura kukarapo kadidi, vanane vakayite mukadona owo va mbandekera].

Oral narratives also point to the central importance of women in the contract labourers' lives. One contract labourer, upon hearing from the police zone that his mother had died returned to ascertain the truth.[120] After he learned that the story was true he informed his father that he had no more reason to remain in Kavango but after the persistent persuasions to stay home he told his father to find him a wife with characteristics and behaviour like his

---

[117] *Ibid.*
[118] Yeboah. (2000), The impact of labour migration on Namibian Women, pp. 21–22.
[119] Frans Tuhemwe Shevekwa interview (2009-07-30).
[120] Bartholomeus Someno Katota interview. (2009-08-12), Mabushe village.

late mother so that whenever he looked at her, he would be reminded of his mother.[121] The women also pounded mahangu cereals and prepared the meal which the contract labourers took on their journey and women performed rituals and observed taboos at home aimed at preventing bad luck to contract labourers during their absence. When contract labourers arrived at home, it was usually the women such as mothers and wives who arranged most activities of the welcoming feast for the returning labourers. In some cases, the women put humanity above profit making and gave a helping hand by providing for free their food originally meant for sale to returning contract labourers who arrived at home starving. As Shikombero narrates:

> We were so lucky when we arrived at Gciriku area that we met some women, the sisters to some of the contract labourers who took their ground nuts for sale at the Portuguese post. They were the ones who saved us from hunger. The women were so happy to see us, to see their brothers and so they took their ground nuts which they intended for sale but gave it to us to eat for free.[122]

> [Lirago ngoli opo twayatikire pa mbongi po, makura vaghunyetu ngoli ava vakaliro navaghuni vavopo, walye kwatwalirepo ndongo, mbo vakatutongoliro ngoli ndjara yakutunda nayo pauKwangali. Makura vakamali pakukatukenga ashi nan! Vagciriku munaya, ntani vanakatupa ngoli ndongo davo kuyota ngoli, avatupa ngoli, ndjara, ghayarashi namakoli ngogha kwato ashi kukuvereka? Vintje twakashimbireko, vi-pepa-pepa tupu vene navinguvo vyavidona vya vinyime vyavo vinya vya ntjanko].

In some cases when contract labourers left home for contract labour, it were their mothers that escorted them a distance from the homestead.[123] This indicates the attachment of love and care that women had for their sons and husbands who left as contract labourers.

Women hid returning contract labourers from the reaches of the Portuguese officials who, since the liberation war of Namibia and the cooperation between SWAPO and UNITA were accused of being SWAPO agents. At a more general or political level, women were instrumental in the political mobilization of contract labourers especially within the police zone. The case of SWAPO activist Maxuilili provides an example. He would sometimes be arrested, but in his absence women took over his work. As Bernhard Limbangu Shampapi recalls:

> Every time even after he was arrested, the meetings were continued daily by others. His members continued to call up the meetings. The wife of Maxuilili with the Herero and Ovambo women continued it together, goodness! It was every day.[124]

---

[121] *Ibid.*
[122] Mathias Ndumba Shikombero interview. (2009-07-28), Rucara village.
[123] Frans Tuhemwe Shevekwa interview. (2009-07-30).
[124] Bernhard Limbangu Shampapi interview. (2009-07-28), Rucara village.

[Ntjene Maxuilili vanamukwata, vigongi shimpe kuvitwikira vapeke. Vamembers dendi kutwikira kuyitapo mbongarero. Mukada Maxuilili navakadi vavaWambo navaherero kutwikira kutulita vigongi, nane! Keheliyuva!]

Women in Namibia therefore have not just been central to the lives of the contract labourers but played a role in the political mobilization among contract labourers. Kihato has made a crucial argument about assessing women's role as agents or victims. She argues that victimhood and agency are not mutually exclusive categories as these distinctions collapse and become intertwined.[125] They cannot be boxed into either categories of victims or agents. Binaries are simply unhelpful. This is borne out by an analysis of women's role in the contract labour system brief as this discussion is.

Conclusion

The contract labourers' view and experience of the contract labour system in Namibia have not been given adequate attention. Studies have mainly focused on Ovamboland whereby labour migration has been traced to an unstable environment, seasonal food shortages and subsequent hardships. The Kavango, another supplier of contract labourers in Namibia, has been neglected but unlike the unstable environment or seasonal food shortages in Ovambo, colonialism was the central reason for labour migration from the Kavango.

According to the contract labourers' own views, the contract labour system was a process through which they were bought as paid slaves by white employers and were delivered to them by the colonial administration through the recruiting organizations. They indicate that the colonial administration was the central agent and beneficiary of the contract labour system. Contract labourers from Kavango provide the lack of clothing as the central factor for labour migration. This must be understood in the light of the colonial activities that reduced acces to clothing at local level and thus exerted pressure on the communities and compelled men to migrate as contract labourers. It is important to understand people's perspectives on why migration occurred.

The implementation of the law on wildlife protection prevented the Kavango people from the previous easy access to these local resources to make skin clothes etc. and they were thus compelled by the situation to turn to migration into contract labour. Parents no longer provided for most of the needs of their children and this caused children not to adhere to the instructions of their parents to look after livestock and instead migrated as contract labourers in the hope of creating wealth and catering for their needs and those of

---

[125] *Ibid.*, p. 413.

their elders. The Kavango people's introduction to European goods made them prefer European clothes and they began to regard their skin dress as old fashioned and backward and as a sign of poverty rather than as culture. They began to regard the acquisition of European clothes as a sign of wealth and civilization and this was a cause for migration of men as contract labourers to work and acquire such European goods. Although there were cases where some men, especially underage ones, escaped to go on contract work, all contract labourers usually left with the knowledge of the parents as these were usually discussed at their family social platforms.

Many contract labourers worked as far as Djwaini (Johannesburg) mines, in Salisbury (Harare) and in Angola before enlisting for contract work in Namibia. Djwaini was their preferred choice as they believed the pay was better and although they regarded it as a destination of death it was also regarded as a destination for "strong men" and this made their sojourn there a worthwhile experience. Salisbury (Harare) in Zimbabwe was seen as the destination for the unwanted and the weak, Angola as a destination of misery and Portuguese mistreatment, while Namibia was regarded as a destination site where labourers were sold as slaves to needy employers for disappointingly marginal wages.

The agency of women under difficult conditions created by the impact of the contract labour system on them and their families has been discussed Women were not just the beneficiaries or victims of the contract labour system; they were central to the lives of contract labourers. They prepared the journeys and the homecoming celebrations of the contract labourers, they were central in the marriage decisions for contract labourers and in the political mobilization of the contract labourers in their new places of work. The next chapter discusses these new work and living experiences.

3 Living and Work Experiences

Introduction

The oral stories of Kavango contract labourers indicate that many of them worked on both the farms and mines and this makes it imperative to address their experiences in both settings. The number of contract workers in Namibia supplied to the farming sector exceeded the number to the mines for the first time in 1934 and remained so during most of the 1940s.[1] After 1948, SWANLA adopted a compelling strategy to be able to meet the demands for farm labour by making it compulsory for all new recruits to spend at least one contract as a farm worker before they would be able to travel to the mines.[2] Despite the unwillingness of most contract labourers to be sent to the farm rather than mines the restrictive labour practices since 1948 forced workers to work on farms before they could go to mines and this explains why so many had experience of both.

Kavango recruits destined for farm work lived on farms. Contract labourers had living and work experiences in countries as far as Angola, Zimbabwe and South Africa before working in Namibia. This chapter explores the experiences of contract labourers on farms, mines and compounds both outside and inside Namibia through oral narratives, archival and written sources to explain where they worked and lived and how they adapted in these places.

The contract labourers on farms

Contract labourers from the Kavango worked as far as the farms and plantations in Angola and Zimbabwe and their working experiences on the Namibian farms were a continuation of those experiences. In Angola, contract labourers from the Kavango met and worked with labourers who came from as far as Zaire/Congo and, together, they cut down trees for timber with sawing machines which, in their view, was dangerous work.[3] Although the Kavango men left for contract work to Angola in the 1950s, some literature on Angola indicates that Africans from the Kavango and Ovambo had worked as slaves on the Angolan plantations since the 1850s after the traders from Mocamedess penetrated the Kavango and Ovambo to acquire slaves.[4] During the 1950s, however, the contract labourers from the

---

[1] Silvester, 'Black pastoralists, white farmers', p. 335.
[2] Ibid.
[3] Shintango Karenga interview. (2009-08-05), Korokoko village.
[4] W.G. Clarence-Smith. (1979), *Slaves, peasants and capitalists in southern Angola, 1840–1926*. London, Cambridge University Press, pp. 15–19, 67.

Kavango mainly worked on railways and timber cutting farms etc. and they speak of insects in Angola called "mutakanye" (tick) which used to bite them. These were small insects like the insects that bite chickens. When the mutakanye insect entered one's feet it started off like a small pimple and soon turned into a large sore.[5]

Contract labourers were paid one rand and twenty cents a month and got the rest of the money as deferred pay upon their return home, but they were disappointed because the Angolan currency was of little value and could buy very little. As with all oral history the challenge is to connect memories to a time frame and many contract labourers found it hard to remember how much they got paid at a specific time. But what is of importance here is what their narratives about the payments reveal about the perception of work in Angola. It shows their belief that their hard work was not equally translated into monetary terms as the wages they received could buy them almost nothing.

The contract labour period to Angola usually lasted for two years or more and gave reason for complaint. Some labourers got beaten by the Portuguese employers for daring to demand to be returned home when they were kept at their workplace long after their initial contract period had expired.[6] Yet others accused the Portuguese officials on the ships at Luanda of killing a contract labourer on each occasion of the New Year's festivals.[7] There are no written sources to confirm or deny the death claims but the narrative shows how contract labourers made meanings of the mysterious disappearances and deaths of fellow workers and this speaks much to the mistrust and the brutal image contract labourers assigned to the Portuguese. The contract workers in Angola were maintained at subsistence level and many died or failed to return to their villages.[8] The employers cared little if contract labourers became incapacitated or died, for they could always ask that other labourers be furnished.[9]

The contract labourers from the Kavango also worked on tobacco farm plantations in Zimbabwe and there they met African labourers who spoke Chinyandja.[10] There is no documented evidence of the number of men from Kavango who worked in Zimbabwe. Those who ended up in Zimbabwe were those who were rejected in Botswana en-route to South African mines. Since there was no official recruiting of contract labourers from the Kavango to Zimbabwe, it is difficult to quantify as by definition such recruiting was

---

[5] Shintango Karenga interview. (2009-08-05), Korokoko village.
[6] Mathias Ndumba Shikombero interview. (2009-07-28) Rucara village.
[7] Ndumba Shirengumuke interview. (2009-07-03), Hoha village.
[8] M.R. Bhagavan. (1986), *Angola's political economy, 1975–1985*. (Uppsala, Scandinavian Institute of African Studies), p. 11.
[9] Bhagavan. (1986), *Angola's political economy, 1975–1985*, p. 144.
[10] Shintango Karenga interview. (2009-08-05), Korokoko village.

unofficial and therefore not legal. The contract labour period was usually for twelve months. The payments were one rand per month, and it was only after six months of work that it was increased to one rand and twenty cents.[11] The narratives of Kavango labourers working on the farms in Zimbabwe show they experienced bad living and working conditions with low pay.

In Namibia, the farms were mainly owned by German settlers and Afrikaners from South Africa. In these new places of work there was a tendency for labourers to be given European names by their farm employers and for contract labourers to also give African names to the employers. The farmers claimed that the African names were too long and difficult to pronounce and thus gave labourers new European names for identification. Shintango, who worked on Zimbabwe farms in 1948 and in Angola in 1951 before going for his first contract in Namibia in 1953, explains his transformation to Jims:

> At that time I was always not recorded by the name Shintango, I was Jims. The whites found my name Shintango to be too slow and called me Jimtango and it was Jims whom they used in my record and was the name which passed me in the police zone. The name Jims means 'your name Shintango is difficult and too slow for a white man and therefore as a short cut we will begin to call you Jims'. That was the name they wrote on my papers and therefore I just continued to use that instead.[12]
>
> [Ame ngoli pashiruvo shinya kapi kavantjangitanga ashi Shintango ame panya ame ngoli Jims. Vamakuwa vavone maranga ngoli Shintango ashi Jimtango. Jims ndyo kavantjangitanga ngoli pakuyenda mushivanda ngoli ndyo kalipitango. Nkoko nakahovire kukaruwana ku Rhodesia nko vakalimpire. Jims kutanta ashi lidina lyoye lidito ngudu ove shintango kumukuwa ntani maranga, makura nkondomoke ngoli shiwapo nkwandi tukuyitange ngoli ashi Jims. Mmo vakantjangire pashimbapira makura kuruwanitanga tupu ndyolyo ngoli].

Other examples include Frans Tuhemwe Shevekwa who narrated his new name calling experience of 1970:

> The white person used to call me Timo. To call me Tuhemwe was difficult for her. But at that time, I was not yet baptized. They called me Timo as they could not manage to pronounce Tuhemwe and so they shortened it to Timo. Since then they called me Timo to imply Tuhemwe (Tuhemwe laughs). I also use to respond to it because I got too tired of correcting them and so I said to myself I will just respond to the name.
>
> [Meshi uye mukuwa kandjitanga ashi Timo. Kuyita ashi Tuhemwe udito, amenka ruvede runya shimpe kapi vandjogha. Makura vavone vavene ngoli morwa lya Tuhemwe nakulivhurashi makura kuliteta ngoli ashi Timo. Makura mbyo kavakandjitanga ngoli ashi Timo! Ashi ndyo Tuhemwe ngolishi (Tuhemwe kunakushepa). Name nko

---

[11] *Ibid.*
[12] *Ibid.*

ngoli kupura morwa narorokire ngoli kuvatantera makura me kunipuranga tupu ngoli ndyolyo].

Harries' view that names that carried a specific meaning at home and provided their bearers with a temporal and spatial identity were met with incomprehension on the South African and Mozambique mines is thus also true of the Namibian context.[13] Although the Kavango labourers adhered to the European names they thought of it as an inability of their employers to pronounce their African names. But they also felt that a European name acted as a pass around the police zone and therefore they agreed to the new names. In South Africa, the black worker's practice of permanently adopting a European name given to them by white employers seems to have started on the diamond fields. According to Harries, these names ranged from terms for local coins, such as Sixpence and Shilling, to popular brands of liquor like Cape Smoke and Pontac, to expletives such as Bloody Fool and God Damn. Harries indicates that while there is truth in the argument that one can ascribe what is perceived as the absurdity of these names to the practices of racist whites seeking to infantilize blacks and legitimate their exploitation it ignores the way in which workers constructed their own vision of the world. He regards the adaptability of migrant labourers to new names as a process in which the labourers created a new situational social identity and as a mark of their passage through life that signified membership of a new and assertive community.[14]

While the practice of giving oneself a European nickname was the case among migrant labourers in South Africa, no evidence could be established from oral interviews if this was the same for the Kavango contract labourers. Unlike Harries' interpretation where the contract labourers derived pride and constructed a new way of looking at the world through their given European names; it was different in the case of the Kavango. Here contract labourers were unhappy as the European names were imposed on them and, although they continued to use them, it was not their choice and was simply a means to relate easily to their employers. The given European names were mainly used at contract work and were hardly used in the Kavango upon their return.

The contract labourers also gave new names to the farmers but unlike the farmers who informed the labourers of their new names the labourers dared not do the same. These names were usually laden with negative connotations and could make their masters furious and only lead to severe punishment, all of which speaks to the politics of power relations

---

[13] P. Harries. (1994), *Work culture and identity: migrant labourers in Mozambique and South Africa, c.1860–1910*. Johannesburg, Witwatersrand University Press, p. 60.

[14] P. Harries. (1994), *Work, culture and identity: migrant labourers in Mozambique and South Africa, c. 1860–1910*, p. 59.

between the labourers and employers at that time. Contract labourers usually gave farmers African names to describe their physical features such as kapunda (stomach) for one who had a huge stomach or katwekatoka (white head) for one who had grey hair. The names also described the behaviour of the employers such as Shimbungu (hyena), which was given to Harold Eedes because contract labourers believed he was cruel.[15] The practice of name-calling among the Kavango people was that a name given to a person was related to either an event during birth, or the physical appearance of the person. Therefore, African names that were given to employers were related to the characteristics or physical appearance of the employer and were always meaningful. Most of these names were loaded with humour and, therefore, name-calling helped the workers to come to terms with the mistreatment they endured from their employers. The term "Ovambo" used by colonial authorities to refer to all the contract workers is interpreted in different ways by the Kavango contract labourers. Some believed that the white employers were too ignorant to identify them properly or to differentiate between black people and therefore used the word Ovambo to mean "black persons". As one interviewee, Muyenga Shintunga, pointed out: "Do whites make a difference? To them, everyone was an Ovambo; we were all black and so then Vambo".[16][Vavo vanya vamakuwa ashi vapongora ndi? Vavo keheghuno ashi Vambo, natuvantje tuvashovaganisha! Makura ashi Vambo].

An unpublished autobiography by a Kavango contract labourer suggests that the term "Ovambo" was a corruption of the Kavango words "Vambo" (those of axes) or "Vambu" (those of reeds) by SWANLA recruiting officials in the police zone.[17] According to this version the words were used by Langhals Kanyinga (a recruiting labour escort from the Kavango during the German and the early South African period in Namibia) but that the colonial recruiting officials utilized the term "Ovambo" to all the contract labourers from Ovamboland and the Kavango.[18] This view by Ausiku is less convincing because the term "Ovambo" appeared on written records as early as 1851.[19] It is also contrary to the view held by scholars who assert that the term "Ovambo" is a Herero term derived from "Aayamba" (rich ones) or from "eumbo" (homestead).[20] Ausiku's view nevertheless is helpful as it shows

---

[15] Bernhard Lipayi Linyando interview. (2009-07-27), Ndiyona village.
[16] Muyenga Shintunga Unengu interview. (2009-07-31), Rucara village.
[17] David Kudumo Ausiku. (2005), My own life stories: is this God's work or Satan's scheme? Unpublished work, Canada, copy right no. ISBN 0-1038934, pp. 1–4.
[18] *Ibid.*
[19] Frieda-Nela Williams. (1991), *Pre-colonial communities of South Western Africa: a history of Owambo kingdoms, 1600–1920.* Windhoek, National Archives of Namibia, p. 53. The word Ovambo was first recorded by a European traveler Galton in 1851 and by Anderson in 1861.
[20] Harri Siiskonen. (1990), Trade and economic change in Ovamboland, 1850–1906. Helsinki, HSH, pp. 20–21.

that the term "Ovambo" held different interpretations for Kavango contract labourers and helped some to accept it as their word.

The term "Ovambo", however, was not accepted or used by many other Kavango contract labourers who fruitlessly corrected their white employers. Tuhemwe is a case in point:

> The white man said to me 'be careful you Vambo! You Vambo will get beaten'. You think there was Kavango there? At that time in the past, they called all of us as Ovambo. It was rare that you were called a Kavango. You were either an Ovambo-Kavango or an Ovambo-Ovamboland; yes, that was how they use to refer to us. Then when I told him that I was not an Ovambo, he retorted, 'you are a Vambo, do you not come from Kavango?' To them, since we all came from the north and others out of Namibia, they thought it were only Ovambos who came from that side. But there were Kavango and Ovambo combined but yet we were all just Ovambo.[21]

> [Ghuye shirumbu ashi takamita muVambove! Ove muVambove ngaunya tupu. Ashi uKavango ko? Ameshi panya pakare vavo natuvantje kavatutwenyanga ashi vaVambo.Rusheshu kukutwenya ashi umuKavango, Ovambo-Kavango ntani Ovambo-Ovamboland, yii ngoweyo vene kavatuyitanga.Makura ame pakumutantera ashi ame kapishi nimuVambo, ghuye ashi ghumu Vambo, ameshi kuKavango watundave?Vavo morwa ameshi ashi natuvantje kwatundasha ngoli kunya ku noorde, vamwe pandje ya Namibia ashi Vavambo tupu vatundangoko.Mara mpovalimo vene vaKavango, ntani mpovalimo vaVambo mara navantje vaVambo].

An official explains the convenience of counting and naming the Kavango as Ovambo:

> The Okavangos [Kavango] can for statistical purposes be classified with the Ovambos, as they come from the eastern portion of Ovamboland. The latitude in which they live is the same as that the Ovamboland lives in.[22]

There are certainly references to the categories that were used for counting purposes by SWANLA and other official institutions where the identities of the Kavango and Ovambo were compounded.[23]

The contract labourers felt very uneasy about being identified incorrectly but some nevertheless accepted it as they felt their constant correction of employers fell on deaf ears. Colonial officials' inability or unwillingness to differentiate labourers from the Kavango from those who came from Ovamboland continued up to the 1950s. From the 1950s onwards, however, the administration officials were becoming worried about the lack of proper identification of the labourers from the Kavango and were encouraging all colonial officials to identify labourers properly as the following shows:

---

[21] Tuhemwe Shevekwa interview. (2009-07-30), Sharughanda village.
[22] The Administrator. (1935), The Union of S.A annual report. Windhoek, NAN, JX 0220, p. 75.
[23] See C.G. Courtney-Clarke. (1941-10-02), The 1927 to 1939 statistics for the recruitment of Ovambo/Kavango migrant workers and `Angolans' to South Africa (SWAA A521/8/2/2404).

> It is felt that something should be said about the habit of the public and also some of the departments of administration refering to all Northern Natives as Ovambos. This can lead to confusion and often to needless correspondence and waste of time. Besides the Okavango [Kavango] natives and the Okavango [Kavango] Native Territory should be accorded their due recongnition. In all police documents Northern Natives are refered to as Ovambos.[24]

This new urge by colonial officials to identify a Kavango labourer correctly was therefore aimed at making administration work easier and not as a response to their previous pleas to be identified properly. Although the colonial administration officials encouraged all white employers in the police zone to identify the labourers from the Kavango as Kavango some continued to use the term Ovambo.

The colonial authorities and employers reminded labourers of the fact that they were in new places different from their home and had to abide by rules and regulations. As Tuhemwe narrates:

> We found a white man who was nicknamed Katoka-toka who was extremely cruel. If you heard him calling on you twice and you still did not seem to hear your name called, oh, trouble! He would first take you around into his office and question you where you went to and inform you that you have come in search for work and that this is the police zone, not your home![25]

> [Twakawaninemo ngoli shirumbu shimwe varukire ashi Katoka-toka shaghukenya wadjanyi. Ntjene ntjo unakuyuvha shinakukuyito ruviri ngoli kapi unayuvhu lidina lyoye, Aah, nkango! Kuyakupinukita tanko ayakupure mumberewo yendi ashi kuni unayendi. Ashi oku waya kwaya kukushana viruwana kapishi mwenu muno, omunone mu benneland kapishi kukwenu ku.]

The harsh treatment and vulgar language of white officials at the Grootfontein recruiting depot filled new labourers with doubt as to their future in new working and living environments. Contract labourers who worked on farms lived on those farms. The labourers on farms usually slept in small rounded houses called pondoks that were usually situated in the backyard of the main house of the farm. The labourers did not receive blankets from the farmer but used those which they received at the Grootfontein recruiting depot. Since there was no bed or a mattress the labourers usually slept on the floor as is indicated by Tuhemwe's experience in 1970:

---

[24] Native Commisioner. (1955-02-16), Northern territories: Okavango [Kavango] natives described as Ovambos. Windhoek, NAN. SWAA 2387, A519/1. 16 Feb. 1955.
[25] Tuhemwe Shevekwa interview. (2009-07-30), Sharughanda village.

> There were no beds; we just spread our blankets on the floor. The blankets were those that were given to us at Grootfontein. You just took a blanket to spread on the floor and another to cover yourself. What sleep did we get? Really nothing![26]
>
> [Mbete kundereko kuyara tupu mbyovyo vinguvo vyetu momo musamente mu vloer. Nguvo detune ndodo da mbendeka vatupire mushivanda. Kughupa shinguvo shakuyara oshino shakufufuka, ashi turare vintje ngoli? Hawe-kwato!]

Tuhemwe indicates that the poor sleeping arrangements resulted in inadequate sleep. During the cold seasons, labourers suffered from extreme cold and it was worse for labourers who worked in the cold mountainous farm areas of Namibia. This was the experience of Shintunga during his third contract in the 1930s:

> Upon my return home, I stayed just a little and then went to Usakos. Oh no! That side was extremely cold! So many mountains there, my goodness! No-no-no-no! Sometimes you would not see the sun until when it was setting down. It was extremely cold there![27]
>
> [Kukavyuka kuyakarapone atuyayendi nka ngoli ku Usakosa (Usakos). Okunyane, hee! Oyinya mpepo yako yakurenka! Mamundundu okunya kuninke nani, um-um-um-um! Liyuva ngoghonya pamweya nakulimonashi dogoro mpopanya linakageha. Okunyane utenda!]

Some of the pondoks were old with leaking roofs and cracked walls and were not usually renovated or fumigated and became the breeding ground for "ntjanya" (bugs) which tormented the labourers during their sleep and it was worse when it rained. Tuhemwe further explained his experience in 1970:

> All the workers slept in pondoks. And then there were bugs my dear? Goodness! No! That was plain suffering. The bugs were in the rooms within the cracks of the wall, all red-red-red-red! But there was no other place for you to go and sleep except there! They did not even disinfect the rooms, there were no such things. You just stayed like that. At times when it was fitting we slept outside otherwise you slept inside turning around your body in pain from the stings. During the rainy season, you had nowhere else to go and the water from the roofs again leaked on you and you woke up in mud.[28]
>
> [Kurarane kuvi Pondoka natuvantje varuwani. Odo ntjanya ove hewa? Nani-nani! Hawe runya ruhepo. Ntjanya momo mushindjuvo mo, omunya mwatavaghuko kukadiwana da ge-ge-ge-ge! Ngoli kwato nka kumwe oko ukarara ashi kuninko, nkwandi momo. Kwato nka ashi vayapomberemo, kwato! Ngoweyo makura. Pamweya ntjene vinakayane murare ngoli pandje, pamweyane mo mugetauka vene momo.

---

[26] *Ibid.*
[27] Muyenga Shintunga Unengu interview. (2009-07-31), Rucara village.
[28] Tuhemwe Shevekwa interview. (2009-07-30), Sharughanda village.

Nange ruvede rwa kurombone kwato vene oko muyenda memanka kumushonyena kukarambuka mulitata.]

Some interviewees tend to use "you" rather than "I" to refer to their personal experiences. "You" was in many cases used when referring to bad experiences. For example, "you were beaten" rather than "I or one was beaten". In this way they transferred their personal bad experiences to an anonymous "you" rather than the personalized "I". This could be regarded as a narrative strategy to deal with past bad experiences.

The number of labourers per pondok depended on the availability of pondoks and it could range from one to as many as five labourers in a pondok. Apart from using pondoks as a form of accommodation, the contract labourers could also be assigned any available structure such as a storage room as was the case with Shindimba Shihungu during his first contract to Outjo farms in the 1950s: "And then they gave me a simple excluded storage room where he use to store all his things, every material that he used was stored in there, where else did you think you could sleep?"[29]

Some labourers did not expect the large work load they received upon arrival at the farms as they had different preconceived ideas about what they would do on the farm. Some thought, for instance, that they would do light work such as gardening. Such preconceived ideas were usually based on the belief that they were minors and also on their prior experiences of farm work at the Catholic mission stations in Kavango. Matamu who left for his first contract after 1936 and worked at a farm in Okahandja refers to his own expectations:

> When I went on contract, I thought they were going to give me easy work since I was a child. I thought it would be work such as cleaning or sweeping the yard or even those which we were taught at mission school by the nuns of planting cabbages. That was what I thought and not that of herding cattle.[30]
>
> [Opo nayendire kukontraka ame naghayalire ashi mpovili vyaureru tupu ngavakampa ame morwa nimwanuke, mpili vyakukomba-komba tupu ndi mpilindi ovinya vatushongire vasosta pa mbongi vyakutapayika makovi, ovinya mbyo naghayalire ngoli, kapishi mukulita ngombe.]

The designations of duties for farm labourers at the Grootfontein recruiting depot were not an assurance that farm labourers would only perform those designated duties at their respective farm destinations. Upon arrival at the farm, the farmer had a final say and allocated any work to the labourer. This meant that a labourer who was contracted to work in the kitchen could end up working as a herdsboy on the farm.

---

[29] Shindimba Shihungu interview. (2009-08-06), Shipando village.
[30] Matamu interview. (2009-07-12), Rundu town.

The Kavango contract labourers on farms worked along with the Ovambo contract labourers, the local Herero and Damara/Nama people. When a new labourer arrived on a farm, they usually inquired from the other farm labourers about their way of life on a farm so as to familiarize themselves with their new places and determine how they would fit in.[31] Since Kavango labourers usually worked with labourers from other ethnic groups they established friendships across ethnic lines. The contract labourers from Kavango usually learned Otjiherero or the Damara language as a lingua franca but some also learned to speak Oshikwanyama. The Kavango labourers could easily learn the Otjiherero language as they could relate to many similar words in their own Kavango languages. As Shindimba Shihungu indicated:

> A Damara came and said 'let us go and look for the cattle'. I said, 'o.k. let us go'. He spoke in Otjiherero saying 'let us go and look for the cattle'. I understood the word 'let us go' and the word 'look for the cattle' sounded like in our language. The word 'let us go' is clearly understood to be the same as the 'let us go' in our language. I also understood 'the cattle'. So then we left to look for the cattle.[32]
>
> [Makura muDamara naye anaya ashi tuyende tukashane ngombe, ame oyaa tuyende. Ghuye kughamba mu Ruherero ashi 'Ngatuyende tukatare othongombe'. Ngatuyendene kughuyuvha, tukatare othongombe meshi yira mwetu ngoli mmo. Natuyende meshi kughuyuvha ashi 'tuyende'. Othongombe nayo unayiyuvhu, makura kuyenda kukashana ngombe.]

Labourers acquired utensils such as a plate, a pot, a cup etc from their master which were later deducted from their wage. At the end of each week the master provided supplies of food. They usually received tobacco, salt, sugar and maize meal, beans and soup while meat was only given occasionally.[33] Many contract labourers on farms surveyed the area to find grass for grazing, checked the fences for repairs, herded the livestock, milked the cows, separated cream from the milk, trained dogs to watch the goats, branded cattle and did other jobs around the farm that were given by the farmer.[34]

Contract labourers related work on contract to that at home. In the Kavango a man herded cattle and milked the cows, he cut down poles to build the fence for the cattle kraal or the homestead and he cut down the reeds to make reed mats, he worked in the field and assisted his elders in any other duties where he was required.[35] During contract work at farms men herded cattle, goats, sheep and other livestock, fixed the fence around the vari-

---

[31] Bernhard Lipayi Linyando interview. (2009-07-27), Ndiyona village.
[32] Shindimba Shihungu interview. (2009-08-06), Shipando village.
[33] G.M. Weka interview. (2009-07-29), Rucara village.
[34] Ausiku. (2005), My own life stories: is this God's work or Satan's scheme? p. 28.
[35] Nyambe Merecky interview. (2009-08-06), Shipando village.

ous cattle camp sites where they herded the cattle for grazing, worked in the garden or field or simply waited to be given any other duties by the master to perform.[36] A herd boy also milked the cows and ensured that he followed the required steps by applying the required medicine on his hands for the milking process.[37]

At home, while a young man learned by practical examples from the elders to perform various duties such as cattle herding and clearing the fields on the farms he was instructed and at times compelled by force. On the farms, labourers were often shouted at and forced to work, while at home they had some form of independence to carry out the task. At home, the men could decide to visit neighbours with no limits of what time to return home or else they sat around shinyanga (social gathering place around the fire in the evening) to discuss their experiences during the day and their plans for the next day. For contract workers, visiting days were only on Sundays and they only visited friends at the various camp sites situated within the same farm and labourers felt there was nothing to do with their limited free time.[38] Unlike at home where cooking was regarded as the women's responsibility, contract labourers on farms had to cook for themselves. They usually prepared breakfast only after they completed their early morning work of cleaning the yard of the farmhouse or after finishing the morning work of cattle milking.

The contract labourers on farms, unlike at home, worked in the kitchen to help to cook for their masters. On the farm the kitchen area, unlike at home, became the central space for a labourer as it was the space in which food for the farmer was prepared. Labourers who worked there felt closer to farm authority than others in the sense that they developed a closer relationship although it at times also meant they felt the authority more directly. Some labourers, for instance, were excited to cook for their employers and this gave them an everlasting honorary feeling of achievement as can be deduced from the following case of Ndumba Shirengumuke who worked at a farm in Gobabis during his first contract after 1936:

> The master of that farm was mister Houjaart. We did milking work there for three weeks and then the fourth week I was taken to work in the kitchen. In the kitchen I washed the utensils to assist the Madam. I was also trained to cook. Yes, I was cooking for the whites. I myself use to cook for the whites. They say apparently whites do not eat the food which is cooked by a black person? That's wishful thinking! They eat! They use to ask me to cut up the meat, cook, constantly observe the pot on fire and put water into the pot. He shall eat![39] (Shirengumuke is laughing).

---

[36] *Ibid.*
[37] Shandini Shiviru interview (2009-08-15), Ndiyona village.
[38] Mbamba Djami Ndara interview. (2009-08-19), Divundu.
[39] Ndumba Shirengumuke interview. (2009-07-03), Hoha village.

[Opo pafarama muhona wapone Mista Hauyara (Houjaart). Atukandako nyuku ntatu, oghu waghune ame avangupuko nikare kukambisa ngoli. Mukambisa kuyoghayogha vyuma mukuvatera misisi ngoli. Kuterayika vakurongita ngoli. Yii, niterayikire vamakuwa, kaniterayikirangame vamakuwa, ashi mukuwa nakulyashi ndya dakutereka mutipu? Vhaavo kulya! Vavone pakundenkanga ashi tetaghura-tetaghura nyama, tereka, konkera, nko alya!] (Shirengumuke kunakushepa).

Shirengumuke's laughter indicates how much fun he derives from thinking of his experience but also the everlasting honour he seems to attach to his past experiences of preparing the food for a white.

Although working in the kitchen was highly regarded among labourers it contained problems especially since it meant dealing with the farmer's wife who was referred to as the "Missis".[40] Labourers point out that although some farmers were likely not to bring trouble on them, it was always their wives the "missis" who in many cases incited their husbands to do so. The wife of the farmer usually reported every mistake of the labourer to her husband and expected him to deal with the respective labourer. The short temper of the "missis" lingers on in the memory of some contract labourers. The prominence of this memory of the missis reflects on the gender roles in the Kavango region in which women were expected to be submissive to their men and listen to their commands and therefore Kavango contract men might have found it more difficult and traumatic to be shouted at by a woman. The constant reporting of a labourer by the missis left him open to acts of victimization from his master. Shirengumuke relates his experiences:

> At the farm we found a labourer Thomas whose "missis" was short tempered. This time she will beat you and then soon afterward she will beat you again. She always quarreled with her Kwanyama labourer in the kitchen. And then we asked, 'our friend how is your master?' He said, 'fellows, whoever is going to replace me in my position will come to see'. That missis was a difficult person unlike the man who was kind.[41]
>
> [Opo pafarama twakawaninepo ngoli Thomasa ano ogho misis wendi ngoli ogho, nane ugara! Weno vanakutoona, weno tupu nka vanakutoona kutanguranga vene nogho mukwanyama mukambisa kendi. Makura atwe ashi weni ngoli ove ghunyetu ogho muhona woye? Ghuye ashi vahewa keheghuno ngapinganenomo mulivango lyande ngavimona. Mudito ghunya misisi, kapishi murumene hawe wamunongo].

The central issue that usually made the "missis" in the kitchen angry was when a labourer broke a cup or plate or spilt anything on the floor and her anger was aggravated when the labourer dared speak back.

---

[40] Missis is a phonetic version of the English abbreviation Mrs.
[41] Ndumba Shirengumuke interview. (2009-07-03), Hoha village.

Other oral histories have found that when people endured trauma as a group, they tended to speak of the hardship of others but were silent about their own suffering.[42] The discourse in the oral narratives that it was always others who were mistreated makes it worth asking why some people present others as the victims and themselves as the survivors and what this says of the politics of self image construction. It is a narrative strategy to deal with pain and humiliation. This tendency to speak more easily about others than about oneself is also displayed among the Kavango contract labourers with the exception of Tuhemwe Shevekwa.[43] They presented others as helpless victims but presented their individual stories as those of triumpth. Ndumba Shirengumuke, for example, points out:

> I was never part of the beating; it was rather my friends who always use to scream from the pain of the smacks. They were usually beaten that one did not know how to skim the milk or that he has spilt the milk from the bucket, then a Boer will surely beat you for that.[44]
>
> [Amene kapi vakantooghonineko oko, vaghunyande ntani mbo kavakatakumango ku marukushi. Kuvatooona ashi eshi shimwe kapi shayiva kukweya mashini kumahina ndi shinateta mashini mumahemere makura mburu yayo opone kukutoona vene].

In their narrations of experiences in the kitchen, some interviewees are careful to represent themselves differently in contrast to other labourers who got into trouble. Shirengumuke is a case in point:

> When I finally entered the kitchen I was never beaten. Even when she got angry she would come and just stand. At times when one was holding something and then it slipped from your hands and broke down, hey! She would come with force and say, 'you broke my cup I am going to beat you'. And then I would respond 'just beat me, have I not told you before that I did not come on contract to work in a kitchen? I came for milking cows but then you said, no, just hang up with milking and come in here until such a time that we find someone for the kitchen, I was not the one who chose this'. After that then she would stand and stand until she gives up and goes away. When she was standing in anger, I would be silent, busy doing my work; she would also just stand there until she turns and goes away. This was unlike the case with my friend who spoke back when she spoke that was why they could not understand each other.[45]

---

[42] U. Dhupelia-Mesthrie, 'Dispossession and memory: The black river community of Cape Town' *The Journal of the Oral History Society*, volume: 28, number 2, 2000, pp. 41–42. Her work focuses on victims of forced removals.

[43] The exception of Tuhemwe Shevekwa to speak freely about his personal sufferings to me could partly be based on the fact that he relates to me as his grandson as we are all from Shikonga lineage and since in the Gciriku tradition, a grandfather is suppose to be open to his grandson, his openness was therefore not surprising.

[44] Ndumba Shirengumuke interview. (2009-07-03), Hoha village.

[45] Muyenga Shintunga Unengu interview. (2009-07-31), Rucara village.

[Ame opo nangenine mukambisane, hawe nakuntoonashi, mpilindi anagarapa kuya-kuya anayimana, pamweya mposhili unakwata makura shinatomponoka shinataghuka ghuyene kare taat! Anaya! Ashi unataghura nkinda kunikutoona ame ashi toona tupu ameshi ame nakutantera ashi kapi nayera kukambisa kwayera vyakukanda ngombe, anwe ashi hawe tanko dogoro ngatushane muntu wakukambisa. Ame kapishi me.Naye kuyimana-kuyimana dogoro kuvyuka.Ghuye anayimana opo anagarapa, ame teete kunakuruwana viruwana vyande, naye kuyimana opo dogoro kuvyuka.Kapishi ghunya ghunyandene oghu kupakamo oghu kupakamo makura nakukuyuvhashi].

His strategy was to be quiet while his friend spoke back and angered the missis further. Some labourers, therefore, developed a survival strategy by being silent whenever abusive words were showered upon them. These were acts of agency. Being silent though could also be related to the earlier traditional education that children received from their parents to never respond negatively to an elder or anyone senior. As Kamenye Likuwa explains:

> The elders taught me that when an elder makes me angry I should not respond badly. Even when that elder was not my parent it was the same and one did not respond badly to them. One was taught to know that bad attitude towards the elders could result in the young one getting bad lucks in life.[46]

[Vakurona vantjongire ashi nange mukurona anakugarapita, nakumuvyutashi mwamudona. Nampili ntjene ogho mukurona kapishi vakondi vande napo mushikwavo nakulimbururashi mwamudona. Kukushonga ghuyive ashi nkedi dadidona kuvakurona kuwana lihudi muliparu mwanuke].

Although there were exceptions, generally, farm employers were regarded by labourers to be cruel. The oral narratives indicate examples of physical abuse of contract labourers on the farms. Some labourers were beaten for failing to greet the "baas" as he passed by and were kicked in the buttocks by the mistress as they pushed the car of their master to start the engine.[47] They were also beaten for beating a calf during the milking process, for the death of livestock and the negligence of work by a fellow labourer, for not being able to operate water pump machines and for speaking out as the farmer speaks. In some cases the farmer called the police to come and beat up his contract labourers for what he believed was the cheeky and disrespectful attitude of contract labourers towards him. Tuhemwe narrates his experience of the beating during his second contract to a farm in Outjo in 1972:

> Early in the morning, the white man rang his bell and we all came and assembled at his house. He told Shikukutu to go to work but ordered that I and Shinyemba should wait as the real men were coming to meet us apparently because I and Shinyemba

---

[46] Kamenye Likuwa interview. (2009-08-13), Kangweru village.
[47] Martin Maghundu interview. (2009-08-19), Divundu.

were full of nonsense and that we seemed to not have come for work at his farm but to want to take over control from him-especially me. By the time we realized it, the police vehicle was already driving to a standstill on the farm. There was one Herero and a Boer policeman. We were called in front. The African policeman was translating for the Boer policeman who asked us why we were refusing to work. I told him we were not refusing to work and that if we did we would have gone back home or we would have broken contract and escaped. Then the master interjected 'alright! That's exactly the person I told you about. He always has something to respond and he is the one teaching the others bad manners.' 'That's it,' said the policeman. 'What else can I ask for? It is evident enough.' The white policeman went to the police car and collected a 'rotang' [sjambok] and gave it to me and said we must beat each other up as they were standing smoking their cigarettes. If one did not beat harder, the police will notice and beat him even more, and so we beat each other up harder in turns.[48]

[Ngurangura katenda kare, makura hoyi, anarambuka ngoli nko kutuyita kumundi wendi. Makura ashi nove-nove. Ovepo Shikukutu kayende ukaruwane, an ova Shinyemba na Tuhemwe, anwe tatererenu varume djuni kunakuya mbyevishi new anwe mwakaro ndino, anwe mwakaro ndino pano pafarama, kunakushana yamuntjakane farama yande. Anwe mwakaro ngoli varume ashi mughupe yinya ndjuwo yande., Yii, mara mwene-mwenepo ne ghu! Ashi me ngoli. Ameshi napa tunavhurukili ove muholi, vaporosi, limbamba olyo linayayimano pano. Natwe tunatetura ashi hee, nani vyashiri? Yira vintje ngoli? Opo navo shine, oko vanakara kuninko? Pakalire muherero ghumwe ayiroko na mburu yimwe. Vavo ashi oku vanakara kuni? Vavo ashi, kuyuvha rumburu ndi? Atwe ashi yii kuyuvha tupu kadidi. Ashi Ruherero? Atwe naro kuyuvha tupu kadidi. Yaa, makura ashi, vatantere ashi vintje vanakushwenena kuruwana? Mburu yitantere ngoli ghunya mu Herero.Makura atwe ashi, atwene kapi tunakushwena viruwana, vyavyone ovi tunakuruwana. Ndi tunashwene meshi ndi tunavyuka kwetu of ndi twa hena, kapishipo mpotuli mpopanone ameshi mbyo viruwana tunakuruwana? Ashi hey! Ashi yaa! Ndjegho ngoli ndje namutantere ngoli! Ndje waupote vene ndjegho anakumulimbururo ndjegho. Ogho ghunyendi kwendi anakuviwana. Makura vanya ashi atwe kwatonka ovyo tughambako. Kukashimba ngora, kudamuna kuyitambeka ogho ghunyande, kurenka naghumwenu mukushepure. Ashi vantu vapeke vamushepuro? A-aa! Naghumwetu na naghumwetu! Vavo vanayimana kunakukoka usekereta. Ntjene kapi unakudameka kuvayikuvyutira. Kunakukengerashi vyashiri kunakutoona ndi kapi unakutoona. Ntjene kapi unakutoona unene vaporosi kuvayikushaana vakutoone nka ngudu].

This was probably a much more traumatic experience than had the police beaten them. Contract labourers believed that they were purchased and taken as possessions by the employer and that it was this idea of possession that made the farmer feel justified at mistreating and beating them. The worst that could happen to a farm contract labourer was to be killed and contract labourers believed that those labourers who disappeared under mysterious circumstances without a trace were in fact killed by the farmer. The farmer could get away with the

---

[48] Tuhemwe Shevekwa interview. (2009-07-30), Sharughanda village.

crime by reporting to the police that his labourers had absconded from work. It was useless for labourers to lay complaints against the farmers' mistreatment of the labourers at the law enforcement units as labourers were always sure to find themselves on the wrong side of the law and always with serious punishment served upon them. As Ndadi explained:

> White farmers could get away with anything; treat their workers just as they pleased. Many times we heard about men being shot dead by their baas (boss) just for talking back. The law did nothing, of course – it was made for the whites! We couldn't resist or even complain without being beaten or sent back to Owamboland with no pay. We had to learn to survive; keep quiet and finish our contracts.[49]

The continued mistreatment of farm labourers with no legal recourse to their problems usually made some farm labourers wish they had never come on contract work at all and it led many of them to resort to the action of absconding. This was, however, a dangerous decision as a labourer was legally breaking contract and could be imprisoned. The estimated number of desertions from farms within the Police Zone over a period of twelve months ending in 1947 was over 600 and at the end of this period 297 arrests had been made within the Police Zone and 21 beyond, but 282 of those who had escaped remained free.[50] Labourers who were caught while escaping were beaten up by the police at the police cells before being returned to their former masters. Ausiku, for example, wrote about how in 1955 after he broke contract work he eventually gave himself up to the police and was sentenced to six strokes of lashes and was returned to his previous employer.[51] In cases where the old master was no longer interested in such labourers, they were usually deported back to the Kavango so as to be eligible for re-contracting.

There were exceptional cases where farmers displayed kindness to some labourers but this selective favouritism from farmers usually created tension, suspicion and conflicts among farm labourers. The tension and conflict was usually between the long-serving labourers and the newcomers. What created discontent at times was when a newcomer was placed in charge over the long-serving labourers or was favoured above them in other aspects. Such discontent led to suspicions on the new labourer which put him in a vulnerable position, sometimes to a point where he felt his life threatened and where the only solution was to leave the farm. This was Tuhemwe's experience in 1970:

> At that farm where I worked, I was the only person from Kavango and the only minor; all of them were from Ovamboland. Then the white madam liked me greatly

---

[49] Ndadi. (1974), *Breaking contract: the story of HelaoVinniaNdadi*, p. 21.
[50] Silvester. (1993), Black pastoralists, white farmers, p. 350.
[51] Ausiku. (2005) My own stories: is this God's work or Satan's scheme? p. 34.

so that whenever she went shopping, I was always taken along in her car. I use to be paid R6.00 a month while those other friends of mine use to be paid R.4.00, others R.5.00 and this is what made my other friends to question why I the recent new comer was getting R6.00 than them who have been there for long. Since then tension began to build up between me and my friends. They were complaining that why was it so that despite the fact that they were the first one to work on the farm, the white madam did not take one of them to do the work that I was doing? And why is it that every time she went shopping, she would only pick me to go with her? So, that was the way it continued to be and every time she went out, she took me along until later I also began to notice that my friends were really not happy. It was then that a thought began to develop in my mind that perhaps one day my friends would be tempted to do something bad to me, I really began to panic, I got scared. Finally, my days for end of contract were nearing and the twelve months were soon over. But then the master asked me not to go back but to add additional months, but I refused. But I did not tell them the truth about why I feared staying.[52]

[Opanya pafarama nakakalire navantje vaVambo, muKavango pentjandepo ti! Amenka nimwanuke. Awe makura ashikahora osho shirumbu kuyenda kudoropa nkwendi name mutukara. Ameko ngoline kani kawanangako ses rand. Vanya vaghunyande ngoli vavo vamwe kutambura vier rand, vamwe fyf ngoli. Ovyo mbyo vyakavatetukitiropo ngoli vantu ashi weni – oghuno yona kaya mara kunakutambura kare ses rand. Makura kutunda opo ameshi kushana ngoli kukunyenga navaghunyande kadidi.Vavo ashi ntje ngoli, atwene twe twahovo kuya pano.Ntje apira kughupapo umwe pano papetu aruwane viruwana vinya unakuyaruwana ve?Vintje vya karera ngoweyo?Ntani nka vintje varenkeranga ashi ntjene kunakuyenda kudoropa nkwendi kukushimbave uyende naye?Mmo katukaranga ngoli, kehekuno name dogoro aniyavikenge ngoli ashi vaghunyande kapi nka vinakuvahafita.Makura ame aye, evi ngavitwalita tupu dogoro vaghunyande kuvhura ngavanduwane namo peke, natukukire vene name kadidi.Mayuva nagho hawe mwedi twalf nado dinatikimo. Vavo avandeke ashi vyenevyene ndi kapishi uyende, ame ashi- a-aa! Ngoli kapi nakuvatantera ashi vintje vyene-vyene nakutjira].

It was an invitation of more problems for a labourer to be loved and favoured alone above others by a farmer as this usually led to suspicion and jealousy from fellow labourers and put the life of that particular favoured labourer at risk. The attitude of suspicion among labourers about selective, favoured individual labourers indicates a demand for equal treatment at work by labourers from the farmer.

Tuhemwe's account shows that contract labourers got paid different salaries at different times. The contract labourers provide differing accounts of wages they received, and this could be a result of the fact that the recommended wages for contract labourers in Namibia given inflation varied over time and within various employment sectors. After the Second World War in 1945, the farm labour commission, for instance, recommended wages

---

[52] Tuhemwe Shevekwa interview. (2009-07-30), Sharughanda village.

for various farm workers as follows: the first four months at 8/- per month, the second four months at 9/- per month, the third four months at 10/- per month, the fourth four months at 12/- per month, the fifth four months at 13/- per month and the last four months at 14/- per month.[53]

By 1966 it was stated through an official publication that a contract worker with no previous experience working on commercial farms in central and southern Namibia started at R7.50 per month, raised to R8.25 per month after 12 months, to R9.00 six months thereafter, and to R9.75 another six month later.[54] The wage that was paid to a contract labourer working in the urban area varied from his place of work and time on contract. The official monthly average wages for mine workers in 1967 for instance was R45.34 for skilled workers, R23.03 for semi skilled, R31.14 for the clerks and R17.58 for unskilled workers'.[55] Gordon has presented examples of the wage rate for contract labourers after the 1971 to 1972 general workers' strike, which show that labourers at a mine could be paid anything between R24.00 to R56.10 per month.[56]

The oral narratives about wages indicate that the wages were disappointingly low and that wages were not fixed. What matters more is not the factual truth or falseness about the wages that contract labourers received, but what meanings their oral statements about wages provide. While they could be paid monthly, others got their wages only at the end of their contract and yet others complained of not having been given their full pay and dismissed unfairly afterwards as was the case for Kativitji in 1929.[57] Some of the labourers got as low as R0.90c per month for the first eight months and then got R1.00 per month for the remaining two months as was the case for Ndumba Shirengumuke in the mid 1930s during his first contract at a farm in Gobabis. Others got R6.00 per month as was the case for Tuhemwe in 1970 at a farm in Grootfontein. Mathias Ndumba Shikombero, who worked in Walvis Bay in 1970, also speaks of his wages:

> This time around I was sent to Mbahe [Walvis Bay]. When I arrived in Walvis Bay at work, I was again paid the same six rand which I had protested at my previous employment. I worked at the municipality at the railway lines. I still could not accept the six rand pay and so I escaped from work that day and went to a nearby mine at Rio Tinto to look for a job where I heard they paid better. I got into a train from

---

[53] The Administrator. (1939-08-30), Circular on farm labour commission. Windhoek, NAN, SWAA 2412, A521/13/3.
[54] G.M. Bauer. (1994), The labor movement and the prospect of democracy in Namibia. PhD Thesis, Wisconsin Madison, p. 49.
[55] Ibid.
[56] Ibid.
[57] The Administrator, (1928-05-05), Returning labourers-complaints, Kativitji, pass No. 370/28 (Windhoek, NAN, SWAA 2397, file A521/2.

Walvis Bay to Rio Tinto train station where I met some people from Kavango. I was lucky and got recruited immediately and was informed I would be paid eighty rand per month.[58]

[Avakantuma ku Mbahe. Pakukatika ku Mbahe kuviruwana, avakamfuta nka ndjoyo ses rand nashwenine pamuhovo. Kwakaruwanine kwa munispality kurutenda. Kapi nakutambura oyo six rand makura ani hene kuviruwana niyende ku mina ya pepi ya Rio Tinto nikashaneko viruwana morwa nayuvhire ashi vavo kufuta hasha. Ani rondo lihina kutunda Mbahe dogoro pa stasie ya Rio Tinto opo nakakugwanikilire navaKavango.Nakalire lirago, avakankuta ndyolyo liyuva nakuntanterashi ngavamfutanga tagtig rand mu mwedi].

The general feeling of contract labourers was that the wages were low and many complained that the whites were tricking them out of their supposed wages. An interviewee, Shikiri waNkayira, went for his first contract before 1936 and worked at Raison farm in Grootfontein district for twelve months and accumulated only R10.00 by the end of his contract. He explains:

I stayed there for twelve months and then my contract ended. Oh no! The money which I brought from there was only R10.00. I did not even come with that money rather I used it to purchase goods right there in the police zone which I brought along home. When I left the police zone and arrived in the Kavango I had no money.[59]

[Anikakarako mwedi murongo nambiri makura kontraka yinapu. Hawe vimaliva nakashimbirekone viponda vitano tupu. Ashi vyakuya navyo ndi kuvighurapo vene tushuma omo mushivanda makura ughurumuke nato. Pakutunda mushivanda niyatike kuno kuKavango ame kwato maliva].

In some cases, farm labourers worked for the entire duration of the contract period and only received their pay at the expiry of contract after the farmer had usually deducted all that was owed to him by his labourer. Tuhemwe Shevekwa explains his 1970 experience:

What the mistress used to do is that whenever a labourer needed something from a shop she was going to buy it for you and then at the end of contract work, all your credit were deducted and you were paid the remaining salary. I worked for twelve months without pay and it was only at the end of my contract that I was given twelve rand. Maybe it was different from my other friends on other farms, I will not know, but I tell you what I experienced, I saw my pay only at the end of my contract period.[60]

[Mbyevishi vavo nange unashana shininke, kughupa tupu vavo ngavayakughulire kushivanda makura opo ngoli ngauyenda ntani kudamuna kashilinga koye kahupoko ukayende, kwato vyakukupa kumwedi-kumwedi. Kapi nakavimonineme,

---

[58] Mathias Ndumba Shikombero interview. (2009-07-28) Rucara village.
[59] Shikiri waNkayira interview. (2009-08-08), Ndonga-linena.
[60] Tuhemwe Shevekwa interview. (2009-07-30), Sharughanda village.

walye ngoli vaghunyetu kuvavirumbu vamweya. Atwene dogoro unakamana ntani unakukenga ngoli shilinga yayikukutu. Amene kwakampire tupu twalf rand].

With the low wages therefore, labourers could only afford to purchase goods in the police zone and usually arrived in the Kavango without a cent left. They felt that they were only making all the money for the whites and did not receive a fair share.[61] Many contract labourers stayed longer on contract because it became difficult to save money in their given period because of the insufficient pay they received and most were concerned about not being able to spend more on their families due to the low pay.[62] But since labourers had no other choices, they continued to work on the farms and made the best use of the little amount of wages they received. Shikiri waNkayira articulates his 1930s experiences explicitly:

> You think we saw any kindness of high wages there? No! The kindness in high wages to which we are now impressed is that of today whereby people are now getting so much money, it was not the case in our times, no kidding! But we nonetheless never threw the money away, we use to be thankful and say let it just be this bad but we are still going back.[63]

> [Ashi ghunongo twakamonineko kunya wavimaliva? Hawe! Unongo tunakutetukane wantantani vano vanakukamato maliva, kapishi panya pashiruvo shetu, hawe vhatwetwe! Ngoli ne kapi katuvivhukumanga, kupanduranga vene ashi vikare mpilindi ngoweyo atwe kunakuyenda tunakuyenda].

In general, therefore, many contract labourers were always short of money and although many extended their contracts in the hope to accumulate much more, this remained more an everlasting hope than a reality as the continuous low pay made it difficult. The duration period of contract labour changed over time, but it was never less than six months. Based on the recommendations of the farm labour commission in the 1940s, the duration of contract labourers contracted through a recruiting organization to farms was extended to two years at one stretch.[64] Despite these changes some labourers stayed longer than usual and in some cases married in the African locations and settled permanently in the police zone. Such labourers became known as "mbwiti", which is a person who stays away for long and does not like to return home. It was, however, the policy of the colonial administration that the contract labour system should not lead to detribalization and, as such, the influx population laws ensured that contract labourers returned after the contract labour period expired.

---

[61] Gordon. (1977), *Mines, masters and migrants*, pp. 80, 145–185.
[62] R. Voippo. (1981), Contract work through Ovambo eyes. In R.G. Green, K. Kiljunen, M.L. Kiljunen, (eds.), *Namibia the last colony*. Essex, Longman. pp. 116–120.
[63] Shikiri waNkayira interview. (2009-08-08), Ndonga-linena.
[64] D.D. Forsyth. (1940-02-26), Recommendations of farm labour commission. Windhoek, NAN, NAT 1/1/54, S/U14, file 13.

Proclamation No. 29 of 1935 dealt with the control of the Extra Territorial and Northern Natives which included the Angolan, Zambian, Ovambo and Kavango contract labourers. Under this proclamation all contract labourers at the expiry of contract had to be repatriated and the police on patrols had to ensure that all contract labourers produced their non-expired employment permits or passes.[65] Those contract labourers who tried to settle permanently after the contract period faced deportation and jail sentences. Oral narratives indicate that the colonial administration carried out some clean up campaigns in the police zone to induce some "mbwiti" people to return home. Kamenye Likuwa who worked for his first contract at a farm in Keetmaanshoop in the 1950s narrates:

> When I wanted to extend my contract, they began calling upon all the 'mbwiti' who have gone away for so long to go back home. Apparently, their mothers and fathers were angry and that they were accusing that the Boers have killed their children and so they demanded everyone to return home. So then all the mbwiti were thrown out and returned but I returned home on my own after seeing that the mbwiti were being rounded up and sent home.[66]

> [Opo nashanine ashi niwederereko nka mpo vatamikire ngoli ashi-a-aa! Vambwiti ovo vayendo kare, kunakuvashana kuno ku Kavango vanyokwavo na vashavo vanagarapa, kunakughamba vanakughambashi vakamana kudipagha vamburu makura ashi ndi vaghurumuke. Makura kwavafaghire, kwavashanine vene ashi vambwiti vaghurumuke-ghurumuke. Makura opo name panaghumwande ngoli ashi, aye ntjene ngoli name kunakuyenda ngoli kumundi].

The end of the contract was usually referred to as "kukutuka" (to be set free from) and it was indeed regarded by labourers as the temporary end of their bondage to contract work at least until their next contract. Many contract labourers returned to contract work more than once although possibly to different employers or employment and some like Ludwig Kudumo Kamenye were engaged in contract labour for a consecutive eight years.[67] The question of adding more months to a contract after the expiry of a previous contract was possible and the specific labourer and employer usually went to the magistrate's office for such permission. Silvester shows, however, that migrant farm workers seldom renewed their contract on a farm or returned to the same farm twice.[68]

The oral narratives from Kavango indicate that although re-contract to a cruel employer after expiry of contract was highly unlikely a labourer did not usually divulge the truth to his master for his unwillingness to return. Instead the labourer gave false reasons or simply

---

[65] Ibid.
[66] Kamenye Likuwa interview (2009-08-13), Kangweru village.
[67] Ludwig Kudumo Kamenye interview (2009-08-13) Kangweru.
[68] Silvester. (1993), Black pastoralists, white farmers, p. 345.

falsely promised their employers that they would return after a break of resting. This was the case with Shirengumuke in the 1930s:

> When the time for our contract came to an end, our master went to Gobabis to want to arrange for a possible extension of our contract. We refused because his wife had bad manners. He asked, 'well, will you not re-write your names for extension of contract? We said 'just hang on; let us first return home for a while and then we shall come back after that.' Then he asked, 'how are you going to know how to get back to me?' We told him 'we will tell them we want to be sent to Gobabis to Mister Houjaare'. Immediately he also knew that this people have refused and that they will not return.[69]

[Makura pakuya ngoli ashi tunakutuka ngolipo, makura kuyenda ku Gobabis muhona anashana ogho mukuwa ashi akatutjangitenka ashi ngatuvyukire nka kwendi. Atwe atushwena morwa mukadendi ghunya mudona.Ghuye ashi "ee kapi mukutjangita nka?"Atwe ashi awe! Tanko ngatukaya tupu ghumwetu. Ghuye ashi weni omu nga-muyivako, atwe ashi ngatutwenya tupu ashi ku Gobabis kwa mista Houjaare. Naye anayiva ashi, awe vanashwena vano, kapi ngavakayanka].

It was not wise or helpful for labourers to tell the whites the truth for leaving as this only put them into more trouble. Contract labourers preferred to work on mines and the next section will explain their mine experiences.

The South African mines and compounds

The history of the development of mines and compounds in South Africa is not the focus of this section as this is a very well documented history.[70] Rather, this section is about the narratives the Kavango contract labourers tell about their experiences on the South African mines and compound.

---

[69] Ndumba Shirengumuke interview. (2009-07-03), Hoha village.
[70] More has been written about the history of mining and compound development in South Africa. See, S. Moroney. (1978), The development of the compound as a mechanism of worker control 1900–1912', *South African Labour Bulletin*, (4); J.M. Smalberger. (1974), I.D.B., and the mining compound system in the 1880', *The South African Journal of Economics*, 42(4); C. Van Onselen. (1980), *Chibaro, African mine labour in Southern Africa Rhodesia, 1900–1933*. Johannesburg, Ravan; P. Harries. (1994), *Work, culture and identity: migrant labourers in Mozambique and South Africa, c1860–1910*. Johannesberg, Witwatersrand University Press; T.D. Moodie with V. Ndatshe. (1994), *Going for the gold: men, mines and migration*. Johannesburg, Witwatersrand University Press; R.V Turrel. (1987), *Capital and labour on the Kimberley diamond fields, 1887–1890*. London, Cambridge University; D. Yudelman. (1984), *The emergence of modern South Africa*. Cape Town, David Philip; A.J. Jeeves. (1985), *Migrant labour in South Africa's mining economy: the struggle for the gold mines' labour supply 1890–1920*. Johannesburg, Witwatersrand University Press; W.G. James. (1992), *Our precious metal, African labour in South Africa's gold industry, 1870–1990*. Cape Town, David Phillip.

Out of a total of twenty-eight former contract labourers from the Kavango who were interviewed for this research, sixteen of them (about 57 percent) also worked in South Africa.[71] Although one contract labourer mentioned the name of the mine where he worked, the rest did not and simply spoke of their experiences on those mines. During their sojourns to South African mines contract labourers from the Kavango faced the hardships that existed there. What stands out, however, among their experiences of the South African mines are the painful medical injections they received and the sending of rejects to the Rhodesian (Zimbabwe) farms, the assembly of contract labourers from other parts of Africa, the experiences of dangers and death situations in the mines, the ethnic separation of sleeping sections and the fear of the maPondo labourers within the compounds.

Yudelman indicates that foreign contract labourers for South Africa came from countries such as Botswana, Malawi, Zimbabwe, Mozambique, Lesotho, and Swaziland and although contract labourers were also drawn from Namibia and Angola, they do not feature among the supplier countries.[72] This could be because for many years until after 1944, recruitments by WENELA in Namibia were done unofficially as there was no agreement. Even after the agreement between WENELA and colonial officials in Namibia, only the Mbukushu ethnic group from the Kavango were allowed on contract together with Angolans and many left for South Africa pretending to be Angolans.

The contract labourers from Kavango were identified as "Mambukushu" [the Mbukushu] and those from Ovamboland were called "Mangwenyama" [the Kwanyama], the names of the ethnic group from Kavango and Ovamboland respectively. In the case of the Kavango, the ethnic label Mbukushu was used because at least until 1937 when Mbukushu territory was declared to form part of the Kavango Native Territory, it was only the Mbukushu people who were mainly recruited from the Kavango to South Africa as they were very near to the WENELA recruiting depot of Shakawe in Botswana.

There was a notion of viewing the compound as a fictive chiefdom of a tribe and mine management resorted to ethnic division of the African labour force. These strategies were aimed at ensuring better control of the work force.[73] In general, labourers slept in the same quarter as others of their ethnic group. However, this was not strictly applied to labourers from Namibia as labourers from the Kavango at times slept in the same section with the Ovambo and Angolans. As George Mukoya Weka explains:

---

[71] They include Anselm Likuwa, Mathias Shikombero, George Mukoya Weka, Muyenga Unengu, Ndumba Likuwa, Shintango Karenga, Shindimba Shihungu, Nyambe Merecky, Shikiri waNkayira, Kavengere Mutero, Jonas Kuyonana, Maghundu Martin, Mbamba Ndara, Kapinga Muhero, Konrad Mbote and Ngonga Katjire.
[72] Yudelman. (1984), *The emergence of modern South Africa*, p. 269.
[73] Harries. (1994), 'Work, culture and identity, pp. 73–74.

In those rooms, sometimes the Vagciriku and Kwanyama would be allocated in the same room. Sometimes, especially those of us who came from this side [Gciriku territory] would be mixed together with the Kwanyama or with the Ovimbundu and the Mbukushu and our rooms would all be in one row. Those of us from here [Gciriku territory] were refered to as Mbukushu even when we were Gciriku or Kwangali. The Kwanyama were referred to as Mangwenyama while the Vimbundu were called Mangola [Angolans] and that was how we lived there.[74]

[Kukaranga omo mundjuvo ne pamweya Vakwanyama, nanwe Vagciriku. Pamwe yira atwe vakuno kumupakerera ngoli navakwanyama, pamwe navavimbundu natwe ngoli Vagciriku navaMbukushu ngoweyo kumupaka ngoli mundjuvo denu mumurayini. Atwe ngoli vakuno kututwenya ashi Mambukushu, ukare ashi umugciriku ndi umukwangali. Vakwanyamane ashi Mangwenyama, Mangola ne vavimbundu, ngoli mmo twakakalire ngoli].

It is possible that this allocation in one room of different ethnic groups from Kavango or Angola was due to their fewer numbers. The various ethnic groups from the Kavango and those from Ovambo were placed together in one row on the basis of their country of origin. The sleeping sections were in rows and there were between ten to fifteen men per room; the beds were simply cement built in a rectangular shape and were usually very cold.[75] Jeeves indicates that there were usually twenty to fifty people per room and each labourer was given one of the tiered concrete bunks and many of the compounds remained dark, unsanitary, overcrowded, bleak and cold.[76]

The inter-ethnic violence among African contract labourers existed in the South African mines even by the 1970s and mine management thought this was partly a result of the poor living conditions of the compounds.[77] Inter-ethnic tensions or conflicts at the mines and compound were a common occurrence. The Ovambo and the Kavango contract labourers usually came to each other's rescue in situations of ethnic fights with groups from other countries.[78] The management of the mines and compounds used ethnic differences and jealousies of one tribe against another to maintain division among the workers to protect European interest.[79]

---

[74] G.M. Weka interview. (2009-07-29), Rucara village.
[75] *Ibid.*
[76] Jeeves. (1985), *The migrant labour in South Africa's mining economy, the struggle for the gold mines' labour supply 1890–1920*, p. 22.
[77] W. G. James. (1992), *Our precious metal, African labour in South Africa's gold industry, 1870–1990*, p. 110.
[78] Ngonga Katjire interwiew. (2009-08-21), Diheke village.
[79] S. Moroney. (1978), The development of the compound as a mechanism of worker control 1900–1912, p. 35.

Kavango contract labourer engaged with "stiki" (stick fighting) competitions where contract labourers participated across ethnic divides. "Stiki" was a fighting game for entertainment which was usually organized during weekends and in which some Kavango men also participated. While off shift the miners could leave the compound as they were not "closed" in the sense of the Kimberley diamond compounds but movements in and out were carefully monitored by the compound police.[80] On weekends, especially Sundays, contract labourers usually left the compound to visit friends at other compounds using electric trains which were called "stimela".

The Kavango narratives indicate that the maPondo men were feared. It was believed that if one moved around the compound alone at night one risked being murdered by the maPondo who needed men's private parts for the ritual processes of marriage in their communities.[81] The labourers from Kavango were therefore careful not to move around alone around the surroundings of the compound, let alone when visiting friends at other nearby compounds. These views contrast with Ndaoya's observation that men from Ovamboland in South African mines met and made friends with the Xhosas, Shanganas (from Mozambique), Nyasas (from Malawi), Pondos etc and that there was very little violence in the compounds.[82]

According to the Kavango contract labourers, upon arrival in South Africa, they underwent what they referred to as school mine for at least a week or two before they eventually went to work underground. Here mine labourers learned about the safety and security measures for underground mining. They were taught about what was expected of them when working underground especially with regard to relations with other labourers and were given some practical training related to underground work.[83]

Fred Cooper has argued that "colonialism in Africa was not just about space but also about time, as the colonial powers compelled African workers to adapt to the work rhythms of industrial capitalism that is to the idea that work should be steady and regular and carefully controlled. The African notion of 'task time' where effort varied seasonally was read as the laziness of the African and was replaced by European notions with a focus on wages and work discipline from above".[84] This colonizing of time was applied in most South African mines and compounds. Bells regulated the lives and times of workers on the mines and

---

[80] *Ibid.*
[81] G.M. Weka interview. (2009-07-29), Rucara village.
[82] L. N. Ndaoya. (2000), Oshiwambo-speaking migrant workers on the Witwatersrand gold mines from 1940 to 1969. B.A thesis, Windhoek, UNAM. pp. 13–14.
[83] G.M. Weka interview. (2009-07-29), Rucara village.
[84] F. Cooper. (1992), Colonizing time: work rhythms and labor conflict in colonial Mombasa In N. Dirks (ed.), *Colonialism and culture*. AnnArbor: University of Michigan, pp. 209–211.

black workers had to adapt to whistles and sirens as a concept of time. Contract labourers woke up for work at four in the morning and it did not matter how long one slept one was certain to wake up as the lights went on automatically when it was time. Labourers believed that someone at a central point had a watch and usually had the lights switched on.[85]

Some labourers worked day shifts while others worked night shifts. The contract labourers carried lights as they worked underground as it was extremely dark. They went underground in an elevator which the Kavango labourers called "limbamba". Usually they walked to their work point, although at times they also used rail transport and were under the supervision of a white man who gave daily attendance tickets.[86] The ticket system ensured that miners completed all work required from them in a given time and the failure to complete work meant the ticket was not signed and the work was not paid for. In some cases it also meant that the food rations for the day were lost.[87] The labour legislation of 1889 stated the centrality of a white supervisor over black labourers as the following shows:

> No native shall work or be allowed to work in any mine, whether in open or underground workings, except under the responsible charge of some particular white man as his master or "baas".[88]

There is a negative feeling about the working relations in the South African mines and some contract labourers referred to the white boss and his bossboy as Satan as they overworked and treated the contract labourers especially "munyowani" (new ones) inhumanly.[89] A contract labourer could only hope to be treated with a little respect if he had worked at that mine for a longer period and had become a "Madala muntu" (experienced person).[90] The white supervisors and his "boss boys" frequently assaulted the African labourers.[91] The sjambok was used on the African labourer to force production and reduce loafing or sleeping on duty. Other reasons for assault ranged from lack of skill of the worker but sometimes it was simply unprovoked violence.

The contract labourers felt unsafe underground as they feared that the mine could collapse anytime. Many labourers got injured from the chips of the stones that fell from the mine roofs.[92] To prevent these, "mapaka" (wooden planks tied with fences) were usually built to hold up the roof of the mine. It was the task of a "timber boy" to fasten 'mapaka' in

---

[85] Mathias Ndumba Shikombero interview. (2009-07-28), Rucara village.
[86] Turrell. (1987), Capital and labour on the Kimberley diamond fileds, 1871–1890, p. 153.
[87] Cooper. (1992) Colonizing time: work rhythms and labor conflict in colonial Mombasa, p. 143.
[88] Smalberger. (1974), I.D.B and the mining compound system in the 1880s, pp. 153–154.
[89] G.M. Weka interview. (2009-07-29), Rucara village.
[90] Ibid.
[91] Ibid.
[92] Mathias Ndumba Shikombero interview. (2009-07-28), Rucara village.

the mine's roof top to prevent chipped stones from hitting the labourers.[93] There was also the 'ncara boy' whose task was to ensure that whenever a stone stood in a dangerous position, he would remove it before it collapsed and fell on labourers. The "ndjini" boy's task was to bore shafts or squares in rocks with a machine with the help of a "spanera" boy who assisted to remove the bore machine from the stone.[94] After boring dynamite was placed to explode the site after which a large heap of ore would accumulate and this was the ore which contained the stones they used to make money, so explains Shikombero the process of gold mining.[95]

The use of machines in mining came later but in the early days, for example, diamond diggings in Kimberley, the claim holder and a handful of workers used a pick, spade, wheel barrow and sieve to extract the precious stones.[96] Later, when some rotary machines were introduced to wash the diamonds, these were driven by horses and later by steam power. Some mines in South Africa made use of animals such as donkeys to pull the "ngorofoni" (the trailers full of this stone sand of money). A strong donkey could pull as many as four filled trailers.[97]

The lingua franca Fanakalo which dominated the mining industry in most of southern Africa was used on the South African mines.[98] Everyone, including the whites spoke Fanakalo at work but contract labourers in the compound switched to their various languages. Many African labourers did not master Fanakalo language and the misunderstandings which resulted from not knowing the language caused much friction and workers were assaulted by the white supervisors.[99] Fanakalo was also known by the men from Kavango as "runguboy". To contract labourers "rungu" meant white person and "boy" meant black person and therefore "runguboy" meant the language of the white and black persons.[100] While white management viewed the labourers as children and infantilized them by calling them boys, the Kavango contract labourers had a different understanding and meaning of the word "boy" to imply "black persons" rather than to mean "a child".[101] There was fear among contract labourer which they expressed in a Fanakalo slogan that "shipukupuku shamulungwani shikuhamba kandjani"[102] [the ghost of the white men can do you well]. This means that

---

[93] Ibid.
[94] Ibid.
[95] Ibid.
[96] Harries. (1994). *Work, culture and identity*, p. 49.
[97] Mathias Ndumba Shikombero interview. (2009-07-28), Rucara village.
[98] Cooper. (1992), Colonizing time: work rhythms and labor conflict in colonial Mombasa. In N. Dirks (ed.) *Colonialism and Culture*, p. 152.
[99] Ibid.
[100] G.M. Weka interview. (2009-07-29), Rucara village.
[101] Ibid.
[102] See *ibid*.

if by chance a contract labourer was forgotten behind at the site after hours it was feared that the ghost will overwork him during the night so that the next day he would be found lying like a "zombie" (dumb person) at the entrance of the mine with an amount of money encrypted on his body. Such a labourer was taken to the hospital for treatment and was paid by the mine and repatriated.[103] This story of the ghost points to the real fear of the men at being left behind at the site after work.

Although a view exists among Namibian contract labourers that the pay in South Africa was better compared to Namibia, Mpondo mine labourers complained that wages were bad and that they simply continued to go and work for the sake of pride.[104] Similarly, some Kavango contract labourers such as Mathias Shikombero and George Mukoya Weka indicated that the pay in South Africa was low.[105] However, wages that were paid out were put in their helmets. Many came to view this act in high regard, and it became a common expression in Kavango that in Djwaini one got paid in a helmet full of money. Part of the salary by contract labourers was received as deferred payment at Shakawe in Botswana upon the end of contract work in South Africa. George Mukoya Weka who went for his first contract work to South Africa in 1948 claims that contract labourers had to be naked as they received their salaries and this he understood to be part of the working culture of the South African mines.[106] Except for George Mukoya, all the other interviewees to the South African mines did not mention this practice of stripping naked during the pay process. The South African literature on mines indicates that the practice of stripping African contract labourers naked was practiced in the 1880s on the developing diamond mines but only as a means to control illicit diamond theft and during the medical examination process.[107] The assertion by Mukoya of being stripped naked during the wage payment process however helps to indicate how the memory of exploitative acts by employers lingers on the memories of some of the Kavango contract labourers. But the fact that others did not speak of it could indicate suppression of this act of humiliation. The experiences of working on South African mines and living on those South African compounds helped the Kavango contract labourers to adapt to Namibian mines and compounds.

---

[103] *Ibid.*
[104] Moodie with V. Ndatshe. (1994), Going for gold, men, mines and migration, p. 88.
[105] See interview with G.M. Weka interview. (2009-07-29), Rucara village and Mathias Ndumba Shikombero interview. (2009-07-28), Rucara village.
[106] G.M. Weka interview. (2009-07-29), Rucara village.
[107] Smalberger. (1974), I.D.B. and the mining compound system in the 1880s, p. 411.

Namibian mines and compounds

The early compounds in Namibia developed in the southern part and around the northern copper mines of Otavi, Tsumeb and Grootfontein area.[108] After the discoveries of diamonds in southern Namibia after 1908 the various mining companies soon began to look to Ovamboland for work on the diamond mines. Despite lack of information on the diamond mines in Namibia we do know that by the 1920s, the diamond mine of Luderitz in southern Namibia experienced high death tolls from influenza and other cold weather-related diseases. This became a notorious labour destination for contract labourers.[109] The contract labourers from the Kavango were mainly sent to the non-diamond mines of Namibia such as the copper mine of Tsumeb and Kombat. A Native commissioner explained the work destination for the Kavango labourers: "These recruits are concentrated at Grootfontein and distributed to mining concerns in the north and to farmers. None of these recruits is sent to the Diamond Mines".[110] By the 1920s, the northern mines of Tsumeb and Kombat areas had compounds for contract labourers. Namibian compounds had as a purpose the inculcation in contract labourers of western notions of labour and to maintain good discipline. The need to discipline African labourers was based on the Eurocentric thinking that when "black tribes men were separated from their domestic economy and culture they were contaminated by the aggressive individualism and cupidity of industrial society and dragged on the ladder of evolution which resulted in a demoralized, decadent and degenerate work force".[111] This Eurocentric thinking among white employers in South Africa also existed in Namibia as can be identified from the following source:

> My experience of natives such as Swazi, Shangaan, Msutu, Mvenda and others, with whose home life I am particularly well conversant is that the moment he arrives in a labour centre he is entirely different to what he is at his home kraal, where he is law abiding, decent and well behaved, always ready to give ear to sound reason. It is the changed environment, contact with other nationalities, separation from his homeland and kith and kin, also the life such as appertain in compound that has such reverse influence almost transforming him into another being. From my observation on the Fields in this area, the Ovambo is not in any way different from other tribes in this respect.[112]

---

[108] O. Kohler. (1958), *A study of Karibib district, South West Africa* (Ethnological publication, no.40. Pretoria, Government Printers, pp. 21–22.
[109] Native Commisioner. (1919), 'The Union of South Africa report' (JX/0220), p. 6.
[110] A.J. Rossouw. (1939-08-30), 'Farm Labour commission. Windhoek, NAN, SWAA 2412, A521/13/3, p. 8.
[111] Harries. (1994), *Work, culture and identity: migrant labourers in Mozambique and South Africa, c. 1860–1910*, p. 72.
[112] Assistant Native Commissioner Hartman. (1931-09-14) 'disturbance of Ovambo labourers at Orange River Mouth. Windhoek. NAN. SWAA 2434, A521/31/ v.2, p. 3.

The Namibian compounds were viewed as places with a civilizing mission to raise blacks from backwardness and as institutions of disciplining contract labourers.

SWANLA had various recruiting depots in the police zone from where labourers were picked up by their employers to be taken to their work places and these included areas of Otavi, Tsumeb, Outjo, Otjiwarongo, Windhoek, Omitara, Seeis, Steinhausen, Gobabis, Rehoboth station, Kalkfeld, Omaruru, Usakos, Okahandja, Mariental, Kub, Maltahohe, Keetmanshoop, Karasburg, Bethanie and Uis.[113] All contract labourers in the urban area had to live either on the premises of their place of employment (a situation which was more unlikely due to stringent racial and labour laws) or in a compound.

Oral interviews indicate that novice contract labourers arrived in the early morning hours (usually seven o'clock) at the train station which was usually situated in close proximity to the compound. They were led by a police officer or guards to the compound entrance from which the labourers were usually led to the hall by an African foreman who was given the title "kamukomboni" (a compound man) where contract labourers were immediately introduced to strict compound rules.[114] This practice of providing the rule of the compound to new arrivals was similar to the South African compounds where umteto (Nguni word for law) was provided to new contract labourers.[115] Since labourers came from Kavango, Ovambo and outside Namibia such as Angola, there were usually translators depending on which language was spoken by "kamukomboni" (compound headman). After the gathering for the compound rules, labourers were allocated their rooms. The compound manager allocated rooms to labourers and labourers were not allowed to change to other rooms without the permission of the compound manager. In some of the early compounds, accommodation for labourers was primitive and the pondoks were unhealthy providing ideal conditions for diseases to spread.[116] Contract labourers faced health hazards resulting from the cold conditions and also overcrowding conditions. The following 1970 description of the single quarters for contract labourers at Grootfontein compound provide a general idea of the state of accommodation:

> A dormitory type building with doorless brick partitions separating sleeping units from one another. There are four beds per unit and approximately eight units per dormitory, four each side of the central dining/living area. The building is a basic structure with no frills. There are no ceilings, bagged wall plaster, and concrete floors.

---

[113] Oliviers. (1961), Inboorlingheid en administrasie in die mandaat gebied van Suid Wes-Afrika, p. 288.
[114] Benhard Limbangu Shampapi interview. (2009-07-27), Rucara.
[115] Moodie with Ndatshe. (1994), *Going for gold: men, mines and migration*, p. 84.
[116] E.L.P. Stals. (1967), 'Die aanraking tussen blankes en Ovambo's in Suid Wes Afrika 1850–1915' (M.A Thesis, Universiteit van Stellenbosch, 1967), pp. 222–223.

Its biggest fault is that, except to a limited extent in the last unit, there is no privacy for the individual as it is necessary to pass through the front sleeping units to get to the end ones. The ablution block is a very poor structure, both in quality of construction and convenience. The building is divided by separating toilets from showers. Low walls 4.5 feet high separate the two rows of closets that face each other.[117]

Since many compounds in Namibia were owned and run by municipalities, all employers paid fees to the municipality for the accommodation of their labourers. While there were separate sleeping sections at the labour recruiting depot compound at Grootfontein on an ethnic basis some labourers, especially in the Walvis Bay compound, indicated that this was not the same everywhere but that, rather, labourers were placed in a room in accordance with the place of employment or employer. If, for instance, six labourers were destined to work for one employer such labourers were usually allocated in one room. Benhard Shampapi explained:

> At that time in the compound each white employer had a section of rooms for his labourers who were usually not mixed with others. At times if you were many, he could be provided with two blocks.[118]
>
> [Ameshi kavakaranga mukomboni, kehe shirumbu kukara nandjuvo davantu vendi, hambara nakuvhonga-vhongashi. Pamwe ntjene muvangi kuvhura vamupe bloka mbiri].

The above comment indicates the possibility of the existence of the different types of compounds such as single or multiple employers' compound. There are indications that at the Katutura compound in Windhoek, accommodation sections were divided along ethnic lines as there was a row for the Ovambo contract labourers and another row for the Kavango contract labourers. But even in this case, there were no clear-cut ethnic divisions as members of the Angolan ethnic groups were accomodated either among the Ovambo or the Kavango ethnic groups. Katema Frans Kudumo who worked in Windhoek in 1970 and lived in the Katutura compound explains:

> In that compound, the rooms were built in rows. In our room we were six. Two of us were Gciriku; the other two were Mbukushu while one was a Nyemba and another was aChokwe. The row for the Ovambo was on the eastern side.[119]
>
> [Munya mukomboni, ndjuvo kwadidikire mudimurayini. Mundjuvo yetu tuva hamboumwe. Vavili tuvagciriku, vavili vaMbukushu ntani ghumwe muNyemba ntani namushivokwe. Murayini wavVambo kughupumeyuva].

---

[117] C.J. Speir (town engineer). (1970-10-23), Report on trip to Grootfontein to inspect the single quarters. MTS 9, N1/18, pp. 1–2.
[118] Benhard Limbangu Shampapi interview. (2009-07-27), Rucara.
[119] Katema Frans Kudumo interview. 2009-07-30, Sharughanda.

In the Walvis Bay compound, each room usually consisted of twelve occupants in which six slept on the right while the other six slept on the left hand side with a long table implanted in the middle of the room which separated the two sections of the room.[120] The table was used for sitting and discussion purposes by the room occupants and was long enough to provide sitting space for visitors from other rooms. The beds, however, bear resemblance to some of those in the South African mines as these were made of cement. Contract labourers did not regard these as beds as the following indicates: "There are no beds. The so-called beds which are there are just walls which are built to the height of a bed, two rectangular walls. Within those four walls, there is a hole, like a grave, where somebody has to keep his property".[121] While most compounds were owned and run by the various municipalities there were certainly compounds that were owned by some mines. The compound management consisted of the compound manager, the African headmen (locally known as kamukomboni) and the African police and together they ensured that all contract labourers followed the compound rules. If a contract labourer had problems, he had to report it to the headmen (kamukomboni) who reported it to the compound manager. Some compounds such as the Pokkiesdraai compound in Windhoek is remembered to have become chaotic by 1961:

> They sent me to Grootfontein. When I got there, S.W.A.N.L.A. sent me to Windhoek, the capital of Namibia. There the Municipality had a compound on the outskirts of the city for Africans. This Ovambo Compound was called Pokkiesdraai. I was given a job as Clerk in the single men's hostel. It was now May, 1961. There were between one and two thousand African men living in the Compound. The majority of these men were from the Ovambo Homeland and most others, like me, were from the Kavango Homeland, while some were from Angola. Although there were many tribes represented in the Compound, the Europeans called everyone 'Ovambo'. I found that the people in the Compound were mistreating one another. When they were drunk, they were stabbing and sometimes killing one another. They were stealing from one another. The European police had to come often to arrest people for major offences. The European Manager, Mr. Potgieter, use to whip the people with a sjambok for minor offences. He was a very large and powerful man. All the windows had been broken and there was a lot of vandalism. There was complete disorder.[122]

Alcohol brewing and consumption among contract labourers was cited as one of the major causes for this disorder in the compounds and the compound manager worked to prevent it. Alcohol was, therefore, prohibited in Namibian compounds and it became a serious offence for labourers to introduce, brew or drink liquor including "kaffir" beer in the

---

[120] Benhard Limbangu Shampapi interview. (2009-07-27), Rucara.
[121] N. Hishongwa. (1992), *The contract labour system and its effects on family and social life in Namibia: a historical perspective.* Windhoek, Gamsberg Macmillan, p. 63.
[122] Ausiku. (2005), *My own life stories: is this God's work or Satan's scheme?* pp. 63–64.

compound.[123] Although alcohol brewing was deemed illegal by the colonial administration, some contract labourers continued to sneak or simply brew alcohol within their sleeping sections and buried the gallons underneath the ground out of easy reach of the authorities. Others simply went to drink alcohol in the nearby African locations. Kamenye Likuwa who worked and lived at the Catholic hospital premises in Windhoek in the late 1950s explains:

> We used to drink our alcohol from our rooms. We used to dig and hide the gallon of alcohol in our rooms because if it was left in the open the police would arrest you saying that you are breaking the law because one was not allowed to sell alcohol. The blacks were prohibited from drinking alcohol. We also use to go and drink alcohol in the old location at some chosen homes. If those people in the old location were caught selling alcohol they were jailed too, and so they too had to hide it.[124]

> [Katunwenanga marovhu ghetu mundjuwo detu. Kutima nakuhoreka matenga ghamarovhu mundjuvo detu morwa ntjene kughashuva paukenu ne vaporosi kukukwata ashi ghunatjora veta morwa kapi vavapulitilire kughulita marovhu. Vatipu vavashwenikire kunwa marovhu. Katuyendanga murukanda kumandi ghamwe-ghamwe. Ntjene vantu vamurukanda vanavakwatere marovhu kuvatura mudorongo, mposhi vanahepa kuhoreka].

Some municipalities constructed bars within their compounds to encourage labourers to remain inside after hours. In the case of the Walvis Bay compound, the bar usually sold local brew such as Tombo, Jabula, and also cool drinks. This did not, however, stop labourers from leaving the compound to visit the nearby location for more entertainment. Outside the Walvis Bay compound for instance, labourers visited a municipal bar at Kuisebmund area which at that time was simply referred to as the municipality bar where contract labourers intermingled with men and women from the location.[125] Since women were not allowed in the compounds, the only time and place when contract labourers intermingled with them was at the bar or other drinking spaces outside the compound.

Many municipalities in the police zone constructed beer halls where they sold African brews and encouraged the Africans in the urban areas to buy at the beer halls while they prevented and jailed those Africans who sold African brew within the location. The prohibition of alcohol brewing for Africans led to political mobilization and African boycotts against the beer halls which led to the shooting and killing of Africans as was the case in the Windhoek old location in 1959.[126] Since labourers usually arrived at the compounds in the

---

[123] The inspector of mines, (1939-05-25), 'Compound regulations, Otavi mine native compound. Windhoek. NAN. SWAA 2434, A521/30/4, p. 5.
[124] Kamenye Lishuro Likuwa interview (2009-08-13), Kangweru village.
[125] Benhard Limbangu Shampapi interview. (2009-07-27), Rucara.
[126] B. Lau. (1991), *An investigation of the shooting at the Old Location on 10 December 1959*. Windhoek, Academy printing department.

morning, those whose job destinations were in easy reach of the compound usually located their place of employment with the assistance of a mundambo (a person with whom one is familiar with).[127] A mundambo did not have to be a person from the same area but any person with whom one had established previous social links or had worked together somewhere. Mundambo therefore played an important role for the labourer at the compounds and helped to socialize the novice labourer into all aspects of the compound.

Each labourer was provided with a card number which was used to receive meals. Each labourer received a metal plate, cup and a spoon which was used during his sojourn in the compound and returned at the end of his contract. Unlike on the farms, at the compounds, labourers did not cook but were served with breakfast, lunch and supper. A labourer could collect the meal tickets of other colleagues, usually placed on the table in the evenings, and go to collect breakfast for them.[128]

Gordon's account of meals in the mine compounds in 1973 details a single daily meal consisting of half a loaf of bread, mealie-meal and either meat or fish with occasional serving of vegetables.[129] This was the case in the municipal run compounds as well. Although interviewees spoke of sufficient food in the compound, the menu lacked variety, and this became a cause for discontent among some labourers. Benhard Shampapi who worked for his first contract at a construction company in Walvis Bay and lived in the Walvis Bay compound explained:

> But surely, wherever there are human beings there are complaints. At times we longed for meat but instead they gave us fish. We mainly ate porridge in the compound. It was porridge every day. In the morning we ate bread and coffee and in the evening, we also got bread and coffee but with porridge and meat or at times fish. From Monday up to Wednesday, we ate porridge and meat. On Thursdays we got mince meat for lunch and supper. Friday and Saturday was the same again, just porridge and meat. When it was Sunday, they changed a bit. On Sundays they cooked the meat in such a way that it tasted the best compared to all the other days. I do not understand why that was so but on Sundays they fried it in oil, they put curry and the meat smelled so nice with all the vegetables. Even if you were unhappy of eating the same kind of food almost the whole week to whom will you complain? They told us that this was the food that our white employers paid for us.[130]

> [Ngoli mwakukara vantune nakupirashi runyeghenyo. Atwe pamwe tunashana ashi ndi vanatuyitiri nyama vavo mbyo vanayita ntwji. Atwene ruvede runya vitima katukalyanga mu komboni. Keheliyuva vitima. Ngura-ngurane mboroto- nakofi, ngurova, mpoyiliko nka kofi, mara na vitima namberera pamwe ya ntjwi tupu. Yira muliyuva

---

[127] This is a word in Rumanyo language from the Kavango.
[128] Benhard Limbangu Shampapi interview. (2009-07-27), Rucara.
[129] Gordon. (1977), *Mines, masters and migrants*, p. 58.
[130] Benhard Limbangu Shampapi interview. (2009-07-27), Rucara.

lyaune kumupa ngoli mince, oyinya nyama yakukweya. Kutunda mandaha dogoro utatu, kunya vitima nanyama. Ntjene yira shitenguko ntjwi yakukanga, mu Une mpo katulyanga ngoli mince ku metaha nangurova. Mu utano momo mwakare, nyama tupu yakutereka nantjwi dakukanga. Namumapeghu namo ngoweyo. Ntjene mu Sondaha kutjindja ngoli, kuwananka ninke nyama yakurenka ashi kuyitereka yipitakane ngoli kuutovali woyo twalyanga kehepano. Kapi niyiva ashi morwa nke, ngoli musondahane kumu tuliramo maghadi ghamangi, keri kuyayiwana rupekwa ashi yiwape nawa. Kutura-turamo navigroente navintje. Mpili uvinyeghenye vyakukalyanga ndya dakukufana hanbara shivike mudima kuninko ngoli uvighambera? Vavo ashi ovo vamakuwa venu mbyo vafutiranga mbyovyo].

Those labourers who worked in close range to the compound could return for lunch but the majority of them only reported back for supper after five in the afternoon. With regard to mine work times, the working hours for the general labour force underground in mines did not exceed forty-eight hours per week.[131] The maximum time for which employers and workers were initially allowed to enter into contract was 309 shifts for workers on the mines or industry.[132] Work on some mines, such as the smelter plant at Tsumeb commenced as follows: Morning shift was at 7.am, midday shift, 3pm and night-shift at 11p.m. A bell was rung in the compound one hour before the commencement of each shift to enable contract labourers to have enough time to be ready and be punctual for work.[133] In Namibian mines, workers found employment as boss boys, machine boys, spanner boys, drivers and lashers.[134] Inside the mine, each contract labourer had to carry his numbered metal disc around his neck. This was a useful way to identify a contract labourer by the supervisor at work but it was also easy to identify the labourer in case of death from the collapse of the mine. All injured contract labourers had to report to the manager to obtain documents to enable them to consult the company's medical officer. As part of safety measures, mines such as Tsumeb provided each contract labourer working underground with a jacket and he also received a lamp at the workplace which was surrendered to the issuing depot at the end of each shift. Gordon further indicates that the mines took safety measures for miners by, for example, ensuring that after holes have been drilled, the whole gang had to withdraw to safety zone before the ganger detonates the charges and that after fifteen minutes he declared it safe and the procedure was repeated, the working ends being reversed.[135]

---

[131] Native commissioner. (1950-09-15), Native labour on Mines: hours worked underground: over time: Sunday labour. Windhoek, NAN. SWAA 1/1/46, 2426, A 521/26.

[132] Marcelle Kooy. (1973), Contract labour system and the Ovambo crisis of 1971 in South West Africa, *African Studies Review*, 16(1), p. 91.

[133] Native commissioner. (1950-09-15), Native labour on Mines: hours worked underground: over time: Sunday labour. Windhoek. NAN. SWAA 1/1/46, 2426, A 521/26.

[134] Gordon. (1977), *Mines, masters and migrants*, p. 50.

[135] *Ibid.*, p. 150.

Despite an indication of safety measures in some mines, contract labourers still had some experiences in some Namibian mines which did not take satisfactory safety measures. Shikombero explains:

> I went in that mine [Rio Tindo] and worked for that one day. I immediately saw that they did things differently from what I got used to Djwaini (Johannesburg mines). In this mine, unlike in Djwaini, they began to explode the ndilimani (explosives) on the stones while the labourers were still inside. In this mine, while the ndilimani were exploded people jumped in the air in fear. It was done so near to you and you felt as if all the stones above were going to collapse on you. I said to myself, 'no way! There is no way I am going to remain here'. As soon as I got out of that mine, I was on my way back to Walvis Bay. I worked at that mine only that one day that I had arrived. I left the next day in the morning back to Walvis Bay as I could not stand their safety measures inside the mine.[136]
>
> [Makura aningene, kukaruwana ndyolyo liyuva. Nikakenge ngoli veta yamo nayinye nakayikire ku Djwaini yapeke. Yavone, vantu vavo shimpe mpovalimomo, kare kunakutameka kushora ndilimani dicuke anwe mpomulimo. Ano kunya ngoli ku Djwaini kurupukamo ntani vashora. Ani mwamo mone yakuhoverera mpuli muwiru, yauviri ve mpuli kunya, yautatu ve mpouli kunya! Ashi Cu! Ani pepi-pepi vene yira kughakumbandukira mamuwe. Ame, naan-naan! Twakayika Djwaini kuno nani ngoli nkaNkwandi kapinirupuka. Tupunarupukamome kukakuyogha namana makura parupadi nivyukenka kuMbahe. Kwako oko ame kwakaruwanineko tupu ndjolyo liyuva ame pakukamona vinya, kurara matiku lyakukyako narongere nivyuke nka nkokunya ku mbahe kuviruwana vyande vya kare].

In some Namibian transportation companies and factories in Swakopmund and Walvis Bay the ticket system was practiced and a contract labourer stated that he worked according to the ticket system where after each day's work a stamp was put on his ticket.[137] The ticket system was developed to control absenteeism and dodging of labourers from work and it ensured that contract labourers were only paid for a job they had worked for and for the completion of the day's task. Absenteeism was discouraged and all labourers were registered by their work headmen before the start of work. A labourer who arrived late was sent back to the compound and was not paid for the shift missed. Food was only given to a labourer who produced a ticket book received so a labourer who missed work did not receive his ration for the day.

There were means of accumulating extra money. One was to work "arutaima" (overtime), this was an option which was possible with work in the urban area such as on mines and construction companies. In the case of the mines such as Consolidated Diamonds Mines (hereafter as CDM) R3.00 per hour was given for overtime and all employees were bound

---

[136] Shikombero interview. (2009-07-28), Rucara village.
[137] G.M. Weka interview. (2009-07-29), Rucara village.

by contract to work overtime if called upon, while at Tsumeb Corp. Ltd. and SWACO Ltd, over time was voluntary and the hours counted towards the completion of contract.[138] On Sundays, especially on mines, labour was restricted to essential services, which involved the employment of only a small fraction of the labour force. Since labourers received small wages their other option for accumulating money came from what Gordon termed as "quick money" and "business money".[139] The quick money included stealing, while business money came from doing business such as tailoring or selling goods etc. The labourers worked across ethnic lines at various work destinations. Inter-ethnic relations were generally good, but this did not exclude occasional cases of individual conflicts. An interviewee indicated that the relationship that existed between the Kavango and Ovambo contract labourers was that of a brotherly relation:

> We had very good relations between the Ovambo and Kavango, all of us were brothers. We never quarrelled. You could at times with your friends-even if you were alone as a Kavango with your three Ovambo friends – relax around the compound or at times out of the compound.[140]
>
> [Hawe twakakutekwire vene, navaVambo navaKavango, navantje vantu namukurwendi vene. Nakutangurashi. Kuvhura navaghunyoye mpilindi muvatatu ove pentjoye navaVambo kushapuka mupasione vene, murupuke mundjuwo mukayendaghure mu komboni ndi pamwe kuvhura vene kurupuka pandje].

While this was so there were some tensions that another interviewee revealed:

> It was alright except for our colleagues the Ovambos who always wanted to get rid of other colleagues regardless of the fact that we all came to work. They were worried that we were taking over their positions at work since they had first arrived there. When we were going to a shop the Kavangos have to always move in groups. They would call on us 'come!' And you will respond 'are you calling me?' They will say, 'no, we are calling that one whom we work with'. When you go to them then they would stab you. That is the truth, some of them use to run away and return to Kavango because of that. The Ovambo were the ones always feeling jealous of us saying that we must leave so that they can work alone. They did not like it that a labourer from the Kavango should also be in a position above them.[141]
>
> [Aye mukombonine thiwana vene thingwa awa ghayendhetu gha Vambo, ghokuninga karone kukupagha-pagha mumwenu omu mwakayera. yii, eshi ghanakutupiterera muyiruwana, yatwe hanawanamo. Ngeshi kuthitora munakuyenda, ghaKavango ne kuyenda kukukutha vene ngeno. Eshi "yila", owe ashi yamendi awo eshi awe yoyo vene twaruwananga naye, Owepone pakuyendakone awone akakukeke. Yoshwemwa

---

[138] Gordon. (1977), *Mines, masters and migrants*, pp. 80, 145–185.
[139] Ibid.
[140] Benhard Limbangu Shampapi interview. (2009-07-27), Rucara.
[141] Martin Maghundu interview. (2009-08-19), Divundu.

vene ghamweyane ngaghakatjiranga vene kukathiya yiruwana kukahuka ghaKavango.Havambone woghokutupakerangapo nya vene eshi ghashwayemo turuwaneneko pithetu. Mbadi ghahakire eshi ghaKavango nagho ghavapitire kughutho akare kuwiru].

The labourers were not allowed to bring any animal in the compound enclosures unless with permission from the compound manager. Contract labourers in the compounds engaged in various social activities during their free time. They could play "wera" (traditional game with stones) or dance the Kavango and Ovambo traditional dances. As Katema Frans Kudumo narrates:

> The Ovambos use to dance their traditional dance of jumping on each other at their section and all of us use to go and watch them play. We [the Kavango] also had our own drums and use to dance the 'shiperu' traditional dance. Hey! That was something, you could see those boys – it were the elderly men who used to do the singing while the rest of us assisted them. We all used to dance our culture and the Ovambo too use to come and see how we were dancing. That was how we lived there.[142]

> [Vavambo kavadananga udano wavo wakukuvatauka kuruha rwavo, natuvantje kuyenda tukavakengere. Atwe natwe twakalire nangoma, katudananga udano wa shiperu. Hawe vinyane! Mona ngoli vamati- vakurona mbo kavayimbango atwe vakuhupako kuvavatera. Natuvantje katudananga mpo yetu nava Vambo navo kuya vayatukengere omu tunakudana. Mmo twatungire ngoweyo].

Athough African labourers in the compounds engaged in singing and dancing all singing and dancing had to cease after 10pm except with permission from the compound manager.[143]

Contract labourers in the compounds were not restricted in their movement and could leave the compound after hours and return late. In the case of a mine compound, labourers could leave the mine compound provided they got permission and a pass from the compound manager.[144] But in compounds such as Tsumeb and Otavi all were expected to return to the compound between 9pm to 10 pm, unless with the permission of the compound manager. Contract labourers usually left the compounds to go to town for small shopping or simply to visit the communities in the nearest African locations.

W. Pendleton has shown that the Ovambo contract labourers were disliked by the black location residents as "most Katutura Africans try to avoid coming into contact with them. Apart from the shops, primarily the only place in Katutura where they go is the municipal

---

[142] Katema Frans Kudumo interview. 2009-07-30, Sharughanda.
[143] The inspector of mines. (1939-05-25) 'Compound regulations, Otavi mine native compound. Windhoek. NAN. SWAA 2434, A521/30/4, p. 5.
[144] Gordon. (1977), *Mines, masters and migrants*, pp. 53–54.

beer hall".[145] While such a negative community attitude towards contract labourers could have been the case in Windhoek, oral narratives from the Kavango present a different view of relations between contract labourers and others. In Walvis Bay, for instance, the relationship between contract labourers and residents of the location was generally good although this did not exclude room for differences. For instance, despite frequenting the municipal bar for alcohol, contract labourers also visited the location to buy and drink local brew known as "mbauko" which was made by both the Damara and Herero communities but if a contract labourer caused trouble during his visit to the location, he was surely bound to get a heavy beating from the location residents. As an interviewee explained:

> If you went to the location, especially to the Damara location and caused trouble, you know very well that those people will beat you. They used to brew their alcohol in the locations and so we the contract labourers use to go and drink there. It was alright if you were not troublesome. If you were not troublesome and was a regular customer in that house, they accepted you as a 'mundambo' (someone familiar). If you were drunk and you were not troublesome, they would even provide a room for you to sleep. The relationship with the location people was good as if you were in Kavango.[146]

> [Vakarukanda, nange omunya murukanda mmo unayendi shinenepo kunya kuvaDamara kunya, nange aghukatindane vanya Vacu meshi mwavayiva vanya ashi kukurangura vene.Vavo navo kavadunganga marovhu ghavo mumarukanda makura kuyenda natwe vaka kontraka tukanwe.Hawe kuyenda tupu nange kapi watindangane nawa tupu.Nangeshi wakudira kutinda ano omo mumundi mmo wanwenanga kukutambura vene yira mundambo vene.Nange unakorwa umwe nange kapi watindanga, kukupa vene nkonda yimwe vakuyarere ghurare.Ukaro navone uwaawa vene kutimwitira yira muKavango unakara].

Mass meetings except for religious, educational or sporting purposes were not allowed in the compound without the permission of the compound manager, an act which was intended to curb political mobilization among labourers. Under conditions of continuous hardship in the mines and compounds and, as a result of information about better conditions in other countries, many contract labourers began to listen to the political activists who mobilized for an end to the contract labour system which eventually came in 1971–72. The next chapter will explain the economic, social impact of the contract labour system on the workers and the political mobilization of workers against SWANLA and the contract labour system.

---

[145] W.C. Pendleton. (1974), *Katutura: a place where we do not stay* (California, San Diego State University Press), p. 87.

[146] Benhard Limbangu Shampapi interview. (2009-07-27), Rucara.

Conclusion

The travel by Kavango contract labourers outside Namibia shows they were desperate to find employment anywhere to address their family hardships. The Namibian mines and compounds where Kavango labourers worked had similarities to those in South Africa. In both cases compounds were aimed at controlling African labour; mine management viewed black labourers in a Eurocentric way as eternal children. Treatment at the compound could be brutal. The compound management provided accommodation on a tribal basis and supported the practice of traditional dancing because they viewed contract labourers as tribal in nature. In both countries, alcohol was not allowed in the confines of the compounds yet alcohol consumption in the compounds continued illegally through various strategies adopted by contract labourers such as hiding alcohol gallons underground. The experience of working in South Africa made adaptation to the mines and compounds of Namibia easier.

This chapter has shown that workers were compelled to work on farms before enlisting for the mines. Here they were given names. They, in addition, gave their employers new names. Their new names had little significance for them after they left work. Oral narratives suggest that while all contract labourers experienced hardships, there was a tendency to speak of other people's hardship than one' own. Where one did speak about oneself it was mainly a story of triumph or agency rather than as victim, and all these relates to how people speak about their experiences in daily life. This chapter has shown that the tendency of colonial officials to label the Kavango labourers as Ovam, despite the attempts of the Kavango workers to correct this has led to the invisibility of labourers from the Kavango in the contract labour history of Namibia. Although some enlisted for contract work for more than eight years while others found alternative means to make extra income through the informal economy, many were still short of money and could do very little to address their family hardships as they had hoped. Many contract labourers, therefore, began to respond to political mobilization. This and the social and economic impact of the contract labour system form the focus of the next chapter.

4 Returning Home: Economic, Social Impact and Worker Mobilization

Introduction

This section explains the economic and social impact of the contract labour system and worker mobilization against SWANLA and the contract labour system. The literature on this issue neglects the Kavango. Further, there is one argument where the contract labour system has been seen as presenting the Ovambo people and kings with new opportunities and advantages for family survival in the midst of the falling ecology.[1] Such an approach places the contract labour system in some good light but neglects the personal voices of the contract labourer on their view of the impact of the contract labour system. By focusing on Kavango oral histories, this chapter seeks to probe the question as to whether the contract labour was a progressive step in their lives, or whether the paradigm of exploitation and suppression remains the dominant one. It firstly draws on one life story to illustrate an engagement with the system and then moves to make a more general discussion.

Mathias Ndumba Shikombero's life story

It is useful to take the life story of one contract labourer to illustrate some of the impact that the contract labour system had on workers. The following is an oral life narrative of Mathias Ndumba Shikombero. He was born in 1933 and was, therefore, seventy-six years old at the time of the interview. Since he left for his first contract in 1949 and only stopped in 1971, he engaged in contract work for 22 years. He was interviewed on 28 July 2009 at Rucara village where he lived with his wife and grandchildren. He is unemployed and he said he survives by catching fish from the Kavango River. His homestead consisted of thatched roof huts built with river reeds and others with clay mixed with stones, cans and bottle on their sides. Similarly, the yard of his homestead was surrounded by a wall made of the Kavango River reeds. The interview took place in the morning around 10 a.m. and lasted for about 1h52 minutes. Shikombero spoke not just about his life story as a contract labourer but also about the history of Vagciriku people. He explained the family tree of his father by way of informing how the interviewer is related to him.

---

[1] R. Moorsom. (1996), *Under development and labour migration: the contract labour system in Namibia*, pp. 19–20.

What is presented in this section, however, is his life narrative as a contract labourer. The aim is to provide readers with oral narratives to get to know better some of the contract labourers referred to in this study and to provide a basis on which readers could make their own interpretation about the impact of the contract labour system. The life story is presented in the first-person format as it was told to me. However, the narrative has been edited. This abbreviated narrative serves to provide a useful basis for understanding the impact of the contract labour system on an individual.

> I belong to my mother's Vakafuma (famous/toad) royal clan. My father Shikombero of Mate was from the Vakankora (parrot/ hunger) clan. My mother's name is Memba, the daughter of Kanyondi. My father lived this side of the river [Namibia] together with King Nyangana but later he left and crossed to the other side of the river [Angola]. It was on the other side of the river at a place called Mashemeno, where I was born.2 After the death of my father I came back to this side of the river to live with my grandmother Kanyondi at Makena village where I finally grew. I never attended school ... When I was of age (about 16 years of age) I went to Djwaini (Johannesburg) after I heard that Djwaini was open to people. In the past, they use to catch the lorries of WENELA in Shakawe area ... Later on the lorries were introduced to Rundu and so we waited for them at their overnight resting stop at Shamvhura village where we were taken to Rundu for medical examinations. When we left for contract work, we did not escape, parents knew of our intentions. When I left for contract work I was not yet married and it was only after my return that I got married. We left for Rundu where we got medically examined. At Rundu we lived in a compound which was situated not far from Mangarangandja area.
>
> [A]ll contract labourers from Ovamboland and Kavango who were destined for Djwaini (Johannesburg) came to that compound. It was in Rundu compound that labourers for Shivanda (Grootfontein) and for Djwaini (Johannesburg) got separated ... When we arrived in Shakawe, we waited for the plane to Djwaini as during our times we had a plane. After we arrived in Shakawe we climbed and flew to Francistown for a refill of gas from where we were transferred into trains. It was also in Francistown that one was given a painful injection. One did not want a friend to stand nearby in fear that he would touch one on his sore. We moved by train the whole day and reached Mafikeng in the evening. We stopped in Mafikeng for our meals. In Mafikeng, next to one building was a small entrance with some security guards. If one by chance found oneself on the other side of that entrance one would be abducted and taken to Kimberley. The people of Kimberley needed people as labourers, so they would abduct one... We left Mafikeng in the evening and travelled the night so that when the sun rose in the morning, we were in Mzilikazi. In Mzilikazi, the buildings were all very tall and it was here where labourers from various parts of other countries met. There were the maMbogwani, maNdaghu, maZulu, maSwazi, maXosa, maBwatja, maTanganyika, maPedi, maNyasa and maPondo, all of us met there. That is where we were separated to various destinations and those who completed their

---

2   Mathias Ndumba Shikombero was born on 4 August 1933.

contract also came and we all met there. ... The duration of our contract was for seventeen months. We were sent to a mine called 'Welbedag' which was in close proximity to 'Moontabei' mine. We were there for almost a year and then our mine closed down and then we were separated like cattle and sent to other mines to complete our contracted period. We were sent to 'Senderera' mine next to 'Mzinginya' mine where we completed our contract ... In the mine we worked underground, far away from the entrance of the mine. Sometimes we walked on foot and at times on a rail transport. When one woke up one took one's helmet, clothing, shoes and safety shields worn around the knees. We used to crawl down in those mines my dear.

[D]o you see this big scar on me? [Asking the interviewer] A mine is just a mine. This scar is a result of a stone. That stone broke off from the roof of the mine and fell and rolled faster. The 'Ncara' boy tried to alert me with his light about the danger but I was not looking at him and did not see it coming. But what helped me was that on the roof top of the mine, there were 'mapaka' (wooden planks) that were built on there to prevent such stones. But this one, a chip of it hit me and I was bleeding. I was taken to the station where our boss use to stand where some medicine was applied and bandaged after which I was taken to the compound from where I was taken to the hospital ... My hand was given some five stitches and I returned to the compound. When I finally returned to work in the mine, I was not given heavy work anymore but only to collect the water pipe and water down where they had finished boring so that one reduced the dust to being inhaled by labourers as it was feared to cause headache. That was what I did for four days. After that I got a note on my bed that I had to go back to the hospital for the stitches to be removed, now, that is when it was painful ... In the mine where we first worked, they also made use of donkeys. A strongest donkey could pull as many as four filled trailers. So, that is what we use to do there ... One did not speak any other languages in the mine but Fanakalo. The Boss boy was the boss of the group and if he asked 'Hey wena upi una hamba?' which means 'Hey where are you going? One answered 'Nina hambela pa!' which means 'I am going just here'. He could even ask one 'Hey wena, upi una puma?' which means 'hey you, where are you coming from?'

[I]n the later period people got higher pay but in the beginning the pay was too small. I began with sixty rand and after the third month my salary was increased to eighty rand a month. They also deducted money from one's salary which was sent as deferred pay to Shakawe. I stayed there for seventeen months ... The reason that discouraged me from taking on another contract to Djwaini was to have to be transported in a plane again. I could not stand it! That plane was flying out in the sky and could fall down anytime and when it made as if it was getting down one felt as if one's heart was coming out.

When I returned from Djwaini, I slept in Shakawe in Botswana. The next day, I climbed into Wenela lorries and reached Shamvhura village. Since lorries were introduced in our time, we did not need to use boats anymore to carry our goods home, we brought them along in lorries. Some of those who were still interested in returning to contract to Djwaini would drop their goods at home and immediately return to contract ... the past it was like this, when one returned from contract work one did not open one's box of goods on the day of arrival. One slept until at least the third day when one's father would come and bring out the box. He would open it and decide who to give. Usually it was the mother who was the first one to be given goods for her efforts in having raised one up. Then the rest of the family would also be given something, may be share the large piece of cloth. I also did the same.

[A]fter my return from Djawini I stayed for a while at home and then I asked myself what to do next. It was at that time that the Angolan colonial administration also began with contract work in Angola at a place called Bie. When I heard about it I said to myself, I am going there to collect a lot of money. We were many, such as Shamakaka, Shighongo, Magana and Shashipapo, who left from this side of the river [Namibia] and crossed to the Portuguese post from where we walked on foot up to Ukwangali [240km] where a lorry came to collect us with a number of Bushmen who came from Shalirova village.

[W]e worked there [in Angola] for two years and got fed up and wanted to return home. We decided to go to the office to inquire since upon recruitment they informed us that we were only going to stay for twelve months. We were chased away from the office by the Portuguese. We went back to the office again for a second time to inquire about our end of contract and about our day of return home. That office was situated inside a fence with two small gates guarded by security guards. We sat the whole day on the office premise seeking to be informed but to no avail. The Portuguese official did not trouble us that whole day until when it began getting dark and the sun was about to set. The security guards were informed to beat us up at the gate. That is how it happened; every one that passed through that gate was beaten up. The old people among us began to lament and regret why we came on contract in the first place. They said the Portuguese were too cruel and that we shall not survive and return home. So then that attempt failed and we went back to work. It was only after some time of working that the Portuguese finally informed us that our lorry to take us home to the Mbweracountry has arrived. The Portuguese referred to all of us from Kavango as Vambwera. It was a day of extreme joy when we were informed that we shall now be taken back home. We almost broke down into dancing because of extreme excitement......What made us unhappy with the contract system in Angola was the problem of low salary and the long period of contract work. We used to be paid only three pounds a month and they informed us that we shall receive the rest of the pay at the end of contract. We got the rest of the pay later (Shikombero is laughing). It was just a bunch of papers with a sign of a hippopotamus on it. It was such a heap of papers and when one saw it one would think it was money while it was in fact just papers [of no value].

[W]e returned home with a lorry and we were told we shall only get our pay in Gciriku area ... We were so lucky when we arrived at Gciriku that we met some women, the sisters to some of the contract labourers, who took their ground nuts for sale at the Portuguese post. These women saved us from hunger. The women were so happy to see us, to see their brothers, and so they took their ground nuts which they intended for sale but gave it to us for free to eat. Imagine we did not even return with a single hat on our head, how then could one say one had really been to contract? What did we really bring from that contract work? Nothing! There were some simple, ugly blankets with pictures of lions on them. We were given our money the next day which was round about sixty rand. It was after getting paid that those of us on this side of the river [Namibia] crossed back to our place at Makena village.

It was after Angola that I decided to go to Shivanda ... After I arrived [at Grootfontein] I was sent to work at 'Kamunate' (soft drinks) company. We had to distribute the soft drinks in Grootfontein, Kombat and Tsumeb areas. I worked the whole day each day and was so disappointed to get paid only six rand at the end of the month. I said to myself, no way, I will not enslave myself for six rand. I used to be paid a lot of money in Djwaini (Johannesburg). Why then should I work for such little money? That was not right! I made up my mind. I waited for the sun to go down and then I escaped. I escaped at that time when the road from Grootfontein to Rundu was placed with gravel [in the early 1950s]. I drank the same water they were using for the road and would hide every time I heard a car approaching. It took me four days and four nights to reach the Kavango. I stayed here only for a while and again wanted to go for contract and so I went back. This time I was sent to Mbahe (Walvis Bay) when I arrived in Walvis Bay at work, I was again paid the same six rand which I had protested at my previous employment. I worked at the municipality at the railway lines, but I still could not accept the six rand pay.

[I]t was then that they [contract labourers] decided to do something about it. They wrote letters to various compounds that contract labour must be ended. We regarded contract labour system to be a mistreatment. We worked for seventeen months and yet there was little to show of the salary. That is why the labourers decided to end contract work ... When I returned to Kavango after the break down of contract, I never went back again; it was useless to go back. What wealth did I bring along from Shivanda [southern Namibia]? Nothing! I only bought my own clothes to wear. There was really nothing! It is only nowadays that people are getting a lot of money. If I had worked in a time such as this one of nowadays I would not have escaped. Our purpose was to go on contract to get money, but we did not get it ... When I returned from my final contract I settled at Makena village after which we moved to Kayova village. After the death of my uncle then we moved on to Hoha village and finally here at Rucara village. These concentrated homesteads you now see in this village only came later, we were not like this in the past as it was spacious. Most of these homesteads are of people from the other side [Angola] who came and settled here.

[A]fter my final return from contract work, I continued to survive from the Kavango River which they are now prohibiting us.[3] It is in that river where we survived this entire period. There is nothing left any more. I used to go and catch fish for consumption and would sell some extra fish to make an income and that was life. It is only nowadays when they are beginning to make it difficult for us to fish freely that life is now beginning to get shorter [becoming harder to survive] ...

---

[3] The prohibiting measures referred to by Shikombero relates to the post colonial period in Namibia where the ministry of fisheries and marine resource has put up fish conservation measures by controlling community fishing methods through the constant patrolling of the Kavango River by fisheries inspectors who dismantle fish nets and at times fine the culprits.

Mathias Ndumba Shikombero's statement "When I was of age I went to Djwaini (Johannesburg) after I heard that Djwaini was open to people" means Shikombero waited to go on contract work only when he was matured and there were ways of hearing about the availability of contract work. The use of "we" to refer to his experiences is an indication that while his experiences about the contract labour system were personal, they were enmeshed with those of other fellow contract labourers. It also shows that SWANLA brought people from different backgrounds together. Shikombero realized during his contract work to South Africa that the use of blacks as contract labourers for the South African colonial economy was not limited to Namibia but extended to other African countries. Shikombero's use of "we were separated like cattle" paints an image of dehumanisation and mass treatment that made no room for individuality. His expression that "a mine is just a mine" indicates that naturally a mine was a dangerous place where the impossible was to be expected and where many got injured or even killed. Shikombero, like many other contract labourers, learned Fanakalo as a lingua franca and derives pride in his knowledge of it. After working on the mines, he was able to purchase some clothing. Shikombero's statement that "after my return from Djawini I stayed for a while at home and then I asked myself what to do next" shows that contract labour system made Shikombero see the act of staying at home as lazing around.

His account of his journey to Angola indicates that he and other men usually travelled long and dangerous distances to reach their places of recruitment. Shikombero's account shows that contract labourers, such as on farms, were at times forced by the employers to overstay against their wishes long after their contracts had expired and that complaints were usually met with brutal response. Sometimes contract labourers broke contract and walked back to the Kavango and faced great hardship along the way but they continued to enlist for new contracts despite the hated low wages. There was a cycle of entrapment within the contract labour system. His story also provides some indication of agency. Most notably he tried to take action when he realized that the pay was low. Despite his efforts he failed to really improve his work conditions and remained trapped in the system.

Mathias Ndumba Shikombero's life story indicates that the contract labour system was exploitative and evil and that the rewards were not worth the exploitation and the suffering. His most poignant words are "What did I bring from Shivanda [Southern Namibia]? Nothing!" He finally ended his engagement as a contract labourer.

His narrative shows that the resources from the Kavango River became his main source for family survival after the contract labour system. His criticism of the Namibian government in post colonial Namibia about the controlling of fishing along the Kavango River shows his unhappiness over the control of what he believes is his remaining central source for survival. Such criticism puts to the forefront the need for the Namibian government to find ways to address the continuing economic and social hardships of former contract labourers and that this will require an understanding of their historical background. Shikombero's life story is not unusual. The accounts of other workers confirm his perception of the system as exploitative. There were but small rewards for labourers under the contract labour system engagement.

Economic and social impact

Some contract labourers were able to buy clothes for their families. Contract labourers bought boxes that contained clothes and other items which they distributed to the extended family members.[4] The low wages limited contract labourers to the type of goods they could possibly purchase and take home and many purchased clothes. The Kavango people at the time wore "muromba" [skin wear] or the loin cloths exchanged with European and Vimbali traders. The purchasing of clothes under the contract labour system led to the eventual transformation from the wearing of "muromba" to clothes which were regarded as an improvement in their lives. The contract labourers show appreciation for this eventual change:

> We used to wear 'no muromba' [skin wear]. But when we saw what was coming from 'usimba' [police zone] we also began to have an interest, we also wanted the trousers. Are these things not nice [Ronginius pulls on his shirt]? Even if they decide to bring back 'no muromba' today do you really think we will accept them again? We will refuse them, no, these ones are just fine.[5]
>
> [Po nare ngatudwara nomuromba. Apa twamwene eyi yinakatunda kousimba nose tatunyenenesanye, nose twaharako no ranga. Kapishi yiwa eyi? Nampili nsene vaninka asivatengwidirepo nomuromba nayina yilye hena nayitambura? Tatuyinyokanye, hawe, eyi yiwa tupu].

The "magayisa" bought clothing that varied from trousers, shirts, blankets, jackets etc. Contract labourers were happy to purchase clothing for themselves and their families. George Mukoya Weka explains:

> I used to get paid six rand at the farm, apparently that was a lot of money [Weka is laughing]. But it was better, at least one could buy a long bundle of loin cloth and that was exactly what I had always wanted that my mother should also benefit. I felt better during this second contract; I managed to bring something back at home. I brought along my trousers, shoes and a suit so that I could also come and show off,

---

[4] Mathias Shikombero interview. (2009-07-28), Rucara village.
[5] Ronginius interview. (2009-07-12), Nambi village.

hey, no, that was better. I took out some trousers and gave my father. It was only then I felt I had arrived.[6]

[Kanikatamburanga viponda vitatu pa farama, ashi maliva ghamangi ngoli (Weka kunakushepa). Ngoli hasha, kughurapo vene mbandwa yalikeshe. Mbyo nashanine ngoli me vanane ngavayamakereko. Pughuviri pano name hashako ngoli; Nakayitireko vintu kumundi. Nakashimbire ranga, nkaku nasuta name niyakumonikite, hawe panya ne hasha. Ani ghupu ranga kupa vavava. Ntani nakuyatika ngoli].

Mukoya shows a sense of achievement and self esteem with having brought something back home to give to the family. It seems that it was customary in some African communities for returning labour migrants to give their acquired goods upon arrival to their parents and, depending upon their gender, they first consulted either with their fathers or with their mothers. Among the returning Phokeng migrant women in South Africa, for example, "upon their arrival it was customary to give their mother all the money they had worked for and she would then call the father and put the money before him. They gave thanks and asked if she had the bus fare to go back to work and if there was nothing left for her then they would give her something out of that money".[7] Among the Kavango people in Namibia, when a contract labourer returned home he always had to reach the homestead after sunset to ensure his spirit had settled in his village before he was seen and talked about by everyone the next day. He also did not open his metal box of goods until the third day. The contract labourers from the Kavango gave all their acquired goods to their fathers. As George Mukoya Weka indicated:

In the past, after you have arrived from contract, you did not open up your goods yourself. When you arrived and you have slept for a night, then the next day they would provide you with a good meal and when that was over, then your father came and asked you to bring your casket. It was only then that you brought it out so that he could open it. The father then separated the goods, first for himself, and then for you. If you bought a bundle of cloth, he took it out and gave it to your mother who divided it up for the various children in the homestead. Then your father would say, 'This is what I have taken out for myself and this is for your mother'. If you brought along some money you also gave all of it to your father. In fact, he asked you about it. So, if you came with a wallet of money, you also gave that together with all the other goods to your father. What could we do? We were thankful of the practice and did not get angry about it. The parents would take your money afterwards and use it to buy some cattle for you. In the past, you did not go against the wishes of your parents, whatever they decided, that was how it was going to be.[8]

---

[6] G.M. Weka interview. (2009-07-29), Rucara village.
[7] Bozzoli. (1991), *Women of Phokeng*, p. 91.
[8] G.M. Weka interview. (2009-07-29), Rucara village.

[Pakare kundereko kurenkashi uyatikene ndi makura ove naghumoye upaturure-A-aa! Kuyatikita kurara kuyushara vakuyumburepo vikondomboro, nkuku ndi nyama, yaa, vanamana ninke ntani vanakuya ngoli vasho ashi yitenu ngoli tanko osho shikesha. Makura kushirupwita ngoli osho shikesha ne vashipaturure ngoli. Vashipaturure ngoli shikesha ne makura kuvitura panya-kuvitura panya, kuvitura, kuvitura! Makura evi vyendi ovi anasha ghuye sho eshi kughupa kuturaku. Mbyevi anashana mwene. Ndjasha ne kuyighura vene ashi eyi yavavava. Evi vinahupomone vyendi nka navyo atoghororemo tanko nange vanamana vyoye navyo kuvikutulira ku! Vino kuturaku ovino makura vanamana kuvirenka, yii, makura likeshe ntjene shi wakaghura, kulighupa likeshe kulighonyonona-kulighonyonona ashi mbandwa ndi ngashi, kuliteta pakatji vape vanyoko.Vavo vanyoko valitapere ngoli.Makura vasho ashi vino vyande me naghupuko, vino vyoye naghumoye, ovino vyavanyoko ngavatapere navoko.Yii, makura ntjene ashi nakashilingapo makura kuya nayintje kuyighupa.Kukupura vene ashi ndjato ya maliva ne kuninko?Ovene kudamuna ndjato kuvapa makura vavo kuvighupamo.Vyendi venne vyo, kughupanka aturenka pavyuma vyendi panya. Omughuruwana?Kuvipandura.Nakugarapashi, kuvipandura vene. Makura omu kavaruwananga ngoli ntjene ashi mukurona yira wa ngavo, panya pakurenka ngoli kutwara mushiruvo ntjene unayashungiri, ukuharukako tupu kunakukuyita ku hambo ashi he-ee, ntana yoye yo! Mbyo nakupako. Ashi wakaruwana nawa monande, mpandu yayinene. Makura oyo ntana upange kudipagha kwaghumoye, upange kuweka kwaghumoye. Ngoli nakuyidapaghashi, pamwe ngaurenka ngauparukemo].

Some contract labourers, especially those who worked in towns, sent money home to their families through friends. As such the celebration of the return of contract labourers was not only an appreciation of the contract labourers' safe return but was an expression of appreciation of the few goods that were brought for them. Some contract labourers purchased goods like "katishu" (a small gun for shooting birds).[9] Others bought metal ploughs.[10] Previously the Kavango people tilled their land with handmade hoes but with the introduction of the metal plough they ploughed larger fields. During the 1940s it was reported by colonial officials that the fields in the Kavango had trebled in size and that hundreds of ploughs had been bought.[11]

Contract labourers had realistic ideas as to what they wanted. These did not include things beyond their reach such as cars. Instead they purchased cattle. Since owning large herds of cattle was a sign of wealth in their communities some contract labourers indeed became wealthy and made life easier as they used the cattle to plough the fields, drank milk from it and sold the meat when the cattle died. Cattle ownership improved the social standing of the owners and also made one's heart feel at peace at all times and reduced one's

---

[9] Benhard Limbangu Shampapi interview. (2009-07-27), Rucara.
[10] Shintango waKarenga interview. (2009-08-05), Korokoko village.
[11] R. Moorsom. (1977), Underdevelopment, Contract labour and the worker consciousness in Namibia, 1915–1972, *Journal of Southern African Studies,* 4(1), p. 66.

worries.¹² Cattle ownership was, however, complex and in some cases it did not become an everlasting means to family survival as cattle diminished by various means. Nyambe Merecky, for instance, purchased some cattle during his contract work period in the 1960s which multiplied but later he had nothing left. He explains:

> It used to be that whenever one returned from the whites [contract labour system] one bought a cow and had a kraal and that was a life we had. My cattle which I use to purchase upon my returns have all finished completely! Some of them died, others were sold and yet others got stolen by people.¹³

> [Kavikaranga pakare ntjene unakatunda kuvamakuwa, kuyaghura ngombe nakudika hambo, ndyo liparu twapalire twe. Ngombe dande odo naghulire pakukavyuka dapwa nadinye nu! Dimwe dakufa, dimwe kughulita ano dimwe vadivaka vantu].

Some returning contract labourers in the 1950s purchased horses in the police zone which they exchanged for many cattle. Shintango Karenga explains his personal experience:

> In 1953 I left for Shivanda [Southern Namibia]. I heard that the Native Commissioner of Kavango, Mr. Morris [1954–1960] had given people permission to bring into the Kavango horses bought from the southern part of Namibia. I thought to myself, what an opportunity not to be missed! And very soon I was on my way on contract work to Shivanda. When I arrived in Grootfontein I got sick and was admitted in hospital. After that they wanted to send me to work in a kitchen at Outjo and I protested because I heard the Outjo Boers were very cruel. They then told me I would be sent to Okahandja and I agreed. I was therefore sent to work in Okahandja at Osona on a farm. We planted vegetables there. The name of our boss was Adam Lister, he was a German man. I worked there for eighteen months but got paid one rand per month. After one has worked for six months one's salary was raised to one rand and twenty cents, it was similar to Rhodesia. I worked and later bought a packet of sugar and began brewing alcohol and sold to other labourers on the farms.

> Later on, my boss's father-in-law passed away at Omatako farm. He was riding a horse and then unluckily it threw him on the stone, and he was injured and died later. His family wanted to kill that horse but then my boss told them that they needed not to do so because he had a labourer who was in need of buying a horse. So that was how I came to purchase that horse. After my contract, I travelled on foot from Okahandja to Rundu (600km) with my horse from Osona which I had bought for sixty rand. As we travelled onward home, at Omatako I bought another horse for sixteen rand. When I arrived in Kavango I exchanged one of the horses for twelve cows to the late Kamburu of Tambuka while the other remaining one was also exchanged for fourteen cows. I tell you my child; I use to own many cattle. In 1956 I left everything with my uncle Muhembo and returned on contract work; hey one never felt they had enough.¹⁴

---

12   Mbamba Ndara interview. (2009-08-19), Divundu.
13   Nyambe Merecky interview. (2009-08-06), Shipando.
14   Shintango waKarenga interview. (2009-08-05), Korokoko village.

[Mu 1953 aniyendinka kushivanda. Komisari Mare apulitilire vantu kukaghura tukambe mushivanda. Ame shi kunakuyenda mpo nashapukire ngoli niyende nka kushivanda. Pakukatika mushivanda ame avakantaura ngoli mulighuru, kwankaliremo rutipa muno. Avakankondera mushipangero. Munyima naporeke makura shi kukantuma ngoli ku Outjo. Ameshi-aaa-ku Outjo nakuyuvhako mburu dako nashwena. Ashi ntjene unashwena makura weni, tukutume ngoli ku Okahandja, ameshi yaa, ku Okahandja nawa tupu. Mpo nayendire ngoli ku Okahandja pa Osona mwedi murongo namwedi hambo ndatu. Nakatundireko ngoli ne mu mwedi waMei natukambe. Kanikaruwananga pa farama, kukunanga katofuru, vikamudesa, shinuti, vininke navintje, nanyanga. Muhona wetune Adam Lister wamuNdoveshi. Kwakaruwanineko mwedi murongo nahambondatu kumfutane vishilinga murongo mu mwedi. Muruku rwa mwedi ntayimwe ntani vandjerwire ku murongo navishilinga vivili yira mu Rhodesia nka. Makura anikaghura shipaketi sha shuka nitameke kuhangitanga naghulita kuvaghunyande

Kuyakarapo opo makura hawe, muhona wande anafita rukwadi rwendi oko kundudnu da Omatako. Kwamurongitire kakambe makura ashi ndi arondangepo. Kakambe makura nko kumugandera paliwe makura nko kufa. Vanya vanashana vakaroye makura muhona wande ashi-a-aa! Okunya muntu wande washana kakambe, avakangulita. Nko nakaruwanineko ne makura kukatundakone kuyenda kuyatika. Kutunda vene ku Okahandja parupadi natukambe dogoro kuyatika. Kakambe kaku Osona kwakaghulire ngoli R40.00. Ovyo nayatiki pa ndundu da Omatako anighurupo nka kakambe kakarume R15.00. Pakuyatika ngoli kuno, oko kakambe kande kwayakaghulitire ngombe murongo nambiri kuvavava nakufa Kamburu ka Tambuka. Oko kamweya ka R16.00 ovyo nayendi mu sharushashi mu Angola mu 1956 anikakaghulitapo nka nako ngombe murongo nantano nka. Karunga! Opo nakalire ndi? Kughukenga tupu oko kunyima vipururo shimpe mpoviliko. Kanikaranga vipururo hambo ndatu morwa ntoto tukambe. Nko kuyavishuva. Mu 1956 nko kuvyuka nka. Nakuyuvhirako shi! Mu 1956 mpo nayavhukiremo nka, nashuvu ngombe dande nadintje kwankwirikwande Muhembo anivyukanka kushivanda].

Shintango waKarenga seems to have done well and was able to boast about the wealth he acquired from his minimal savings under the contract labour system. The extent of the value for horses in the Kavango is not well established. It seems that before the settlement of the Native Commissioner at Rundu in 1936, horses were greatly valued for hunting purposes. Local people got horses through exchanges with European traders. King Weka, for instance, bought a horse in the late 1920s from a German speaking trader who lived on the Angolan side of the Kavango River. George Mukoya Weka explains:

Weka bought a horse. Its name was Haifi. He bought it from a German who lived at Mpupa. Since then we survived on meat. It was that horse which fed us [helped us survive]. After being well settled we use to go into the forest in Mundumu where a large kraal was built and where we were all taken to go and to kill for meat. The hunters for meat were the late Shampapi and the late Shamate Kangwe, they were two. That was how we survived. If it was during the times of food shortage, then we only survived on meat. That was how we stayed. At that time the wild animals were in our control and there was nobody to prevent us. We could kill any animal and there was no case where it resulted in any quarrels or anything else.[15]

[Weka ghuye kwaghulire kakambe. Lidina lyako ne nko haifi. Kwakaghulire kwa Mundoveshi oghunya akakaliro ku Mpupa. Kutunda ngoli opo makura atwe ovyo katuparukangane nyama, nkoko kakambe katureliro. Kuyarenka opo tuturene makura kuruta ngoli omunya musheli munya muwiya ngoli muMundumu, mmo mwakaliro ngoli vakadikemo limurugumbo makura momo ngoli makura natuvantje kutushimba ngoli tukakare momo tukadipaghe nyama. Wakuyidipaghane nakufa Shampapi na nakufa Shamate Kangwe, vaviri. Mmo twaparukire ngoli. Nangeshi mwaka walirumbu ne a-a-ndjoyo nyama pantjako, ngoweyo mmo twakalire. Opanya pakarene ameshi kwafanine ashi vikoramane yira vyetu, kundereko kukushweneka. Kehe shikorama kunderoko ashi pakarepo vininke ashi pakarepo vininke].

But with the eventual hunting ban, horses became important mainly for long distance travelling and were therefore still exchanged for cattle as was the case for Shintango.

The returning contract labourers also made use of the local means of transportation to carry their goods. This had an impact on the fortunes of local businesspeople. As Shikombero shows, contract labourers paid boat owners to transport their goods along the Kavango River.[16] Before the introduction of WENELA lorries returning contract labourers were dropped off at Muhembo border post with their entire heavy luggage from which they walked home, some more then 230 km away and they experienced great difficulties. They, therefore, paid local people who had donkeys to transport their goods up to Andara Catholic mission station from where they paid for the boat transport for their goods along the Kavango River while they walked home. The father of Andara Catholic mission recruited some men who helped transport the goods of contract labourers by boats along the Kavango River. George Mukoya also explains:

Every time when we returned with our bargains from contract work sufferings began. Some of them sold their goods right there so that they can manage to carry very small bargain. It was so heavy! It was at that moment that people with donkey and sledge would arrive. They were businesspeople who made sure to exploit our vulnerable situation to maximize their profit. They would say 'Yes, bring it here. If I take you from here and take you that side, you need to give me this amount of money'. When one looked at one's heavy bargain, one paid. We all paid. What else could we do?

Then they would transport and bring us up to the place of a policeman Mukoya Ditembero where we dipped our feet in medicine. After that then we would be told 'Yes, there are other people here who can help to transport you from here.' Then we would pay again and get transported up to the Catholic mission station at Andara.

---

[15] G.M. Weka interview. (2009-07-29), Rucara.
[16] Mathias Shikombero interview. (2009-07-28), Rucara village.

At Andara we had to pay again for transport to our villages. Some contract labourers arrived home with no money left. At Andara mission lived Pater Shiroli who use to record us. He had to record us and then we would leave all our baggage with him so that we walked empty handed. Our baggage was then transported along the river by his people and brought to us but we also had to pay Pater Shiroli. He would record us and ask the names of our villages and they would bring our goods to us.[17]

[Anwe munakashimba vintu makura nane ruhepo ngolipo runaya ngoli. Vamwene kughulita mpopo vyuma vyendi ashetekere mpopo kushimba vyavisheshu. Nane udito. Makura mpopone vamweya vanayaa-ya pamweya vakavidongi, pamwe vaka-vireyi, vanangesefa vakuvaka vininke vamushunune ngoli. Ashi 'yaa, yita shi kuno, ntjene ashi anikughupu pano nikutware kunya kuninke, yita vimaliva vyakutika kungandi'. Kukenga ngoli kudimurongerero doye. Natuvantje kufuta, omu ghuruwa-na? Vamuyite ngoli dogoro panya pa Mukoya waDitembero wamu polisa akaliropo. Makura vamurenke ngoli ku mpadi. Makura kutunda opo ashi yaa apano napompov-alipo nka vamweya nange munashana vamughupepo nka mufute nka. Ntjene ashi ghudito unene pamweya vamuyite ngoli dogoro pa Missiona ya Andara. Pa andara shimpenka napokuyafuta. Vamweyane kuyatika kumundi mawo-kowoko. Pa Andara akalirepo ngoli muruti Pater Shiroli makura kumuyita ngoli amutjange, amutjange. Ghuye amutjange mposhi ovyo vyuma makura muvishuve ngoli anwe makura muy-ende ngoli mawoko-woko. Ovinya vyuma makura ngavapereke ngoli vantu vendi mu-mawato ngoli vavimutwarere. Ngoli naye nka kumufuta ogho Pater Shiroli. Vyuma vature ngoli mumawato ashi yaa, ove kuninko kumukunda ghoye ashi pa ngandi vamutjange ngoweyo. Makura ashi yaa, tatererenu ngoli vyuma vyenu. Yaa, makura anwe mupite ngoli yaurundu vavo vaduwe ngoli mumukuro].

Mukoya's narrative is suggestive of the feelings of exploitation and helplessness for he uses words like "suffering", "exploit", "our vulnerable situation" etc to explain their return. Yet the impact of their return was felt by much wider circles than their families. Some women cooked porridge and meat which they sold to the returning contract labourers along the routes and in this way accumulated some profits. When WENELA transport was introduced between Botswana and Rundu later, contract labourers did not need to walk anymore and so this was better for the workers although it cut off the local people from their previous trade activities with returning labourers.

The contract labour system was in general viewed as bad. It was generally seen as an exploitative system and was hated by contract labourers. Many feel the contract labour system did not enable them to gain long lasting wealth as hoped and many of those who left home with great expectations ended up disappointed. Shikombero shows that the acquisition of western clothes made the local people look down on the previous skin wear and saw it as old fashioned and backwardness rather than as part of their culture.[18] It also shows

---

[17] G.M. Weka interview. (2009-07-29), Rucara.
[18] Mathias Shikombero interview. (2009-07-28), Rucara village.

that the contract labour system turned the Kavango people into wage labourers. Money became more important and it detached them from their previous means of exchange through "Mushanga" (shells worn on legs and hands).

Before the German imperial occupation of Namibia, the Kavango people's economic means of exchange was through the barter system and "mushanga" were used as a method of monetary payment.[19] The shells were made from ostrich egg and were used as compensatory payment to a person after a court hearing etc. The Bushmen made these "mushanga" which they exchanged with the Kavango communities which in turn they could exchange for loin cloths with the Vimbundu and European traders who operated in the Kavango. The contract labour system forced the local men to depend on wage work and they began to regard staying at home as a sign of lack of work.[20]

In the past when a young Kavango man wanted to marry it was the duty of his parents to find a wife for him. Parents depended on their sons getting married so that their wives would help them in agriculture activities. The parents of a contract labourer usually approached the woman's parents for the proposal. If the woman's parents agreed to the proposal, the young man was taken into the homestead of the woman's parents to live with them to be observed and once he had proven himself and gave a cow to the woman's parents, he was finally given his wife to take to his parents' homestead. This marriage process changed during the time of contract labour system when young men left on contract work and therefore had no time to live and work for their in-laws. In this case a young man usually brought presents for his future wife and in-laws before he was finally given his wife. The parents whose sons stayed too long on contract work were left at a disadvantage to marry off their sons as soon as possible. Although young men could get a wife to marry without going on contract work, the contract labour system provided a means to purchase some items to be used in their marriages. The aspirant contract labourers usually purchased gifts for his in-laws to boost a good personal image. Contract labourers usually saved from their scant wages to purchase some cooking utensils for marriage purposes.

In Ovamboland one impact of the contract labour system was the loss of male labour to agriculture as women were left alone to deal with family activities, which included the care of domestic animals and subsistence farming.[21] In the Kavango this was felt less. Here the homesteads for married couples were usually built within the boundaries of the homesteads of parents where family members were usually responsible for the welfare of others. During

---

[19] Theresia Shidona Weka interview, (2009-08-11), Guma village
[20] Mathias Shikombero interview. (2009-07-28), Rucara village.
[21] Hishongwa. (1992), *The contract labour system and its effects on family and social life in Namibia, a historical perspective*, p. 95.

the absence of a husband there were usually other adult males left within those homesteads that the wife could use to help her with agriculture work etc.[22] Cattle herding, for example, was an activity for young boys (who usually did not go on contract work) rather than for adult men.

This should, however, not underestimate the impact of contract labour system on women in the Kavango but should indicate that, in the absence of husbands, there were usually other options left that women exploited to complete duties and get along with life. There were indeed some negative impacts of the contract labour system on women: some were bound to contract sexually transmitted diseases from husbands who may have picked it up while on contract. Some women never saw their husbands again as these husbands died inside the mines or joined the SWAPO armed struggle in Francistown, Botswana and died at the war front.

Since the returning contract labourers had seen that women in the police zone had short hair, they accepted the order of the commissioner and missionaries to have all women in the Kavango to cut their "vihiho" (traditional braids) which caused a great outcry from the women.[23] Despite the suffering, women came to play a great role in the struggle of men under the contract labour system by providing the men with both economic and political support and suffered equally as men did from colonial oppression.

Contract labour system bound the labourer to a long period of contract without a chance to see their beloved family members. The duration of the contract labour system was very long (about twelve to eighteen months). In some cases the married (or the just married) contract labourers left their wives for longer periods and in this way felt alienated from their spouses and children.[24] The feeling of estrangement from the family also extended to estrangement from their home areas as they saw their home area as too idle to live compared to the areas away from home during the contract labour period. Some contract labourers indeed felt lost upon arrival in the Kavango and felt the immediate urge to leave and return on contract work just as Tuhemwe felt upon his return in 1971:

> When I reached at Rundu, I felt undecided whether I should proceed home or not. I decided I was going back immediately because when I looked at my area it looked ugly and I felt estranged as if it was not my land. I could not think of what I was going to do at the homestead if I proceeded there.[25]

---

[22] K.M. Likuwa. (2001), Djwaini, a coffin with your recruit number on. The experience of contract workers from Kavango to South African gold mines, 1944–1977', p. 10.
[23] G.M. Weka interview. (2009-07-29), Rucara.
[24] Hishongwa. (1992), *The contract labour system and its effects on family and social life in Namibia, a historical perspective*, p. 89.
[25] Tuhemwe Shevekwa interview. (2009-07-30), Sharughanda.

[Opo nayatikire pa Rundu kapi nakuvhura kutokora shi niyende kumundi ndi.Ani tokora mpopo me kunakuvyuka.Kukenga weno shirongo shande udona-dona yira kapishi mwetu.Kapi navhulire kughayara ashi vintje nganikaruwana kumundi ntjene niyendako].

The return home, which men longed for while away, fell short of expectations. The long duration of contract was a cause for concern as their hard work during that long duration was not equally translated into high wages. Since the wages remained low, contract labourers always felt short of money and therefore spent most of their time on contract work in the hope of earning more and thus spent less time with their families at home. Farm workers, in particular, were unable to save much and were compelled by constant "ushotere" (lack of money) to always return for contract work.

In the 1970s it had become clear that the Ovambo labourers were troubled by not being able to spend more on their families and that many felt they worked for the benefit of the employers rather than for themselves.[26] Among the Kavango contract labourers, the low wages and remittances that some of them managed to send home did not add much to the family livelihood and many lived under continued family hardship.[27]

There were cases when contract labourers did not bring anything back home or brought what they felt were worthless items such as when Mathias Shikombero felt he brought nothing from his contract work in Angola except for a simple, ugly blanket with pictures of lions on it.[28] Some contract labourers were unable to buy anything after contract work and they felt embarrassed to face their expectant family members, a situation that usually compelled them to enlist for new contracts. Bernhard Lipayi Linyando explains his 1960s experiences:

> See the suffering on that farm of Dan Opperman, hey, that Boer was very cruel. That was what we lived with. Those who talk about Colonialism-You people have not seen colonialism! [You have not experienced colonialism in its harshest forms]. We saw how colonialism looks like! One got paid twelve cents; apparently that was now a lot, no! What lots? How could you possibly accumulate wealth in such a situation even if you were us? The tiny suitcase contained only your five trousers with nothing to take home. I asked myself, what will I take home? Will they really think I went on contract work? So I said to myself it was better to re-contract and I returned. I was sent to Outjo where I again met a very cruel Boer.[29]

---

[26] R. Voippo. (1981), Contract work through Ovambo eyes' In R.G. Green, K. Kiljunen, M.L. Kiljunen (eds.), *Namibia the last colony*. Essex, Longman, pp. 120–121.
[27] Bernhard L. Linyando interview. (2009-07-27), Ndiyona.
[28] Mathias Shikombero interview. (2009-07-28), Rucara village.
[29] Bernhard L. Linyando interview. (2009-07-27), Ndiyona.

[Kenga ngoli oro ruhepo ngoli ro! Muhona wetu Dan Opperman.Mburu yidona. Mbyo ngoli twakakalire vyo! Ava vanakutimwitirango ashi ukoloni! Ukoloni kapi mwaghumona! Kapi mwaghumona! Atwe twaghumonine ukoloni ashi weni omu wafana. Ame kwakavarekire navishilinga murongo navitano. Ashi vimaliva vingi ngoli? Ani hawe! Nampili naghumwenu ngoli murongo naviviri ashi vininke mbiliha, nanine ndiro vimweya. Aniyakara mwedi waghuhambo ghumwe avangwederere ayiyakara fyf rand ngoli. Opo nakavyukire nakandjato tupu kanagwana ranga dande ntano, kwato vyakutwara kumundi. Anikupura umwande me hepero kuyenda kumundi vanane kuvakangayarashi kushivanda vene nayenda ndi? Ame, aye, mpo nakuvyukira mpopa! Mpo navyukirenka kushivanda kukawana nka ne mburu yayidito, okone ku Outjo ngoli].

The fear of embarrassment by Kavango contract labourers was similar to what was also observed among the returning farm contract labourers in Ovamboland. A Kwanyama headman Weyulu testified that many of the farm contract labourers usually returned home crying with nothing to show from their long absence and were too shy to face their families and were usually compelled by the situation to return immediately on contract work.[30] The contract labour system thus trapped workers in a constant cycle of re-enlisting.

The former contract labourers previously engaged in alcohol consumption at their work destinations and therefore continued to do so upon their return to the Kavango. The long wait in Rundu compound for transport to take returning contract labourers home resulted in many spending their remaining money on alcohol in Mangarangandja area. This happened to Benhard Shampapi upon his return in 1967:

> While one waited for transport in Rundu, one could visit Mangarangandja area to drink alcohol. When we arrived in Rundu, we just left our clothes in the compound and off we went to Mangarangandja. In Mangarangandja lived the brother of George Mukoya the late Mahupe (Shamakongwa) with his daughter who was married to Murenga and so we went to visit him. We lived there for some days drinking up all our money; after all we only had little money anyway.[31]

> [Pakutatereranga mahauto mu Rundu makura kudingura ngoli mu Mangarangandja ku marovhu. Opo twayatikire mu Rundu, kushuva tupu ndjato detu mu komboni makura vyu ku Mangarangandja. Mu Mangarangandja mwatungire mughunya George Mukoya, nakufa shaMakongwa (Mahupe) namonendi wamukadi oghu akwalire Murenga. Atuyendi tukavadingure. Mmo twakatungire momo mayuva nakunwapo tuliva twetu natuntje twatonkane kapishi twatudjuni].

---

[30] E.H. Kreike. (1996), Recreating Eden: Agro-ecological change, food security and environmental diversity in southern Angola and northern Namibia, 1890–1990. PhD Thesis, Yale University, p. 231.
[31] Benhard Limbangu Shampapi interview. (2009-07-28), Rucara.

When the "magayisa" (returning contract labourers) purchased local brew in Mangarangandja area they eventually got into physical fights with the youth which led to the social breakdown of the once non-violent Mangarangandja area as the following indicates:

> In the beginning Mangarangandja was peaceful. There were only activities and peace. But where it ended, it was very rough because there were many people and single women. So, when Magayisa (returning contract labourers) returned from the mines and dropped off in the compound, they would go into Mangarangandja and enjoy themselves. Most of the boys there were unemployed but needed money; those who were employed needed women, well now, stealing activities started. Life became a life that you would no longer call as a good life because by then, everybody who had 'a broken mind' and was rude came to Mangarangandja.[32]

Many contract labourers, however, purchased alcohol from the Portuguese across the Kavango River and this led many of them to become poor as they ended up exchanging their hard-earned goods or cash for Portuguese alcohol. Contract labourers assert that, although traditional brew was drunk in the Kavango before the arrival of the Europeans, this was only occasionally drunk by parents at traditional dances, such as shiperu. A high increase of alcohol abuse in the Kavango resulted from the Portuguese sale of liquor.[33] Some of the contract labourers speak of how they ended up selling all their livestock for alcohol to the Portuguese. Ronginius, who had been on contract work in Namibia in the 1960s, narrates his experience:

> Upon my return from contract I bought cattle but then later when they began to multiply, we began to eat them up. We finished them to the Portuguese for bottles of "Tindo". Per cow, you could get twelve shillings and that was the way our cattle got lost.[34]

> [Apa nakarugwire, tanidiranda odo nongombe apa daninkire ngwendi tadilivhara tatupiruka hena nyamwetu tudilyepo. Tatudimana kovaPutu nye tudirandesepo komakende vatupenye no Tindu. Mo ngombe pamwe yisilinga murongo nayivali. Nongombe detu yimonye ngoso datuzumbana].

Contract labourers considered the Portuguese businessmen as corrupt because they usually cheated people in business. Ronginius explains:

> If the Portuguese saw that you were drunk, they came and added empty bottles and said that you drank them. You must never drink at their place because they will convince you to have a little nap and then you were sure to pay a very high price afterwards.[35]

---

[32] K. Likuwa. (2005), Rundu, Kavango, a case study of forced relocations in Namibia, 1954 to 1972, p. 92.
[33] Ndumba Likuwa interview. (2009-07-31), Rucara village.
[34] Ronginius interview. (2009-07-27), Nambi.
[35] *Ibid.*

[Nsene kukumonanye vaPutu asi onowoteke, awo kuwiza tavakugwederereko nye makende goyimpepa asi tarasi eyi nyove koyinwine nayinye eyi. Kapi tonwinepo vene ntudi opo morwa navakuninka asi tanko fuwapo nye. Makura nye opo yimaliwa tavakufutisanye yoyinzi].

The Portuguese sold different brands of alcohol. Some of these brand names came to take on a new meaning as Ndumba, for example, explains: "It was from there that the name we gave my son Anisi came from. It was from those bottles of alcohol. He was born during that day when we were drinking it".[36]

Contract labourers believed that the contract labour system was an example of colonial exploitation at its worst because they suffered extreme mistreatment as the Boers displayed the worst cruelty by treating contract labourers as non-persons.[37] This view of the inhumane treatment of contract labourers is similar to the view presented of Ovambo contract labourers in the 1970s that saw contract labour system as the source of destruction of all that was human in a man.[38] The contract labour system instead of helping to bring an end to the hardship of contract labourers became another form of colonial oppression due to harsh working and living conditions and the low wages inherent in it. There are contract labourers who hold an extreme view of the contract labour system and see it as akin to slavery that denied their humanity. Tuhemwe who went on contract work in the 1970s, for example, felt it failed completely to uplift him economically:

There was nothing good about the contract labour system. Nothing! Whoever will claim that there was some good in it, unless perhaps he was educated and was not somebody like me, no! You! The Boers were extremely cruel! The Boers were not the kind of people who could regard one as a human being! Is this not what we have just finished talking about here? Just imagine, one [contract labourer] is angry with him [the Boer] and yet he [the Boer] instructs a fellow farm labourer, with whom one has friendly relations and with whom one use to eat with, to beat each other in turns. Is that not exact slavery?[39]

[Kundereko uwa mu kontraka. Kwato! Keheghuno ngaghambo shine ghuwamo nkwandi walye wakukushonga kapishi wakufana yira me, hawe! Ove! Mburu kwanyanyenine unene! Mburu kapishi muntu wakurenka ashi akumone nove ashi umuntu! Kapishi mbyo tunakumana kughamba ntantani pano? Ghayarashi, ove unakugarapere naye [mburu] ano uye [mburu] arenke nka unyoye oghu mwakara naye ghuholi mwalyanga naye mukutoghoone. Kapishi ngo upika wene-wene wo?]

---

[36] Ndumba Likuwa interview. (2009-07-31), Rucara village.
[37] Tuhemwe Shevekwa interview. (2009-07-30), Sharughanda.
[38] R. Voippo. (1981), Contract work through Ovambo eyes' In R.G. Green, K. Kiljunen, M.L. Kiljunen (eds.), *Namibia the last colony*. Essex, Longman, pp. 120–121, p. 114.
[39] Tuhemwe Shevekwa interview. (2009-07-30), Sharughanda.

Tuhemwe saw contract labour as work for people who were unsettled psychologically and were running around under indescribable circumstances in search of solutions. He creates a powerful image of unsettled, restless people engaged in a kind of defeating activity.

Kapinga Muhero who went on his first contract in Namibia in the 1960s asserts similarly that although the contract labour system was the only means to acquire money one received nothing good out of it. Muhero compares the engagement in contract labour system to a local parable regarding the gathering of wild fruits. He explains:

> I see contract work like the issue of collecting wild fruit. When your fellows are gone to look for wild fruit in the jungle then you too begin to question why you must stay. You then decide that you also have to go there regardless of whether you will die there or survive. Those things [contract labour] was all about sacrificing and suffering and making up one's mind and being aware that whether one dies there or returns alive was up to God to know. There were no benefits there.[40]

> [Yo kontraka ne kuyimona me yira mbuyo thiya thoninga eshi hayethoyene ghana piti ku mbuyo, owe nowene eshi yinyo shokarere, wakona ndani kuyenda, kufa kufa, kupara kupara. Oyina yinunguturene yokukumina vene nokuyipaka mumawo gha nyambi eshi nikafe nikahuke yokudimuka keho mwene nyambi. Mbadi yokuyendera ghuwa].

The "wild fruit collection" parable is a common parable among the Kavango ethnic groups and it is usually interpreted by the local people as follows: people may take a long journey under great hardships to the dangerous jungle and collect the wild fruits but once such wild fruits are collected they only last for a day and still leave families in the same hardship as before and yet one has to make repeated journeys to the jungle for more needed but yet non-lasting wild fruits. Here is once more the image of entrapment. This cycle of entrapment had a powerful effect on workers. Their frustrations led to their political mobilization.

Mobilizing politically

Many contract labourers felt as non-persons as a result of the bad treatment they received and they felt that the contract labour system rendered them as property rather than as humans with feelings and needs. The contract labour system brought Kavango workers in close contact with Africans from other countries and they shared stories of colonial exploitation and about the means to undo colonial domination. Their exploitative work conditions rendered them ready for political mobilization. From among their ranks were political activists belonging to the Ovambo Peoples' Organization (hereafter, OPO) which was formed in 1959 and which by 1960 became the South West Africa People's Organization (SWAPO)

---

[40] Kapinga Muhero interview. (2009-08-19), Kamutjonga village.

with Sam Shafishuna Nujoma as its president.[41] Gordon showed that the Second World War (1937–1945) helped to develop national consciousness among Namibians but delayed national independence for Namibia.[42] Some of the African ex-service men like Andimba Toivo ya Toivo became one of the early nationalist leaders who formed the Ovambo People's Congress in 1957 (which by 1959 became OPO).[43]

The OPO president, Sam Nujoma, clandestinely entered and carried out secret political meetings in various compounds across the police zone to address contract labourers. During such political meetings, money was donated to him and the message was passed on to various compounds among contract labourers to raise funds so that Sam Nujoma would leave for exile. Labourers donated money at secret political meetings in their respective compounds. George MukoyaWeka narrates:

> At a place where I stayed during my first contract, we donated money for Sam Nujoma when he left the country to go and bring those things [independence] that he had brought to us now. It was at that time that people were sent to ask for donations. Then they said whoever had one pound or a fifty cent was also o.k. to donate so that Sam Nuyoma could use it to leave the country. The whole compound of the mine of Uesa [Uis] donated and we were the one who held the donation bowl around. A message was sent to all the compounds where his people were found. It was both the Ovambo and Kavango. That was the way it was.[44]

> [Atweko ne pamuhovo opo twayendire, oko twakakalire kwakatapire maliva pakushapukanga Sema Nauyoma ayende oku anakashimba ovyo vininke. Mpo arenkire pa ngaro ngoli vayende vantu ashi yaa, oghu anakaroko naponda nawa tupu ndi vitano nawa tupu tughupe ngaro mbyevishi Nauyoma anashana kuyenda. Mupongayike ngoli maliva mbyovishi ngaviyende kunya ngakayenditeko. Komboni nayintje kukaturapo ku mina ya Wesa, atwe twakaghumbiro ngaro vene. Kwatumine ashi kehe komboni vene oko vakara vantu vande, vaWambo, vaKavango natuvantje. Ngoli mmo vyayendire].

Although the name OPO seemed to signify a focus on the Ovambo, in reality, it appealed to members across ethnic boundaries. Although OPO mobilized among contract labourers in the compounds, its membership extended beyond contract labourers. In the words of the founding president of OPO, after the formation of OPO people from the Kavango soon joined them and then later people from eastern Caprivi. OPO recruited members very quickly and in large numbers.[45] By 1960, OPO changed its name to SWAPO with a broadened

---

[41] S. Nujoma. (2001), *Where others wavered: an autobiography of Sam Nujoma*. London: Panaf, p. 55.
[42] See R. J. Gordon. (1993), The impact of the Second World War on Namibia, p. 148.
[43] *Ibid.*
[44] G.M. Weka interview. (2009-07-29), Rucara.
[45] Nujoma. (2001), *Where others wavered: an autobiography of Sam Nujoma*, p. 57.

scope of mobilization among all Namibians for political independence. Sam Nujoma left for exile after 1959 but his political campaigns among contract labourers were continued by SWAPO members and supporters. Key among the assembly of these SWAPO campaigners was Nathaniel Maxuilili, an Oshivambo speaker who lived in Walvis Bay's African location. To some of the contract labourers Maxuilili became synonymous with SWAPO. Maxuilili became popular because they believed he was fearless of the police since he held his rallies publicly. Benhard Shampapi explains:

> On Sundays when there was no work, we usually attended meetings of that old man named Maxuilili. On other days the meetings were held in the evenings after work and we would stay there the whole evening. My goodness that was the man! He never used to panic. At those meetings, the police were also in attendance, the Boers also attended, and he used to insult them while they were just shaking their heads in disbelief. That man was never secretive and held his meeting in the open. The Sunday meeting usually began at three in the afternoon and he would talk until perhaps at six after which we would march from the meeting place, singing their Oshivambo language liberation songs, and take him back to his house.[46]

> [Makura katukakaranga ngoli pamwe yira mapeghu, shinenepo mu Sondaha morwa kwato viruwana, makura kukara ngoli navigongi vyaghunya mukondi Mahwilili. Mumayuva ghamwe ghapeke pamwe kuvitulita ngurova morwa liyuva lyaviruwana. Makura mukatokwere ngoli nkoko kushigongi shendi dogoro mpopo shikatweka. Nane-nane! Oghunya kwakalire murume, kwato kutukuka ghuye. Ruvederone navapolisa kukarapo, mburu kukarapo vene nado ghuye pakushwaghura anakudishwaghura, mburu dado tupu dinakupuka kumutwe. Ghuyene kapi kakaranga naka-holya-holya ghunya-a-aa! Ghuye kuruwana mbongarero pakambandjangera vene. Shamusondahane kutameka pa drie uur. Makura shikaree! Kughamba kughamba pamweya dogoro pa ses-uur. Makura mu mashe ngoli, mukaghupe oko munakashitulira, muyimbe ngoli, kuyimbane ndodo ntjumo davo vene dashiVambo dalikondjero manguruko. Muyimbe ngoli pamwe mumutware kundjuvo yendi, name nakamonineko kundjuvo yendi].

Maxuilili mobilized labourers and other Namibians for SWAPO as far as Windhoek, usually with other friends who assisted to organize such meetings. After such meetings, Maxuilili was usually arrested and put in jail but other colleagues continued the struggle. Some contract labourers from the Kavango who were mobilized by Maxuilili later believed the constant flying of planes across the Kavango River into Angola, which they used to see, signified the end of the white men's rule. As Benhard Shampapi explained:

> Before we left the Kavango, during our childhood we use to hear about the politics of 'Rumbumba' plane that it was the plane that was meant to kill the whites. It was only after we arrived there on contract that we discovered that SWAPO was fighting

---

[46] Benhard Limbangu Shampapi interview. (2009-07-27), Rucara.

for the liberation of the country so that they would remove the white rule and install the rule of the black people. That was what Maxuilili use to tell us. That was when we said 'O.k. so then it all has to be related to the stories of the 'Rumbumba' plane and it was only then that we made the connection.[47]

[Opa twatundire kuno kuKavango atwe tuvanuke katuyuvhanga tupu vya upolitika vyakuhamena Rumbumba yinya ndira ashi yakudipaghanga vamakuwa. Opo twakatikire ngoli kunyane ntani tunakayiva ngoli ashine aye, nani SWAPO kunakukondjera limanguruko lya shirongo ngayaghupemo vamakuwa makura lipangero livyuke kuvatipu. Ngoweyo ngoli kaghambanga Mahwilili. Makura atwe ashi ohoo, nani mbyovinya nani vyakuhamena kwa Rumbumba, ntani kuvikwatakanita ngoli kumwe].

A Kavango contract farm worker since 1955, David (alias Davy Lyangurungunda) Ausiku later worked as a black clerk in Windhoek at Pokkies Draai compound in 1961 and eventually became a SWAPO member in 1962.[48] Although during his work as a farm labourer there were no political discussions among them as they were quite isolated from what was going on in the rest of the country, this was different during his work in Windhoek in the 1960s. Ausiku explains:

When I was in the old compound, I started recruiting for the South West African People's Organization (S.W.A.P.O.). When S.W.A.P.O. was formed, it became an umbrella organization which included several smaller ones, including the O.P.O. I became a member of S.W.A.P.O. in 1962 through John Ya Otto in Windhoek. He had known me from Okahandja. My fellow recruiter was John Ya Otto. Together, we recruited many members from within the migrant workers' compound in Windhoek. We encouraged members to steal from the bad rich whites and kill the bad ones ... By the time I had returned to Windhoek after my four-month absence, recruiting people for SWAPO had become spontaneous and included many gang members from outside the Compound. We told them to leave and become guerrillas outside Namibia. Many who left travelled through Botswana and into Zambia where there were training camps.[49]

---

[47] Ibid.
[48] David Kudumo Ausiku was born at Sikondo village, Namibia, in April 1936. His father Liasanga belonged to the Buffalo clan while his mother Mate belonged to the lion royal clan of the Mbukushu people. He obtained his SWAPO membership card from John Ya Otto in 1962. David Ausiku became the SWAPO leader in Kavango. He went into exile to Angola in 1978 to join SWAPO armed liberation struggle and worked at SWAPO radio broadcast in Luanda, broadcasting freedom messages to Namibia. In the early 1980s, he feared that his life was in danger from his own SWAPO comrades who began to call him an 'ekuli' (sell out) as he could not reconcile his Christian beliefs with SWAPO's communism stance. Since the 1980s David Ausiku was based at SWAPO radio broadcast in Lusaka, Zambia. After hearing continuous rumours that he was going to be sent to the war front where he was going to be killed by fellow PLAN combatants, he chose to resign from SWAPO around October 1986 and left through the United Nations in Lusaka as a political refugee to Canada where he lived since then.
[49] Ausiku. (2005), My life stories: is this God's work or Satan's scheme? pp. 75–76.

It was during the mid-1960s when great political tensions were developing in Namibia that Ausiku began to mobilize for SWAPO in the Kavango. Returning Kavango contract labourers faced accusations and assaults from the colonial authorities who accused them of co-operating with SWAPO. Theresia Shidona, the granddaughter of King Nyangana of Vagciriku who was born on the Namibian side of the Kavango River was married in Limbaranda area in the 1960s.[50] She explained the fate of the returning contract labourers and their families:

> They really killed people in Limbaranda! Some; mother-mother-mother-mother! There, they put all those returning from contract work in a queue. They put them all in queues like the way we queue up around here for old age pension. And then the gun shots would ensue 'tau-tau-tau-tau!' They left the corpses in a heap and said, 'let us move on to the next house'. What do you think did the people do next? These ones were fleeing and so were the others there.[51]

> [Ani vadipaghire ngoli limbaranda! Vamwe; nane-nane-nane-nane! Omone kuvapakanga mumutete avavanakatundo Djwaini. Kuvapaka mumutete-mutete yira momu twatamburanga ukurupe, makura tau-tau-tau-tau! Kuvashuva rwaki, ashi tuyendenu nka mumundi ghumwe. Ashi weni vavaruwanine? Avano kunakutjira, vanya kunakatjira].

Shidona explains further why they became victims of the Portuguese:

> It was the Portuguese who made us to flee to this side [Namibian side of the Kavango]. Those Portuguese said we were collaborating with SWAPO [forces]! The SWAPO [forces] came and killed the Portuguese and it was then that the Portuguese in turn came and said 'let us kill the Vagciriku people and wipe them out of here'. That is what made us to flee. But how many of them really managed to flee to this side? The Vagciriku people died there. Where is the Kandambo family who lived in Rwenge area? Finished! They have all perished.[52]

> [Vyatutjwayuro ndjesha ndjegho Muputu. Ovano Vaputu ashi atwe kunakahatanga kuvaviwapo! Ovo vaSWAPO ne vadipaghe vaPutu, makura vaPutu vavo nko kuyane ashi tudipaghe ngoli vagciriku vatundemo, mbyo vyatutjwayuro ngoli twe. Vangashi vatjiliromomu? VaGciriku vafa momo, vakaRwenge vaka Kandambo kuni vanakara? Too! Vanapu].

---

[50] Limbaranda or Mbunda is an area between Kwito and Kwando Rivers. Prior to the Portuguese atrocities in the 1960s it was inhabited by a heterogeneous population many of whom had ties of kinship or ethnic affinities with the population on the Kavango River. The older inhabitants of Kavango regard Mbunda or Limbaranda as the land of plenty and that in earlier days, the local people removed temporarily to Limbaranda during times of famine, returning only in time to cultivate their fields with the first summer rain. See 'Unregistered correspondence 1962–67' (Windhoek, NAN, NAR 1/1/55, group 11, file 20), pp. 4–5.
[51] Theresia Shidona Weka interview, (2009-08-11), Guma village.
[52] *Ibid.*

The contract labourers and their families who already lived in fear of the Portuguese atrocities, frequently fled as the Portuguese armed police forces arrived at their homesteads. Many were shot since the Portuguese believed them to be guilty. Many crossed to the Namibian side of the Kavango where they where sympathetically received by the local inhabitants who were kin and family members. It was during this period of atrocities by both the Portuguese and the South African colonial authorities on the Kavango population that mobilization against SWANLA and the contract labour system intensified. Returning contract labourers continued to mobilize people and therefore families began to express their disillusionment with the contract labour system, especially against the recruitment operator SWANLA which was perceived as exploitative.

The SWANLA shop at Rundu was, for example, a place of political tensions in the 1960s because of the racial discriminatory practices experienced there by the locals. A returning member of the SWAPO combatant trained in Tanzania who clandestinely visited the Rundu SWANLA shop in March 1966 wrote about this in his autobiography:

> I nearly committed an unforgivable mistake in the SWANLA shop. One area of the shop was reserved for whites only and blacks had to point to what they wanted from a distance. Blacks could not hand money directly to the white saleswoman. They first had to give it to the black salesman, who would then pass it over to the white saleswoman after he had 'cleaned' it. People entering the shop were sprayed with fly repellent pesticide. The whole practice infuriated me and, coming from abroad where I had not seen such disgusting behaviour, I just snapped.[53]

David Ausiku believes that it was his confrontation with the white saleswoman at the Rundu SWANLA shop in June 1966 that eventually led to the end of segregated selling points for blacks and whites and to the eventual removal of the white saleswoman from Rundu. He explains:

> At this time the shop in Rundu was using segregation system and it was the only shop to go to. There was a rope dividing it into "Europeans-this side", "Africans that-side". One day in June 1966, I went into this shop but stood on the European's side. The S.W.A.N.L.A. shop owner's wife told me to go to the other side of my kind. I told her, "You can do this in South Africa, but not here in Kavango. If you want to do this, take your shop to South Africa. This is Bantu-Homeland. The law says we can do what we want here in our own land and not what you want to do to us. We can even make our own laws." I told her, "I will talk to the Commissioner about this too. I will tell him to fire you from Kavangoland and I will write to your S.W.A.N.L.A. boss to kick you out from your S.W.A.N.L.A. job." All my kind in the shop stood stunned at my boldness for challenging a so-called "Whiteman's wife." I continued quarrelling

---

[53] H. Shityuwete. (1990), *Never follow the wolf, the autobiography of a Namibian freedom fighter.* Kliptown Books, London, pp. 120–121.

with her and threatened to report her to her boss in Grootfontein which I later did. I wrote a letter to that effect. Not long afterwards, the ropes in the shop at Rundu and Ondangua in Ovamboland were removed. Later, when I was working on the road construction, I heard the woman who quarrelled with me in the SWANLA shop had been removed from Rundu.[54]

The Rundu SWANLA shop also became the scene of physical assaults such as was the case when Dr. Kampungu, a black Catholic priest became violent and assaulted a white person for using bad words on him. Diescho[55] explains Dr. Kampungu's source of dissatisfaction and resentment:

> I have kept all the correspondences of Dr. Romanus Kampungu to the pope in Rome. This man was in great pain. His pain came not only from the white missionaries but also from us who did not lift him up. Dr. Kampungu would march up and down the streets of Rundu with his groceries but we did not understand him, and he became so frustrated. Dr. Kampungu use to drive a car to go and buy groceries from the only shop in Rundu. At one such occasion he went to this shop and one white man pronounced some words that were offensive to Dr. Kampungu and Kampungu broke his arm. Dr. Kampungu's frustrations later on translated into anger and we are to blame for that.[56]

Although an event such as the one of Dr. Kampungu could be regarded as more personal than politically oriented, to the local people it was political and it forms part of their memory of local examples of resistance towards colonial discriminatory practices at institutions that served the well-functioning process of the contract labour system in the Kavango.

At the tribal meetings that were held by the Native Commissioner in the Kavango since the 1960s, complaints were brought forward against SWANLA.[57] People complained that the contracts were not good as the wages were too low, that labourers were mistreated and that those labourers who tried to escape were captured and jailed.[58] They detested the fact that SWANLA chose the place of employment for the labourers and that a labourer who questioned his employment destination at Grootfontein recruiting depot was usually beaten

---

[54] Ausiku. (2005), My life stories: Is this God's work or Satan's scheme? pp. 77–78.
[55] Professor Joseph Brian Diescho is a Namibian academic and political analyst born at Andara village in the Kavango and works for UNISA in Pretoria, South Africa. He completed his standard ten at Rundu secondary school in 1975 and went to study at Fort Hare, South-Africa. He later studied in Germany and USA where he got his PhD in Politics and another in literature. He held a public lecture in Rundu in 2006 at the invitation of Rundu secondary history club.
[56] See K.M. Likuwa. (2006-10-27), Report on a public lecture on potential economic development for the Kavango Rundu Secondary Library, p. 6.
[57] Native Commissioner. (1965-10-27), Klagtes oor SWANLA: stamvergaderings, Okavango. Windhoek, NAN, SWAA 1/1/46, 2426, A521/26.
[58] *Ibid.*

up by the SWANLA police. They were unhappy at SWANLA selling them and of the fact that SWANLA was only interested in making huge profits of the people. The people in Kavango asserted that SWANLA arrived in the Kavango a poor company, accumulated its wealth from the local people and was now becoming deliberately forgetful of the source of its accumulated wealth. This was summed up by hompa Sivhute of the vaKwangali ethnic group at a tribal meeting held in 1965:

> We are very unhappy! Why does SWANLA not thank us? When SWANLA first came to the Kavango, it started with one old ugly small truck. And then it set up one of its ugly buildings, but now it has built up so many buildings and has many big trucks. But now they are not thinking as to where their money came from? Just look: our grandfathers, uncles, and even our own fathers' money have finished on SWANLA and up to now we are still adding on to our forefathers' money. But now we are seen and regarded by SWANLA like dogs or things. What has made them satisfied now, why then are they not telling us that they are satisfied?[59]

The increasing complaints against SWANLA by the contract labourers and their families were detrimental to the colonial state's ideas of continued political hold on Namibia and they feared that such anti-SWANLA feelings could create an explosive situation. As D.F. Maree, the commissioner for Kavango wrote to the administrator:

> SWANLA is in the Kavango with the approval of the state, if it is going to remain here and continue with its current unpopularity then it follows (from the natives' standpoint) that the state supports the actions of SWANLA. The very strong feelings against SWANLA can be a disadvantage to our political gains. The blacks of the Okavango [Kavango] are showing increasing identity awareness and any feelings that he is being regarded as an outsider in his own area can create an explosive situation. In the meantime, SWANLA, whose current activities are still profitable, should see to it that its relationship with the inhabitants of the area should be made healthy otherwise, we will have to take steps to speed up the process of its replacement.[60]

These anti-SWANLA feelings added to the colonial administration's action to speed up the process of replacing SWANLA with yet another form of labour recruitment. It therefore proposed in 1965 for Bantu Bellegings Korporasie (hereafter BBK) to take over SWANLA's trading interests in the Kavango and Ovambolands, and the recruitment of labourers became the direct responsibility of labour bureaus of the envisioned homeland governments of Ovambo by 1968 and of the Kavango by 1970.[61] BBK is directly translated as Bantu In-

---

[59] 'Hompa Shivute. (1965-10-01), To the Natives Affairs Commissioner. Windhoek, NAN, SWAA 1/1/46, 2426.
[60] D.F. Maree. (1965-10-01), To the administrator of the executive committee on SWANLA. Windhoek, NAN, SWAA1/1/46, 2426, A521/26.
[61] For more information see, letter titled 'SWANLA: aanbod deur die Bantu Bellegings Korporasie

vestment Corporation. It was a company that was established with the aim to develop and encourage black persons in the Bantu industrial areas and to provide development, finance and investment opportunities. It should be noted that, although the abolition of SWANLA and the introduction of labour bureaus in both Kavango and Ovamboland has normally been represented as evidence of the partial success of the strikes between December 1971 and January 1972,[62] the plans to dissolve SWANLA had already begun since the mid-1960s and SWANLA was theoretically dissolved by 1 December 1969.[63] The majority of the contract labourers, however, continued to see SWANLA intact and went on strike in December 1971 until January 1972 in which about 13000 workers are believed to have participated.[64]

When the strike began in Windhoek, a meeting was called in Walvis Bay, which was attended by the Chief Bantu Affairs Commissioner for SWA, Gert White, and a group of Ovambo headmen from the Ovambo Executive Council, the workers, and Bishop Leonard Auala in which they tried to discourage the contract labourers from the striking plan.[65] The presence of the Ovambo Executive Council but absence of the Kavango Executive Council at the Walvis Bay meeting are worth noting and speaks much to the colonial view of the centrality of the Ovambo contract labourers and the invisibility of the Kavango contract laboures in the strike. Some oral narratives indicate that the Bishop of the Evangelical Lutheran Ovambo Kavango Church (hereafter ELOC) had a meeting where he encouraged the contract labourers to solve their issue amicably with time rather than rush. Shikombero argues that the Bishop's words fell on deaf ears:

> The Bishop sent the message saying 'my children I would come to address you on the issue of why you want the contract system to be broken'. He was a black Bishop. And the Bishop was true to his words, he came and that day we did not go to work. The Bishop then said 'my children just calm down, I know contract labour system must stop but you must slow down and not rush'. He really spoke those words and we heard him speak them. But then the Ovambos were saying, 'no ways! Where does our money go which you use to purchase us? We do not get any money, we just come and work but we do not get money'. It was then that they said they have decided to break the contract system. They decided that they were going to strike on a particular date and that was true, they really went on strike.[66]

---

van Suid-Afrika beperk om handel belange oorteneem' (Windhoek, NAN, SWAA 1/1/46, 2426, A521/26).

[62] See M. Kooy. (1973), 'Contract labour system and the Ovambo crisis of 1971 in South West Africa', *African Studies Review*, (16) p. 102.

[63] Report number (66) N3/19/2 titled 'Ooreenkomstussenmnrenuwe SWANLA en die department Bantoe-administrasie en ontwikilling' (Windhoek, NAN, SWAA 1/1/46, 2426).

[64] G.M. Bauer. (1994), The labor movement and the prospect of democracy in Namibia, p. 39.

[65] *Ibid.* pp. 60–61.

[66] Mathias Shikombero interview. (2009-07-28), Rucara village.

[Makura Mubisofi kwakatumine liywi ashi 'vanuke nganiya ngani yamughambaghulite ashi vintje yitjokera kontraka'. Mubisofi vene wamutipu. Mara ghushiri ayire ogho Mubisofi, liyuva olyo kapi twayendire kuviruwana. Makura mpo arenkire ngoli mubisofi ashi anwe vana vande, kuworenu tupu, mara kontrakane ngayitundako vene mara kuworenu ngoli kapishi mpuku wande pya wangu nilye ashi kare vene mpopa mutokore vene ashi kontraka yitjoke, a-aa! Oyo nkango ne ayighambire vene atwe natwe kunakuyiyuvha. Mara vavo vavambo shine nan! um-um! Maliva ghetune kuni ghayendanga ogho mwatughuranga, kwato maliva atwe, kuyaruwana mara kwato maliva. Kontraka yitjoke vene! Mpo varenkire ngoli ashi atwene tunatokora, makura avatjanga shimbapira ashi muliyuva lya ngandi ku staka. Ngoli ushili kwa stakire vene].

There exist contestations over whether the 1971–72 strike was well planned or occurred spontaneously but some accept that it was influenced by SWAPO, especially the expelled secondary school SWAPO youths who became contract labourers in Walvis Bay and helped to mobilize the workers.[67] The oral narratives from the Kavango indicate that some contract labourers were responsible for writing letters to other mines to inform and request them to join the imminent strike. They show that, although the strike was mainly the idea of some Ovambo contract labourers, all contract labourers across ethnic groupings supported and participated in the strike. As Shikombero who worked in WalvisBay by the time of the strike indicated:

We began to demand in various places that the contract labour system should be broken down. Letters were sent to various compounds that on the 15th of December, contract labour system must stop. The Ovambos decided that contract labour system should be done away with and all of us including the Kavangos joined hands that contract labour system must stop because it was enslavement. People were asking where all the money goes that they were paid so little. So then they demanded that contract system be done away with so that labourers can be free to search for jobs of their own liking without being limited by contract.[68]

[Mpo twavarekire ngoli turongo natuntjeya ashi Kontraka ndi yitjoke ngoli. Kehe mukomboni kutjanga, kutjanga ashi pakukatika December, mayuva murongo namatano ashi kontraka yitjoke. Vavambo vanatokora ashi kontraka yitjoke yitundemo vene navantje navaKavango kupapakerera navantje ashi kontraka yitundemo vene. Ashi Ruhepo. Vyakurenka kutunda kunya ashi maliva ghenu ogho tunamutete ashi kuni mwaghatwaranga anwe ngoli mwatutetango? Vintje tukatambwiranga ngoli viponda vyakutika pa ngandi? Nkwandi kontraka ntjene ngoweyo nkwandi yitundepo. Nkwandi tukuyendawirange tupu vene ashi kuyenda kuno kuruwana kapishi vya kontraka nka ne ndi kwato vene].

The colonial administration reacted by sending striking workers home. Bauer elaborates:

---

[67] Bauer. (1994), The labor movement and the prospect of democracy in Namibia, p. 59.
[68] Mathias Shikombero interview. (2009-07-28), Rucara village.

As soon as the labor action began, striking workers were deported to the North, to Ovamboland. Special trains were arranged by South African Railways from December 16 from Walvis Bay and Windhoek to Grootfontein, from where other transport was provided. The trains were 'protected' by the South African police, although the striking workers were peaceful.[69]

Although Bauer shows that striking workers were sent to Ovamboland, there is no explanation as to what happened to the contract labourers from the Kavango. Shikombero's interview shows that all Kavango contract labourers were also sent to Ovamboland:

> Then they brought the trains. One trailer was for the blacks and another for the whites. All the labourers were led to the trains like someone herding cattle into a kraal and they were all filled into the trains so as to send them back since they have decided to go on strike. The black labourers were put inside and the whites on the train aimed to ensure that no one of the blacks escaped from the train. When the trains arrived in Grootfontein, the buses which were equally arranged in accordance to the number of all labourers were waiting. As soon as each train arrived, a bus drove nearer to it and all the labourers were immediately shifted into the buses and all were taken to Ovamboland. There was not a single one which was taken to Kavango. Some of them had to make their way from Ovamboland to the Kavango but others remained there in Ovamboland up to this day. Yes! No play! Where else do you think you would be taken since we were all punished for causing trouble? There was not a single bus that went to the Kavango.[70]

> [Makura aghaya mahina kuyimana weno. Shikoto shino shamukuwa, shikoto shino shamutipu. Varuwani kuvashinga yira vakungeneka ngombe, kuvatjokeda momo mbyevishi vanastaka sha ashi nkwendi vavyuke. Avavarondeke ngoli vatipu, vamakuwa vavo vakutakamita ashi nevishi vihenamo vitipu vimwe. Pakukatika mushivanda, dado besa vanamana kare kudirikanyita pa muvaro wovo vantu vanakutundo kuni ndi kuni. Kuya besa kuyayimika vene pepi namahina kurupuka tupu weno navantje kuvangeneka mubesa navantje vavatware ku Vambo. Kwato ogho varenkire ashi hawe ovene ghumuGciriku kayendenu ku Kavango, hawe! Navantje kwakatundilire ngoli nkoko kuVambo. Yii! Nan! Anwe munayita nka ghupote ashi muyende kuni? Kundereko besa dayendiro kuKavango].

The colonial administration's reaction to send all the striking workers, including the Kavango contract labourers, to Ovamboland contributed to the invisibility of the Kavango contract labourers in the strike and created a view that it was mainly the Ovambo contract labourers who were striking. Little is known about how some employers during the strike tried in vain to offer some of their labourers an increase in wage if they remained behind closed doors and did not join the strike and some oral narratives point to such actions.[71]

---

[69] Bauer. (1994), The labor movement and the prospect of democracy in Namibia, pp. 60–61.
[70] Mathias Shikombero interview. (2009-07-28), Rucara village.
[71] *Ibid.*

After the strike, Namibian labourers from both the Kavango and Ovambo continued to report to Grootfontein labour depot but under new agreements with respective homeland governments. The tribal employment bureaus which were established in both areas continued the responsibility to supply the work-seekers to employers in the police zone. Under these new labour arrangements, the director of community affairs was in charge of the new recruiting process and was assisted by labour officers who were responsible for the distribution of the work-seekers. The attesting and checking officer and African clerks dealt with contracts and records of the work-seekers. Very little changed under the new recruiting system and although labourers were now no longer bound to a contract, the features of the old system of low wages, the compound, separation of families and the restriction on mobility of the Africans remained intact and many labourers discovered that most things were the same if not worse.[72]

Conclusion

This chapter has shown that the contract labour system had both significant social and economic impact which eventually resulted in the political mobilization of workers against SWANLA and the contract labour system. The voices discernible from the life narratives of the contract labourers indicate their view that the contract labour system was evil and exploitative. Although there were some positive social, economic impacts these were largely overshadowed by negative impacts and many felt the rewards from the contract labour system were not worth the exploitation and the suffering they endured.

Some of the positive aspects are the acquisition of the clothes which were shared among family members and which was felt to produce a positive transformation. Other goods such as ploughs helped to plough larger fields while the purchasing of livestock from their wages helped some to accumulate wealth. The use of local transport by contract labourers to carry their loads meant the local businesspeople benefitted from the outcomes of the contract labour system. Some men used the contract labour system to purchase items to prepare for their eventual marriage and the construction of their new households. Despite all these, this chapter shows that the contract labour system did not enable labourers to gain long-lasting wealth as hoped and many of those who left home with great expectations ended up disappointed.

The contract labour system led to hatred of traditional dress muromba (skin dress) and imposition of money as an economic exchange in the place of mushanga (shells). It made

---

[72] J. Kane-Berman. (1972), *Contract labour in South West Africa* (Johannesburg, South African Institute of Race Relations), p. 7.

cash more important than older forms of economic exchange such as mushanga (shells). It also had impact on the way marriages were concluded. While in the past, the men who wanted a woman to marry had to stay in the homestead of the parents of the woman to be observed before he was given his wife, this changed and a young man had to provide presents derived from contract work to his parent in-law to promote a good image and to be given his wife. Women had to endure the family hardships to fill the vacuum left by the men and also faced contracting diseases from returning husbands, or at times never saw their loved ones as they had died or settled permanently outside the Kavango. The long durations under the contract labour system led to the feeling of alienation from families and also to one's area of birth and many remained troubled by not being able to bring anything back for the expectant family members at home and therefore many were psychologically troubled by it.

Apart from suffering the humiliating experiences of the medical testing process, the hardship and dangers during the long travel to and from recruiting centres, some labourers wasted their wages upon return on alcohol. This also led to social breakdown as in the case of communities such as Mangarangandja. The cruel treatment and exploitation suffered created the feeling among some contract labourers that they experienced colonialism at its worst, more so than other Namibians. Instead of helping to bring an end to hardships the contract labour system was viewed as another form of colonial oppression due to its failure to uplift many contract labourers economically. Many contract labourers saw the very act of engaging in the contract labour system as an act of slavery practice which was never ending. The engagement in the contract labour system by the Kavango workers was therefore not seen by contract labourers as a progressive step in their lives so that the paradigm of exploitation and suppression remains the dominant one. The significant outcome of the economic and social impact of the contract labour system was that the frustration and the exploitation made contract labourers or workers become politically mobilized and in turn to mobilize their communities against SWANLA and the contract labour system. Workers believed that their ultimate strike brought an end to SWANLA. After the strike things did not change materially and some workers joined SWAPO in exile. There was the hope that only an independent Namibia would finally address their need to address ruhepo (poverty/hardship).

5 General Conclusions and Lessons

This book presented a study of oral narratives of former contract labourers from Kavango about their engagement under the contract labour system in Namibia. Its aim is to put into historical context our understanding of their current complaints about family hardships in post-colonial Namibia. In particular, the book sought to explore what light contract labourers shed on migration, their experiences with recruiting organizations and local recruiting agents, their living and working experiences and the impact of the contract labour system on them and their family life. The central aim was to investigate whether their engagement into the contract labour system was a progressive step in their lives, or did exploitation remain dominant.

Rather than simply repeating that many traditional chiefs after the colonial take over in Namibia became colonial puppets, this book argues that the traditional chiefs got caught up in a precarious situation between two competing colonial powers (South African and Portuguese) and eventually sided with the South African colonial administration for continued survival which entailed supporting the colonial labour extraction from their areas. The intention of the colonial administration to control the local population for labour purposes was clear through the South African negotiations with the Portuguese over the control of the Kavango population on the border, and the seduction of the Kavango traditional chiefs through provision of gifts and the payment of salaries etc.

Unlike the literature on Ovamboland where ecological conditions are emphasized as the main reason for labour migration and where the South African colonial administration arrived and and offered the Ovambo people an opportunity for labour migration as a means of family survival,[1] this book, from the onset, shows that colonial administration was central in the development of the contract labour system and labour migration. Although contract labourers personally decided to leave their homesteads for the recruiting centres, they did so because of the social and economic hardships that resulted from the activities of the colonial administration officials. The colonialists introduced clothes to the Kavango and later curtailed the supply of these through the Native Commissioner and his police who denied local access to clothes through laws against slave trade and game killing. These colonial restrictions left the Kavango with no option but to engage in the contract labour system with the hope of gaining wages to accumulate wealth and address ruhepo (poverty/hardship).

---

[1] See R. Moorsom. (1977), *Under development and labour migration: the contract labour system in Namibia*, pp. 19–20.

Unlike the literature on Ovamboland which indicates that people and their kings embraced the labour migration system and made the best use out of it, the oral interviews from the Kavango indicate that the contract labour system was not embraced but engaged in under compelling social and economic hardship caused by colonialism.

While in Ovamboland, for example, the impact of slave trading and raiding and later ecological disasters played a central role in the underdevelopment of Ovamboland and resulted in impoverishment and the eventual labour migration, this did not have similar results in the Kavango. In the Kavango, despite the similar slave trading and raiding and the ecological problems since the 1890s to the early South African period, evidence shows people were able to find local means to survive without centrally resorting to labour migration. In Ovamboland, more labour migrants were forthcoming from the earliest period of the colonial rule partly due to the early permanent presence of missionaries and colonial officials while in the Kavango these came very late and, therefore, it became hard to get similar results. Unlike Ovamboland, in the Kavango, the lack of clothing was a central factor for labour migration and this factor is part of what Kavango people regarded as "ruhepo"; this however, should always be explained in the historical context of the impact that the colonial restrictive measures had on them.

The colonial officials believed that the availability of food played a crucial role in the labour migration. In this book I argue that the key reason for migration was the contract labourers' economic and social hardship and the belief that the white employers owned the wealth and that Africans could get some of it by working on contract. I show that before the formalization of the contract labour system in 1925, the contract labourer shaped labour recruitment and distribution through, for example, the 1923 protest which saw the distribution of Kavango contract labourers only to the northern farms and mines according to their wishes. The colonial view of the people from the Kavango and Ovamboland as lazy and unwilling to work was used to justify the brutal colonial actions that compelled the local people to leave their home for contract work and was seen as instilling a culture of labour in them.

This book provides information about the actions of contract labourers to avoid dangers on their journey, especially the attacks by the San. They, for example, provided dagga to the San to put them to sleep. It shows the pressure workers put on the labour escorts to protect them, for-example, by mocking them through songs on traditional flutes. The book points to how during their migration journeys, the workers realized the co-operation among colonial officials, the labour recruiting organizations and employers in their exploitation causing their original hope and aspiration of wealth accumulation fade away. Their experiences on farms and mines extended both outside and inside Namibia. Their primary experience was of low pay and bad living and working conditions. This academic work has shown that the term "Ovambo" was used by colonial officials in the police zone to refer to contract labourers from the Kavango and at times the statistics for contract labourers from the Kavango were conflated with those from Ovamboland. This has led to a silencing of the place of Kavango workers in the contract labour system and points to the need for a careful reading of colonial sources.

Contract labourers use the words "people" or "vakakontraka" (the contracted ones) to refer to themselves, which emphasize their assertion as people with human emotions under contract. They viewed their recruitment at Grootfontein depot as a sale to needy employers. Oral histories point to how workers gave their employers new names which they used among themselves. On the farms, given the gender relations they were accustomed to, the role of the "missis" assumed a significant part of their experience.

The working and living experiences of workers can be understood better when placed in their historical context of home as many related or differentiated their experiences at work such as milking cows, respect for the employers to the early milking of the cattle and the respect for the elderly at home. Many contract labourers were willing to speak about the suffering of others rather than their own. There were narrative strategies to maintain their own sense of dignity and self-worth, for example, different appropriations of meanings to terms such as "boy" which was commonly used on the South African mines. While the employers, for example, used "boy" to infantilize the African, to the workers the term meant "black person" and they were, therefore, able to accept it. Although the mine managements in South Africa stripped the African workers to search for diamond thefts, the workers from the Kavango show that on the goldfields of Johannesburg this was done not only during the medical examination of workers but also during the wage paying process and some workers like George Mukoya Weka believed that this was the culture of the South African mines. Various work control measures such as the ticket system, which discouraged loafing and late-coming and linked the day's work to daily food rations, indicate that the mines were eager to control the worker's time to maximize profit. Similarly, the clock time system which came in the form of bells or whistle blowing at work sites was meant to inculcate into workers the western notion that "time is money".

In Namibia, contract labourers from the Kavango and Ovamboland, in general, had good inter-ethnic relations although there was room for personal differences. Personal differences arose when, for example, one labourer was paid more than another or was favoured by the employer above the others. Although the literature speaks of the contract labourers being despised by the residents of the African locations such as Windhoek in the police zone, this was not the case everywhere. There were good social relationships between contract labourers and the residents of the African location at some times and places. For example, in the Windhoek and Walvis Bay areas, contract labourers visited the African locations for alcohol consumption, and were received positively by residents as long as they were not troublesome.

The central view about the impact was that there were but few benefits under the contract labour system but that such benefits were not worth the suffering and exploitation workers endured. Some managed to purchase clothes for themselves and their families. They also purchased horses in the police zone, which they exchanged for a lot of cattle in the Kavango and became wealthy cattle owners. But this wealth was not long lasting as many squandered it on the purchase of alcohol from the Portuguese and still ended up poor. The high consumption of alcohol by contract labourers upon their return led to social break down of the areas in their communities, such as was the case of Mangarangandja in Rundu, which had turned from a once peaceful area to one of violence by the early 1970s. The contract labour system seemed to have stimulated the local economy. Local businessmen provided transportation to returning labourers at exorbitant prices. Although the contract labourers received low wages and knew that they would never receive high wages, they continued to enlist for contract work because of their unresolved economic and social hardships.

The general feeling is that contract labourers engaged in a defeating activity which they similarly related to a local proverb about the wild-fruit collection. Although many chose to leave for contract work and traversed many dangerous pathways with the hope of collecting a lot of money to address the social and economic hardships, many became disappointed with the little rewards, which were non-lasting solutions to their problems, and the realization of their entrapment under the contract system; these frustrations eventually led to their political mobilization.

Contract labourers across ethnic divides listened to and supported OPO and later SWAPO leaders who mobilized among them because they realized the failure of the contract system to address their economic and social hardships. The contract labourers believed that they, in comparison to other Namibians, experienced colonial exploitation at its worst under the contract labour system and this explains their support for the armed liberation struggle for Namibia. This book shows that the political mobilization by workers had an impact on the Kavango itself and led to disenchantment and rebellion against SWANLA and its institutions. While there is a general belief that the workers' strike of 1971 to 1972 led to the end of SWANLA, this book shows that plans to disband SWANLA began in the mid 1960s and that SWANLA was actually theoretically disbanded in 1969. The book calls into question the 1971–72 workers' strike as an "Ovambo strike". It included contract labourers from the Kavango and Angola. The invisibility of the Kavango was not only due to their smaller numbers but was also a result of the colonial authorities' action to transport all the Kavango contract labourers to Ovamboland which created the public view that the strike was an "Ovambo" activity.

Some contract labourers such as Mathias Ndumba Shikombero never returned to work after the 1972 strike and continued to make a living by fishing along the Kavango River. Others believed that only a Namibian led government after independence would address their social and economic hardships and, therefore, supported or joined the armed liberation struggle by SWAPO in exile. In the Kavango the "Muzogumwe" (one move) political party was formed by 1973 with David Ausiku, a former contract labourer, as its president. Its first meeting was held at Sauyemwa village on 31 May 1973 where more than fifty people signed up as members and another two hundred signed up as supporters. "Muzogumwe" acted as a "false front" [pseudonym] for SWAPO in the Kavango. It operated by creating a false impression that it was anti-SWAPO and communism. It held meetings in secret and recruited more members for SWAPO, provided food and other supplies to PLAN combatants until it later leaked out that "muzogumwe" was SWAPO and its leader was arrested and brutalized.[2] But "Muzogumwe" members in the Kavango continued to play the central role in providing support to SWAPO combatants throughout the 1970s and the 1980s.

Namibia got its independence on 21 March 1990. However, two decades after independence the former contract labourers still complain of family hardships and of the continued labour recruiting from the Kavango to the farms (especially the charcoal producing farms) in the former police zone. The Kavango people (this time both men and women) said they continued to go and work on those farms because of poverty and that there are few opportunities locally to earn money.[3] All recruitment to the Namibian farms after independence is done illegally as they are not sanctioned by the government. Individual white farmers continue to send their black workers by truck to convince the local people to work on their farms without the permission of the traditional chief or the village headmen.[4] On the other hand, some former contract labourers, like Mathias Ndumba Shikombero, complain of the new river conservation measures by the Namibian government, which he says are detrimental to his previous main source of income as in the past he could freely catch as much fish and sell these for an income.

I argued that our understanding of the contract labour system can be enhanced through the focus on oral narratives as these personalize the contract workers' voices about their

---

[2]   Ausiku. (2005), My life stories: is this God's work or Satan's scheme? pp. 85–88.
[3]   Bernhard L. Linyando interview. (2009-07-27), Ndiyona.
[4]   *Ibid.*

experiences helping us understand their feelings, dreams, hopes, aspirations and interpersonal relationships. One limitation of the research, however, is that I draw only on male narratives to understand the impact of the contract labour system on women. Although I was able to discern from these labour narratives some of the impact on Kavango women, future research is needed to prioritise women's voices about their experiences of colonialism. Apart from the need for further research on women in the Kavango, the early methods of political mobilization for SWAPO in the Kavango through "Muzogumwe" require further study. This might lead to a better understanding of memorialisation and heritage projects in present day Kavango. It certainly calls into question public perceptions as to who are puppets and heroes as well as acess to rewards for war veterans. There is a need for future research on post-colonial labour recruitment from the Kavango to the charcoal and grape farms in central and southern Namibia which, as the oral narratives indicate, continues.

Some of the lessons can be discerned from the voices of contract labourers for post-colonial Namibia such as that the ruhepo (poverty/hardship) of workers and their families results not just from ecological factors (lack of rain and recurrent drought or animal diseases), but also from political factors (the control and denial over access and distribution of the local resources by the political authorities).

The post-colonial migration of opportunity seekers from former Kavango and Ovambo lands are partly a result of colonial underdevelopment of these areas and fewer opportunities for access and distribution of local resources, which compel many to migrate in the hope of acquiring these opportunities in order to accumulate wealth and address their problems.

The narratives of the experiences of contract labourers provide a lesson that when an existing economic setup such as the contract labour system became oppressive rather than providing a solution to the workers' problems of wealth creation and ending "ruhepo", contract labourers began to mobilise politically to overthrow the colonial system. Therefore, when considering the post-colonial narratives that Namibians must still wage the struggle for economic independence, the migrant workers in post-colonial Namibia must learn to establish viable political partnerships that work to end their suppression and exploitation and instead help them create wealth and end their "ruhepo." It therefore remains a task for future research to compare and contrast the past struggle of workers to the present and analyse what economic reforms have taken place for the workers in Namibia's post-colonial economy and how far such economic reforms remain useful or are detrimental to the workers' struggle.

Bibliography

Private manuscripts

Ausiku, D, K. (2005), My own life stories: is this God's work or Satan's scheme? Unpublished manuscript, Canada, copyright no. ISBN 0-1038934.

National Archives of Namibia (NAN), Windhoek

ADM 30, file 243/3, f1, 'The German Imperial Gazette' No. 168, 21 July 1887.

ADM 30, file 243/3, part 2, the administrator of SWA to the Minister of Defense in Pretoria, 'Administration of the Okavango area: SWA Protectorate', 16 November 1917.

ADM 30, file 243/3, Part II, 'letter from Col. Jose Carregado Vianna to the military magistrate of Grootfontein', 10 December 1917.

ADM 30, file 243/3, Part II, letter from Brownlee, F. 'Patrols to Nkurenkuru', 26 January 1918.

ADM 30, file 243/3, part II, letter from Brownlee, F. 'Resume of arrangements concluded between the Commandant Fort Cuangar and the Military Magistrate Grootfontein district', 27 September 1917.

ADM 30, file 243/3, part II, SWA administrator to minister of defense, 'administration of Okavango area: S.W.A protectorate', 16 November 1917.

ADM 30, file 243/3, part III, Dickman, R., to the Native Commissioner of South West Africa, 'labour: Okavango district', 1 December 1923.

ADM 30, file 243/3, part III, letter from Brownlee, F. 'Patrol to Nkurenkuru', 16 January 1917.

ADM 30, file 243/3, part III, Secretary of South West Africa to the military Magistrate of Grootfontein titled 'Re: Okavango matters', 27 June 1919.

ADM 30, file 243/3, part III, Secretary of South West Africa to the superintendent for native affairs at Nkurenkuru 'Recruiting of native labour', 11 March 1921.

ADM30, file 243/3, part II LTNT Col. 'Jose Carregado Vianna to the military magistrate of Grootfontein', 10 December 1917.

ADM30, file 243/3, part II, letter from Brownlee, F. 'Statements under oath' 24 April1918.

ADM 95, file 2794/8, 'Grootfontein annual report Number 3370', 29 January 1917.

ADM 95, file 2794/8, letter from Brownlee, F. 'Ovamboland labourers from Okavango', 21 May 1917.

ADM 95, file 2794/8, letter from Brownlee, F. 'Ovamboland labourers from Okavango', 11 March 1918.

ADM 95, file no 2794/8, acting military magistrate, 'Ovambo land labourers from Okavango', 20 June 1917.

AKA 552, N1/15, 6-2, 'Labour recruitments, 1938–1940'.

JX/0220, the Native Commissioner 'The Union of South Africa report', 1919.

JX/0220, 'The Union of South Africa report', 1921.

JX/0220, 'The Union of South Africa report', 1923.

JX/0220, 'The union of South Africa report', 1924.

JX/ 0220, 'The union of South Africa report', 1925.

JX/0220, The Administrator, 'The Union of S.A Annual report', 1935.

K.A 12233, file FXIII B4, storage unit 1009, 'Manuscript, Geographische u ethnographische forschungen Caprivi zipfel u Okavango gebiet', October 1902–1906.

LGR 3/3/4, file N3/13/2, 'Vervoer van Ekstra Territoriale en Noordelikke Bantoes tussen Grootfontein en Runtu en tussen Runtu & Katwitwi', 7 March 1960.

MTS 9, N1/18, Speir, C. J. (town engineer), 'Report on trip to Grootfontein to inspect the single quarters', 23 October 1970.

NAR 1/1/55, 11/7, Native recruiters for the Okavango [Kavango] area, 4 February 1937.

NAR 1/1/55, 13/1/1, The Native Commissioner to District surgeon of Runtu, 'Classification of recruits, SWANLA and WENELA', 28 March 1947.

NAR 1/1/55, file 11/1/2, 'Declaration by Langhans Kanyinga', 2 January 1936.

NAR 1/1/55, file 11/1/2, 'Illegal recruiting, administrator to the managing secretary of NLO' 14 December 1935.

NAR 1/1/55, file 11/7, 4 February 1937 'Native recruiters: Okavango recruiters'.

NAR 1/1/55, file N4/3/2, 'The Chief Native Commissioner in Windhoek to the Assistant Native Commissioner of Rundu', 23 January 1938.

NAR 1/1/55, group 11, file 20. 'Unregistered correspondence 1962–67'.

NAR 1/1/55. A579/1, the Native Commissioner, Okavango to the Chief native Commissioner in Windhoek, 'monthly reports for January and February 1952', 24 March 1952.

NAR1/1/55, 11/7. 'Native recruiter, Sambio [Sambyu] area'.

NAR1/1/55, file 11/1/2, 'NLO managing secretary to the secretary for South West Africa', 28 November 1935.

NAT 1/1/54, S/U14, file 13, 26 Forsyth, D. D. 'Recommendations of Farm Labour Commission', February 1940.

NAT 1/1/54, S/U-20, file 25, 'Circular on Control of Extra- Territorial and Northern Natives', 8 January 1936.

NAT, 1/1/54, S/U-14, file 13, The Native Commissioner of Windhoek, 'Recommendations of Farm Labour Commission', 26 February 1940.

SWAA 1/1/46, 2426, 'Hompa Shivute to the Natives Affairs Commissioner', 1 October 1965.

SWAA 1/1/46, 2426, 521/26, V.5, 'Suggested revision of agreement between NLO and SLO for the recruitment in Ovambo land and the Kavango'.

SWAA 1/1/46, 2426, A 521/26, Native commissioner, 'native labour on Mines: hours worked underground: over time: Sunday labour', 15 September 1950.

SWAA 1/1/46, 2426, A521/26, V.6, 'the Native Commissioner of Rundu to Chief Native Commissioner in Windhoek', 11 June 1945.

SWAA 1/1/46, 2426, A521/26, 'Circular letter to agents of SWANLA', 16 October 1950.

SWAA 1/1/46, 2426, A521/26, Native Commissioner, 'Klagtes oor SWANLA: stamvergaderings, Okavango', 27 October 1965.

SWAA 1/1/46, 2426, A521/26, V.5, 'Amalgamation: Northern Labour Organization Limited and Luderitz Chamber of Mines recruiting', 24 November 1942.

SWAA 1/1/46, 2426, A521/26, V.5, 'Rest camps on the Okavango River', 28 June 1944.

SWAA 1/1/46, 2426, A521/26, V.5, 'The draft constitution of SWANLA', 24 November 1942.

SWAA 1/1/46, 2426, A521/26. 'SWANLA: aanboddeur die Bantu BellegingsKorporasie van Suid-Afrika beperkomhandelbelangeoorteneem'.

SWAA 1/1/46, 2426, Report number (66) N3/19/2, 'Ooreenkomstussenmnrenuwe SWANLA en die department Bantoe-administrasie en ontwikilling'.

SWAA 1/1/46, A521/26, 'the secretary for native affairs to the secretary for South West Africa', 20 September 1950.

SWAA 1852 File 2/16/3/6, 'Meetings with Chiefs and headmen, Annual meeting held at Runtu on 03 January 1952 to 05 January 1952'.

SWAA 2387, A519/1. Native Commissioner, 'Northern Territories: Okavango Natives described as Ovambos', 16 February 1955.

SWAA 2397, file A521/2, the Administrator report, 'Returning labourers- complaints, Kativitji, pass No. 370/28', 5 May 1928.

SWAA 2407, file a521/10, Deputy Commissioner of South West Africa Police to the secretary for the protectorate 'native labour supply from Okavango', 29 January 1917.

SWAA 2407/ file A521/10, 'Luderitzbucht Chamber of Mines re: nativesfrom the Okavango', 7 August1920.

SWAA 2407, file no. A521/10, letter from Sgd. M Otzen to the inspector of mines, 23 February 1924.

SWAA 2407, file no. A 521/10, Secretary of South West Africa to the administrator of S.W.A, 'Native labour recruitment-Okavango natives', 2 July 1926.

SWAA 2408, file F/521/11, Secretary for South West Africa to the secretary for Luderitz Chamber of Mines, 'investigation of native Labour resources: Okavango', 31 March 1924.

SWAA 2408, file F/521/11, the general manager of Luderitzbucht to the secretary of South West Africa, 'Re: native labour', 27 November 1924.

SWAA 2412, A521/13/3, letter from Rossouw, A. J. 'Farm Labour commission', 30 August 1939.

SWAA 2423, A521/26, 'S.W.A Administrator to W.N.L.A district manager at Francis town', 3 October 1950.

SWAA 2426, A521/10, the SWANLA Manager of Grootfontein to the Chief Native Commissioner in Windhoek 'medical examinations of recruits at Runtu', 8 April 1953.

SWAA 2434, A521/30/4, the inspector of mines, 'Compound regulations, Otavi mine native compound', 25 May 1939.

SWAA 2434, A521/31/ v.2, Assistant Native Commissioner Hartman, 'Disturbance of Ovambo labourers at Orange River Mouth', 14 September 1931.

SWAA A521/8/2/2404, letter from Courtney-Clarke, C. G. 'The 1927 to 1939 statistics for the recruitment of Ovambo/Kavango migrant workers and 'Angolans' to South Africa', 2 October 1941.

SWAA1/1/46, 2426, A521/26.Maree, D. F., to the administrator of the executive committee on SWANLA.

X0220, 'The Union of South Africa report on labour recruitments', 1924, 1925 & 1926.

Interviews by Kletus Muhena Likuwa in the Kavango

Kamenye Ludwig (Lishuro), Kudumo, (born ca.1938), Kangweru village, August 2009.

Kamwanga Susana Mate (born 15 October 1915), Guma village, 11 August 2009.

Karenga Shintango (born ca.1934), Korokoko village, 5 August 2009.

Katjire Ngonga (born ca.1936), Diheke village, 21 August 2009.

Katota Bartholomeus Someno (born ca.1932), Mabushe village, 12 August 2009.

Kavengere Mutero (born ca.1938), Bagani village, 9 July 2008.

Kudumo K. Frans (born ca.1948), Sharughanda village, 30 July 2009.

Kupembona Theodor (born ca.1932), Guma village, 6 June 2001.

Likuwa Kamenye (born ca.1943), Kangweru village, 13 August 2009.

Linyando Bernhard Lipayi (born 1936), Ndiyona village, 27 July 2009.

Maghundu Martin (born ca.1942), Divundu village, 19 August 2009.

Matamu (born ca.1919), Rundu town, 12 July 2009.

Mberekera (born ca.1934), Kambowo village, 20 January 2007.

Mbote Konrad (born ca.1941), Thirume village, 21 August 2009.

Merecky Nyambe (born 04 August 1936), Shipando village, 6 August 2009.

Muhero Kapinga (born ca.1942), Kamutjonga village, 19 August 2009.

Mukoya Anselm Likuwa (born ca.1942), Ndiyona village, 4 August 2009.

Ndara Mbamba Djami (born ca.1926), Divundu village, 19 August 2009.

Ronginius (born ca.1943), Nambi village, 12 July 2009.

Shampapi Benhard Limbangu (born 24 August 1946), Rucara village, 28 July 2009.

Shevekwa Frans Tuhemwe (born18 August 1946), Sharughanda village, 30 July 2009.

Shihungu Shindimba Ndumba (born 1932), Shipando village, 6 August 2009.

Shikombero Mathias Ndumba (born 4 August 1933), Rucara village, 28 July 2009.

Shirengumuke Ndumba (born 1921), Hoha village, 3 July 2009.

Shiviru Shandini (born ca.1943), Ndiyona village, 15 August 2009.

Unengu Muyenga Shintunga (born ca.1915), Rucara village, 31 July 2009.

WaNkayira Shikiri (born ca.1918), Ndonga linena village, 8 August 2009.

Weka Kandjeke (born 1946), Rucara village, 28 July 2009.

Weka George Mukoya (Shamandimbe) (born 1926), Rucara village, 29 July 2009.

Weka Theresia Shidona (born 14 May 1914), Guma village 15 June 2003.

Government publications

Kohler, O. (1958), *A study of Karibib district, South West Africa* (Pretoria, Department of Native Affairs).

Books

Akuupa, M. U. (2015), *National Culture in Post-Apartheid Namibia: State-Sponsored Cultural Festivals and their Histories.* Basel, Basler Afrika Bibliographien.

Beris, A. P. J. (1996), *From Mission to Local Church: One hundred Years of Mission by the Catholic Church in Namibia.* Windhoek, Catholic Church.

Bhagavan, M. R. (1986), *Angola's political economy, 1975–1985.* Uppsala, Scandinavian Institute of African Studies.

Bierfert, A. (1938), *25 Jahre bei den Wadiriku am Okawango.* Hünfeld: Verlag der Oblaten.

Bozzoli, B. (1991), *Women of Phokeng, Consciousness, Life Strategy and Migrancy in South Africa, 1900–1983.* Johannesburg, Ravan Press.

Breytenbach, W. J. (1972), *Migratory Labour Arrangements in Southern Africa.* Pretoria, Africa Institute of South Africa.

Brinkman, I. (2005), *A War for People: Civilians, Mobility, and Legitimacy in South-East Angola during the MPLA's War for Independence.* Cologne, Rüdiger Köppe.

Brinkman, I. (2009), *Angolan Refugees in Namibia: Remembering Home and Forced Removals.* New York, Springer

Burton, A. (ed.) (2005), *Archive Stories. Facts, Fictions and the Writing of History.* Durham, Duke University Press.

Chadwick, B. A.; Bahr, H. M.; Albrecht, S. L. (1984), *Social Science Research Methods.* Upper Saddle River, Prentice Hall

Clarence-Smith, W. G. (1979), *Slaves, Peasants and Capitalists in Southern Angola, 1840–1926.* London, Cambridge University Press.

Cronje, Gillian and Susanne (1979), *The Workers of Namibia.* London, International Defence and Aid Fund for Southern Africa.

Crush, J. et al. (1991), *South Africa's Labor Empire, a History of Black Migrancy to the Gold Mines.* Boulder, Westview Press.

Duffy, F. (1961), *Portuguese Africa.* London, Oxford University Press.

Emmet, T. (1999), *Popular Resistance and the Roots of Nationalism in Namibia, 1915–1966.* Basel, P. Schlettwein Publishing.

Field, S. (ed.) (2007), *Imagining the City: Memories and Cultures in Cape Town.* Cape Town, HSRC Press.

Fisch, M. (1994), *Die Kavangojäger im Nordosten Namibias.* Windhoek, Scientific Society.

First, R. (1963), *South West Africa.* Middlesex, Penguin Books.

Gibson, D. G.; Larson, T. J.; McGurk, C. R. (1981), *The Kavango Peoples.* Wiesbaden, Steiner Verlag.

Goldblatt, I. (1971), *History of South-West Africa from the Beginning of the Nineteenth Century.* Cape Town, Juta & Company.

Gordon, R. J. (1977), *Mines, Masters and Migrants: Life in a Namibian Compound.* Johannesburg, Ravan Press.

Hamilton, C. et al. (2002), *Refiguring the Archive.* Cape Town, David Phillip.

Harries, P. (1994), *Work, Culture and Identity: Migrant Labourers in Mozambique and South Africa, c. 1860–1910.* Johannesburg, Witwatersrand University Press.

Hayes, P. et al. (eds.) (1998), *Namibia under South African Rule, Mobility & Containment 1915–1946.* Oxford, James Currey.

Heninge, D. (1982), *Oral Historiography.* London, Longman.

Hishongwa, N. (1992), *The Contract Labour System and its Effects on Family and Social Life in Namibia.* Windhoek, Gamsberg Macmillan.

Hofmeyr, R. (1993), *We spend our years as a tale that is told: Oral Historical Narratives in a South African Chiefdom.* London, James Currey.

Hunke, H. (1996), *Church and state, the political context of 100 years of Catholic mission in Namibia.* Windhoek, Roman Catholic Church.

IDAF (1987), *Working Under South African Occupation. Labour in Namibia.* London, Canon Collins.

James, W. G. (1992), *Our Precious Metal. African Labour in South Africa's Gold Industry, 1870–1990*. Cape Town, David Phillip.

Jeeves, A. H. (1985), *Migrant Labour in South Africa's Mining Economy: The Struggle for the Gold Mines' Labour Supply 1890–1920*. Johannesburg, Witwatersrand University Press.

Kane Berman, J. (1972), *Contract labour in South West Africa*. Johannesburg, South African Institute of Race Relations.

Kanyinga, A. H. (2002), *Liparu mu Sancana*. Windhoek, Gamsberg Macmillan.

Lau, B. (ed.) (1991), *An Investigation of the Shooting at the Old Location on 10 December 1959*. Windhoek, Academy Printing Department.

Magadla, T.; Voltz, C. (2006), *Words of the Batswana, Letters of Mahoko a Becwana, 1883–1896*. Cape Town, Van Riebeeck Society.

Miller, L. (2000), *Researching Life Stories and Family Histories*. London, SAGE publication.

Moorsom, R. (1997), *Under development and labour migration: the contract labour system in Namibia*. Bergen, Chr. Michelsen Institute.

Moodie, D., with Ndatshe, V. (1994), *Going for Gold: Men, Mines, and Migration*. Johannesburg, Witwatersrand University Press.

Ndadi, V. H. (2009), *Breaking Contract: The Story of Helao Vinnia Ndadi*. Windhoek, AACRLS.

Ngavirue, N. (1997), *Political Parties and Interest Groups in South West Africa Namibia: A Study of a PluralSsociety*. Basel, P. Schlettwein Publishing.

Nujoma, S. (2001), *Where Others Wavered: The Autobiography of Sam Nujoma – my life in SWAPO and my participation in the liberation struggle of Namibia*. London, PANAF books.

Pendleton, W. C. (1974), *Katutura: A Place Where We Do Not Stay*. San Diego, San Diego State University Press.

Serton, P. (1954), *The Narrative and Journal of Gerald McKiernan in South West Africa, 1874–1879*. Cape Town, Van Riebeeck Society.

Shetyuwete, H. (1990), *Never Follow the Wolf: The Autobiography of a Namibian Freedom Fighter* London, Kliptown Books.

Siiskonen, H. (1990), *Trade and Socioeconomic Change in Ovamboland, 1850–1906*. Helsinki, SHS, 1990.

Stals, E. P. (ed.) (1990), *The Commissions of Palgrave, Special Emissary to South West Africa, 1876–1885*. Cape Town, Van Riebeeck Society, Second Series No. 21.

Turrel, R. V. (1987), *Capital and Labour on the Kimberley Diamond Fields, 1871–1890*. London, Cambridge.

Van Onselen, C. (1980), *Chibaro: African Mine Labour in Southern Africa Rhodesia, 1900–1933*. Johannesburg, Ravan Press.

Wallace, Marion (2002), *Health, power and politics in Windhoek, Namibia, 1915–1945*. Basel, P. Schlettwein Publishing.

Weyl, U. (1991), *Labour migration and underdevelopment in Malawi, late 19th century to mid 1970's*. University of Zimbabwe, Centre of Applied Social Science.

Williams, F. N. (1991), *Pre-colonial Communities of South Western Africa: a History of Owambo Kingdoms, 1600–1920.* Windhoek, National Archives of Namibia.

Ya-Otto, J. (1982), *Battlefront Namibia: An Autobiography.* London, Heinemann.

Yudelman, D. (1984), *The Emergence of modern South Africa.* Cape Town, David Phillip.

Articles, journals and chapters in books

Beachey, R.W. (1962), The Arms Trade in Africa in the Late Nineteenth Century, *The Journal of African History*, 3 (3): 451–467.

Becker, H. (2010), A Concise History of Gender, "Tradition" and the State in Namibia.' In C. Keulder (ed.), *State, Society and Democracy: A Reader in Namibian Politics.* Windhoek, Konrad Adenauer Stiftung, 171–200.

Brinkman, I. (1999), Violence, Exile and Ethnicity: Nyemba Refugees in Kaisosi and Kehemu, Rundu, Namibia, *Journal of Southern African Studies*, 25 (3): 417–439.

Budack, K. F. R. (1976), The Kavango: The Country, Its People and History', Namib und Meer, Band 7: 29–43.

Cooper, F. (1992), Colonizing time: Work rhythms and labor conflict in colonial Mombasa. In N. Dirks (ed.), *Colonialism and culture.* AnnArbor, University of Michigan.209-245.

Cooper, A. D. (1999), The Institutionalization of Contract Labour in Namibia. *Journal of Southern Africa Studies*, 25(1): 121–138.

Dhupelia-Mesthrie, U., Dispossession and memory: The black river community of Cape Town. *The Journal of the Oral History Society*, 28, (2) 2000: 35–43.

Eckl, A. (2007), Reports from beyond the line: the accumulation of knowledge of Kavango and its people by the German colonial administration, 1891–1911. *Journal of Namibian Studies*, 1: 7–37.

Field, S. (2001), Remembering Experience, Interpreting Memory: Life Stories from Windermere. *Journal of African Studies*, 60(1): 119–133.

Fisch, M. (1983), Der Kriegszug der Tawana zum Kavango. *Namibiana*, 4(2): 43–71.

Fisch, M. (1994) Die Kavangojäger in Nordosten Namibias. Jagdmethoden, religiös-magische Praktiken, Lieder und Preisgedichte. Windhoek. *Namibiana*, 5 (1):105–169.

Gewald, J.-B. (2003), Near Death in the Streets of Karibib: Famine, Migrant Labour and the Coming of Ovambo to Central Namibia. *Journal of African Studies*, 44: 211–239.

Gibbons, A.S.T. (1901), Explorations in Marotseland and Neighbouring Regions, *Geographical Journal.* 17(2): 106–134.

Gordon, R.J. (1993), The Impact of the Second World War on Namibia. *Journal of Southern African Studies*, 19(1):147–165.

Hayes, P. (1996), 'Cocky' Hahn and the 'Black Venus': The Making of a Native Commissioner in South West Africa, 1915–46, *Gender and History*, 8(3): 364–392.

Kooy, M. (1973), The Contract Labour System and the Ovambo Crisis of 1971 in South West Africa. *African Studies Review*, 16: 83–105.

Kihato, C. W. (2007), Invisible lives, inaudible voices? The social conditions of migrant women in Johannesburg. In N. Gasa (ed.), *Women in South African History:They remove boulders and cross rivers.* Cape Town: HSRC press, 89–110.

La Hausse, P. (1990), Oral History and South African Historians, *Radical History Review*, 46(7): 346–355.

McKittrick, M. (2008), Landscapes of Power: Ownership and Identity on the Middle Kavango River, Namibia. *Journal of Southern African Studies*, 34(4): 785–802.

McKittrick, M. (1996), The 'Burden' of Young Men: Property and Generational Conflict in Namibia, 1880–1945. *African Economic History*, 24: pp. 115–129.

Moorsom, R. (1977), Underdevelopment, Contract Labour and Worker Consciousness in Namibia, 1915–1972. *Journal of Southern Africa Studies*, 4 (1): 52–87.

Moroney, S. (1978), The development of the compound as a mechanism of worker control 1900–1912. *South African Labour Bulletin*, 4 (3): 29–49.

Portelli, A. (1981), The Peculiarities of Oral History. *History Workshop Journal*, 12: 96–107.

Portelli, A. (1998), What Makes Oral History Different. In R. Perks, P. Thomson (eds.), *The Oral History Reader.* London, Routledge, 63–78.

Rey, C. F. (1932), Ngamiland and the Kalahari. *Geographical Journal,* 80 (4), 281–308.

Sandelowsky, B. H. (1979), Kapako and Vungu Vungu: Iron Age Sites on the Kavango River. *Southern Africa Archaeological Society*, Goodwin series, 3: 52–61.

Scott, J. (1991), Women's History. In P. Burke (ed.), *New Perspectives on Historical Writing* Cambridge, Polity Press, 42–43.

Smalberger, J. M. (1974), I.D.B. and the Mining Compound System in the 1880s. *The South African Journal of Economics*, 42 (4): 398–414.

Stoler, A. L. (2002), Colonial Archives and the Art of Governance: On the Content in the Form. In C. Hamilton et al., *Refiguring the archive.* Cape Town, David Phillip, 87–109.

Thompson, P. (1998), The Voice of the Past. In R. Perks, A. Thomson (eds.), *The Oral History Reader.* London, Routledge, 107–113.

Voipio, R. (1981), Contract Work through Ovambo Wyes. In R. H. Green, K. Kiljunen, M. L. Kiljunen (eds.), *Namibia: The Last Colony.* Harlow, Longman, 116–120.

Wallace, M. (1998), A Person is Never Angry for Nothing. In P. Hayes et al. (eds.), *Namibia under South African Rule.* London, James Currey, 77–94

Weigend, G.G. (1985), German Settlement Patterns in Namibia. *Geographical Review*, 2 (75): 156–169.

Internet sources

Dierks, K. (2005), 'Colonial period: German rule' 52, 1896. http://www.klausdierks.com/Chronology/52.htm Accessed 02 January 2020.

Unpublished theses and papers

Akuupa, M. U. (2006), Checking the Kulcha: local discourses of culture in Kavango region of Namibia (unpublished MA thesis, University of the Western Cape).

Akuupa, M. U. (2011), The Formation of 'national culture' in post-apartheid Namibia: a focus on state sponsored cultural festivals in Kavango Region (PhD Thesis, University of the Western Cape).

Banghart, P. (1969), Migrant labour in South West Africa and its effect on Ovambo tribal life (M.A Thesis, University of Stellenbosch).

Bauer, G. M. (1994), The labor movement and the prospect of democracy in Namibia (PhD Thesis, Madison, Wisconsin).

Bosch, J. L. (1964), Die Shambiu van die Okavango: 'n volkundige studie (PhD Thesis, Stellenbosch University).

Diaz, H. N. (1992), A definitive edition and analysis of the tjakova myth of the Kavango (PhD Thesis, University of Cape Town).

Diescho, J.B. (1983), An analysis of the Odendaal commission of enquiry into South West Africa Affairs 1962–1963, with specific reference to its findings, recommendations and implementation in respect of Kavango (M.A Thesis, University of Fort Hare).

Eckl, A. (2004), Konfrontation und Kooperation am Kavango (Nord-Namibia) von 1891 bis 1921 (PhD Thesis, University of Cologne).

Fumanti, M. (2003), Youth, elites and distinction in a Northern Namibia town (PhD Thesis, University of Manchester).

Hayes, P. (1992), A history of the Ovambo of Namibia, c1880–1935 (PhD Thesis, University of Cambridge).

Kampungu, R. (1965), The concept and aim of Okavango marriage customs (Rome, Doctor of Canon Law, Pontifical University of Propaganda Fide).

Kreike, E.H. (1996), Recreating Eden: agro-ecological change, food security and environmental diversity in southern Angola and northern Namibia, 1890–1990 (PhD Thesis, Yale University).

Karapo, H.K. (2008), Living memory in a forgotten war zone: the Ukwangali district of Kavango and the Namibian liberation struggle, 1966–1989 (MA thesis, University of the Western Cape).

Likuwa, K. M. (2001), Djwaini, a coffin with your recruit number on. The experience of contract workers from Kavango to South African gold mines, 1944–1977 (Bachelors degree research, UNAM).

Likuwa, K. M. (2005), Rundu, Kavango, a case study of forced relocations in Namibia, 1954 to 1972 (M.A Thesis, University of the Western Cape).

Likuwa, K. M. (2006), Report on a public lecture on potential economic development for the Kavango (Rundu Secondary).

Mbambo, S. K. (2002), Heal with God: indigenous healing and religion among the Vagciriku of the Kavango region, Namibia (PhD Thesis, Utrecht University).

Mohlig, W. J. G. (1967), Die Sprache der Dciriku: Phonologie, Prosodologie und Morphologie (PhD Thesis, University of Cologne).

Nambadi, A.H. (2007), The Kavango legislative council, 1970–1979: a critical analysis (MA thesis, University of the Western Cape).

Ndaoya, L. N. (2000), Oshiwambo-speaking migrant workers on the Witwatersrand gold mines from 1940 to 1969' (B.A. research paper, UNAM).

Olivier, M. J. (1961), Inboorlingbeleid en administrasie in die mandaad gebied van Suid Wes- Afrika (PhD Thesis, University of Stellenbosch).

Rassool, C. S. (2004), The individual, auto/biography and history in South Africa (PhD Thesis, University of the Western Cape).

Shiremo, R. S. (2005), The role of Kavango Kings in the anti-colonial resistance: 1903 the year of unity and resistance (Rundu college now as Rundu UNAM campus).

Shiremo, R. S. (2010), The reign of Hompa Nyangana over the Vagciriku and relations with neighbouring kingdoms, politics and challenges to his leadership: an era of hostility and violence, 1874–1924 (M.A Thesis, History, UNAM).

Shirungu, M.J.M. (2010), Cultural and social factors impacting on the programme to prevent mother to child transmission (PMTCT) of HIV in Namibia: a case study of the Kavango (MA thesis, University of the Western Cape).

Silvester, J. G. (1993), Black pastoralists, white farmers: the dynamics of land dispossession and labour recruitment in Southern Namibia, 1915–1955 (PhD Thesis, University of London).

Stals, E.L.P. (1967), Die aanraking tussen blankes en Ovambos in Suid Wes Africa, 1850–1915 (M.A Thesis, Universiteit van Stellenbosch, 1967).

Toivanen, P. (No year), Namibia, Kavango ngapi nare? (Unpublished script, University of Stellenbosch library, TEOL 266.416881 TOI).

Van Tonder, L.L. (1966), The Hambukushu of Okavango land: an anthropological study of a South Western Bantu people in Africa (PhD Thesis, Port Elizabeth University).

Yeboah, A. (2000), The impact of labour migration on Namibian women (B.A., research paper, UNAM).

Photographs of interviewees taken by Kletus Muhena Likuwa

Ludwig Kudumo Kamenye, Kangweru village (13 August 2009)

Susana Mate Kamwanga, Guma village (11 August 2009)

Simon Kandere, Rundu (29 April 2012, courtesy of Elvira Makena Ndara)

Ngonga Katjire, Diheke village (21 August 2009)

Bartholomeus Someno Katota, Mabushe village (12 August 2009)

Frans Katema Kudumo, Sharughanda village (30 July 2009)

Kavengere Mutero, Bagani village (18 August 2009)

Anselm Likuwa Mukoya, Ndiyona village (4 August 2009)

Bernhard Lipayi Linyando, Ndiyona village (27 July 2009)

Martin Maghundu, Divundu village (19 August 2009)

Mberekera, Kambowo village (20 January 2007)

Konrad Mbote, Thirume village (21 August 2009)

Nyambe Merecky, Shipando village (6 August 2009)

Kapinga Muhero, Kamutjonga village (19 August 2009)

Kamenye Likuwa, Kangweru village (13 August 2009)

Mbamba Ndara, Divundu village (19 August 2009)

Ronginius Karupu, Nambi village (12 July 2009)

Benhard Limbangu Shampapi, Rucara village (28 July 2009)

Frans Tuhemwe Shevekwa, Sharughanda village (30 July 2009)

Shindimba Ndumba Shihungu, Shipando village (6 August 2009)

Mathias Ndumba Shikombero, Rucara village (5 May 2012, courtesy of Basilius Haingura)

Ndumba Shirengumuke, born 1921, Hoha village (3 July 2009)

Shintango waKarenga, Korokoko village (5 August 2009)

Ntjavi Shandini Shiviru, Ndiyona village (15 August 2009)

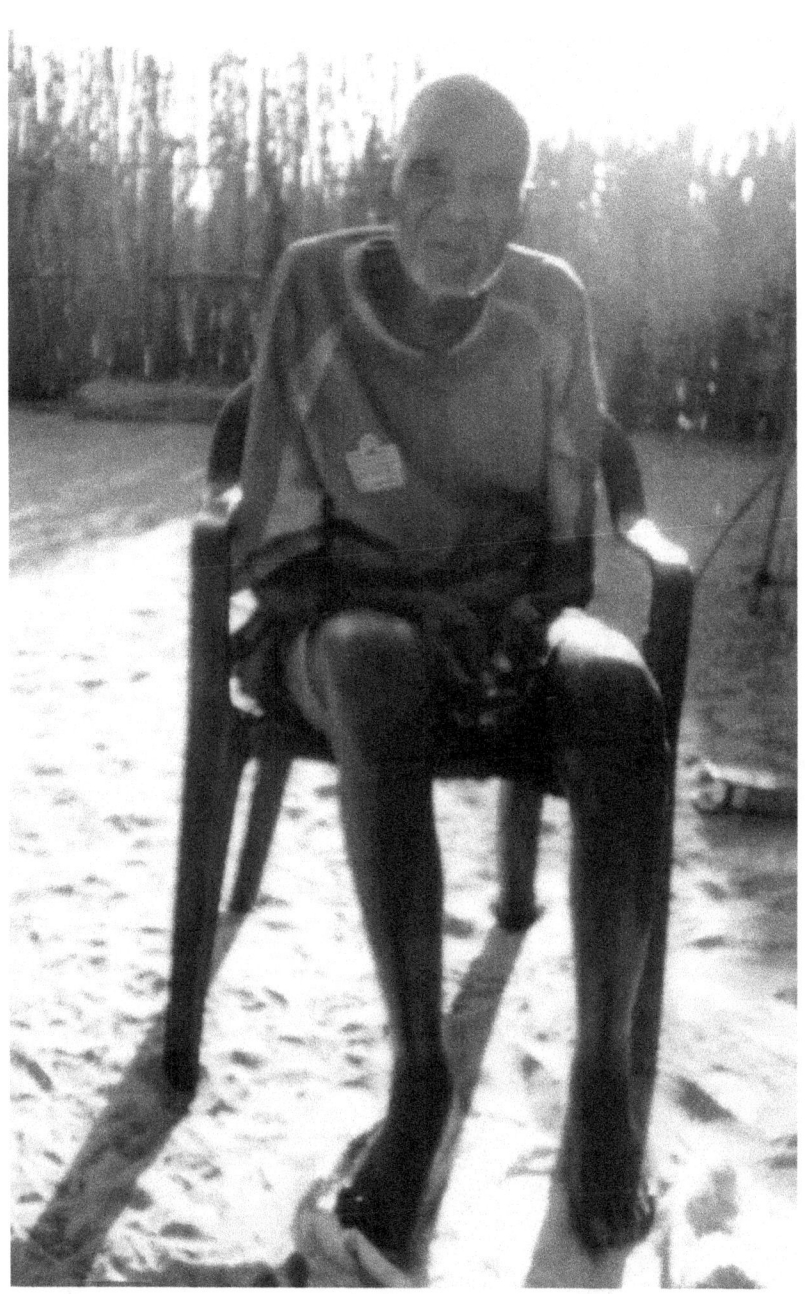
Shikiri waNkayira, Ndonga-linena (8 August 2009)

Kandjeke Weka, Rucara village (28 July 2009)

George Mukoya (alias Shamandimbe) Weka, Rucara village (29 July 2009)

Theresia Shidona Weka, Guma village (11 August 2009)

Index

A
alcohol 9, 147, 154–156, 169, 173
Angola 6f., 13, 64, 66, 72, 77, 85–88, 90, 97–100, 120f., 127, 129, 139, 141–143, 148, 153f., 159f., 174
Ausiku 8, 160–163, 174

B
boys 123f., 132, 135, 152

C
cloth 70
clothes 62–64, 66–71, 83, 92, 97, 142, 144f., 150, 168, 170, 173
colonial xiif., 1–10, 12–15, 17, 24, 29f., 32–49, 52, 54–56, 59–67, 71, 74, 77–82, 86–88, 90, 92–94, 96, 102–104, 117f., 120, 122–124, 130, 137, 141–143, 146, 152, 156f., 161–167, 169–171, 173, 175
compound 6f., 119–137, 139f., 154, 160, 168

D
Djwaini 64, 70, 74f., 77, 81, 97, 125, 133, 139, 142f., 152

E
economic xiii, 138, 144, 151f., 163, 168–171, 173–175
entrapment xiii, 2, 143, 157, 173
experience xii, 2, 16–18, 21, 98, 100, 104f., 109, 111–113, 115f., 126, 137, 171

F
families xiii, 9, 144, 146, 150, 153f., 157, 161f., 164, 168f., 173, 175
farms xif., 2f., 10, 12, 98, 100, 104, 106–108, 111, 113, 115–117, 120, 131, 137, 143, 147, 171f.2, 174f.

G
German 2–4, 15, 24f., 29f., 32–42, 44, 54, 57, 61f., 100, 102, 147f., 151

H
hunters 2, 15, 24–26, 32–34, 63, 148

I
impact xiii, 2f., 7, 9, 11, 17f., 20, 138f., 144, 149–152, 158, 168–171, 173, 175

J
Johannesburg 64, 70, 72–77, 81, 97, 125, 133, 139f., 142f., 152

K
Kampungu 10
kings 25, 27–29, 32f., 36, 44–47, 50f., 56, 58f., 61, 63, 138, 171, 174
kitchen 106, 108–110, 147

M
master 107–109, 111–114, 118f., 123f.
men 1, 6f., 16f., 62f., 65–70, 72, 74, 77f., 82, 86, 88–90, 92–94, 96–99, 107–109, 119, 121, 124, 126, 129, 135, 151–153, 159, 169
migration xiif., 1–3, 6f., 62f., 65–68, 70–72, 78f., 88, 92–94, 96f., 119, 125, 127, 170f., 175
mines 3, 6f., 14, 98f., 101, 119–127, 129f., 132f., 135–137, 140, 152, 166, 171f.
missionaries 4, 10, 24, 34–36, 38f., 48f., 78f., 94, 152, 163, 171
Moorsom 3, 63, 138, 146, 170

N
names 17, 100f., 119f., 137, 150, 172
Northern Labour Organization (NLO) 5, 13, 24, 54, 55, 57, 58, 59, 61, 62, 79, 80, 81, 85

O
Okavango 77, 79f.
oral xii, 14, 16f., 20–23, 80, 93, 95, 110, 118, 127, 137, 172
Ovambo xif., 1, 4–6, 8–10, 14, 17, 63, 78, 87–89, 93, 96, 98, 102–104, 107, 117f., 120f., 126–129, 132, 134f., 137f., 153, 156–158, 164–168, 170, 172f., 175

P
political xiii, 2–6, 8f., 152, 157–164, 168, 173–175
pondok 106
poverty xiif., 1, 6, 63, 69, 97, 169f., 174f.
purchase xii, 1, 143f., 147, 151, 165, 168, 173

R
recruit 74, 76, 85, 152
return xiii, 2, 139, 141–143, 146, 150, 152–155, 169, 173
ruhepo xiif., 1, 6, 63, 69, 97, 105, 169–171, 174f.

S
San 79, 80, 81, 92
Shikombero 138, 139, 141–144, 150f., 153, 166
social 6, 9, 12, 18, 138, 144, 146, 151f., 155, 168–174
South African 2–9, 12,f., 15, 17, 20f., 24f., 32, 39–45, 47–49, 54, 57, 59, 61, 63, 72f., 76–78, 90, 93, 99, 101f., 119–125, 127, 129, 143, 152, 162, 167f., 170–172
Southern Labour Organization (SLO) 5, 24, 54, 59, 61
South West Africa Northern Labour Association xiii, 2f., 5, 24, 59–62, 83–87, 89f., 98, 102f., 127, 136, 138, 143, 162–165, 168f., 173
strike 1, 3f., 8f., 165–169, 173f.
SWANLA 2f.., 5, 24

T
traders 2, 4, 24–29, 32–34, 37, 62f., 98, 144, 148, 151

V
Vacu 80f., 92
vambo 17, 120f., 128, 153, 166–168

W
wages 1, 9, 99, 114–117, 122, 125, 134, 143,f., 151, 153, 156, 163, 168–170, 173
Witwatersrand Native Labour Association 13, 57–59, 74, 76f., 85, 120, 139, 149f.
women xiii, 2f., 14, 16f., 63, 68–70, 92–97, 108f., 145, 151f., 169, 175

Basel Namibia Studies Series

In 1997, *P. Schlettwein Publishing* (PSP) launched the *Basel Namibia Studies Series*. Its primary aim was to lend support to a new generation of research, scholars and readers emerging with the independence of Namibia in 1990.

Initially, the book series published crucially important doctoral theses on Namibian history. It soon expanded to include more recent political, anthropological, media and cultural history studies by Namibian scholars.

P. Schlettwein Publishing, as an independent publishing house, maintained the series in collaboration with the *Basler Afrika Bibliographien* (BAB), Namibia Resource Centre and Southern Africa Library in Switzerland. All share a commitment to encourage research on Africa in general and southern Africa in particular. Through the incorporation of PSP into the *Carl Schlettwein Stiftung,* the series, by then a consolidated platform for Namibian Studies and beyond, was integrated into the publishing activities of the BAB.

Academic publishing, whether from or about Namibia, remains limited. The *Basel Namibia Studies Series* continues to provide a forum for exciting scholarly work in the human and social sciences.

The editors welcome contributions. For further information, or submission of manuscripts, please contact the *Basler Afrika Bibliographien* at www.baslerafrika.ch.

www.ingramcontent.com/pod-product-compliance
Lightning Source LLC
Chambersburg PA
CBHW080358030426
42334CB00024B/2914